LEGENDARY

DUNE: EXPOSURES

GREIG FRASER   JOSH BROLIN

FOREWORD BY BRIAN HERBERT

DUNE: PART ONE AND PART TWO

ARE BASED ON THE NOVEL BY FRANK HERBERT

INSIGHT EDITIONS

SAN RAFAEL • LOS ANGELES • LONDON

The Eyes of Dune by Brian Herbert

Frank Herbert was himself a professional photographer—in addition to his better-known skills as the genius author of *Dune*, which has the mysterious desert world of Arrakis at its core. His classic novel has been read by millions of people around the world and translated into more than forty-five languages.

When Frank Herbert taught me the craft of writing, I listened with rapt attention as he told me he liked to write scenes as if he were viewing them through a camera lens. When he spoke of this, he showed me his first description of the Baron Harkonnen in *Dune*, whom he described over several pages as if seen through a camera lens that was opening very slowly, a little at a time.

As the chapter begins, the Baron is not seen yet, but he speaks from the shadows. Then Frank Herbert writes, *"The fat hand descended onto the globe, stopped the spinning . . . ."* And: "*The fat hand moved, tracing details on the surface."* Dialogue ensues, and narrative, while the Baron moves *"within the shadows beside the globe . . . a shadow among shadows."*

Over several pages, the reader does not see any more of the evil, shadow-immersed antagonist than this, as the Baron, Feyd-Rautha, and Piter de Vries plot against Duke Leto. The reader sees no more of the Baron than his fat hand, and only hears his deep, basso voice. It is not until the very end of the chapter that Frank Herbert opens the camera lens all the way, to reveal his monstrous villain in startling detail.

Frank Herbert captivated millions of readers around the globe with his magnificent novel. Back in 1941, young Frank worked at the *Glendale Star* in California as a reporter and photographer. He went on many aerial assignments and personal flights, and took at least 5,000 aerial photographs. Then, during World War II, he was assigned to the immense Norfolk Naval Shipyard in Portsmouth, Virginia, where he served as a Photographer Second Class V-6 in the US Naval Reserve. After the war, Frank Herbert talked with his best friend, Howie Hansen, about opening a camera supply store, a business project that never came to pass.

By the early 1960s, Frank Herbert was the night picture editor for the *San Francisco Examiner*, and later a wine critic and features writer there, often taking photographs that were published. As his creative writing career reached new heights in the 1970s and '80s, he took many photographs, especially on a trip to Ireland researching his novel *The White Plague*, which became a worldwide bestseller.

My father liked to keep a camera tripod and camera equipment in his study next to his writing desk, and in 1985 he would proudly show me a trove of new camera gear he had purchased for a trip he planned to the Himalayas. On a trek accompanied by a famous Sherpa guide, he intended to become the oldest man to climb Mount Everest, a dream that never came to pass.

But many of Frank Herbert's dreams did come true, including the tremendous success of his great novel *Dune* after a rocky start in which it was rejected by more than twenty publishers. Then in 1983 at Churubusco Studios in Mexico City, near the site of the 1968 Olympic Games, he clicked the clapboard to start the cameras rolling on the initial *Dune* movie, and he got to keep the clapboard from the first take of the first scene.

My father would have enjoyed seeing Greig Fraser's evocative photographs from the set of the new Dune movies, and reading Josh Brolin's inspired poetry. Now, through Greig and Josh's eyes, we see a new interpretation of the filmmaking experience and my father's magnificent universe.

Brian Herbert, Seattle, July 2023.

Brian Herbert, the son of famed science fiction author Frank Herbert, is the author of multiple New York Times *bestsellers. He has won several literary honors and has been nominated for the highest awards in science fiction.*

DUNE: EXPOSURES

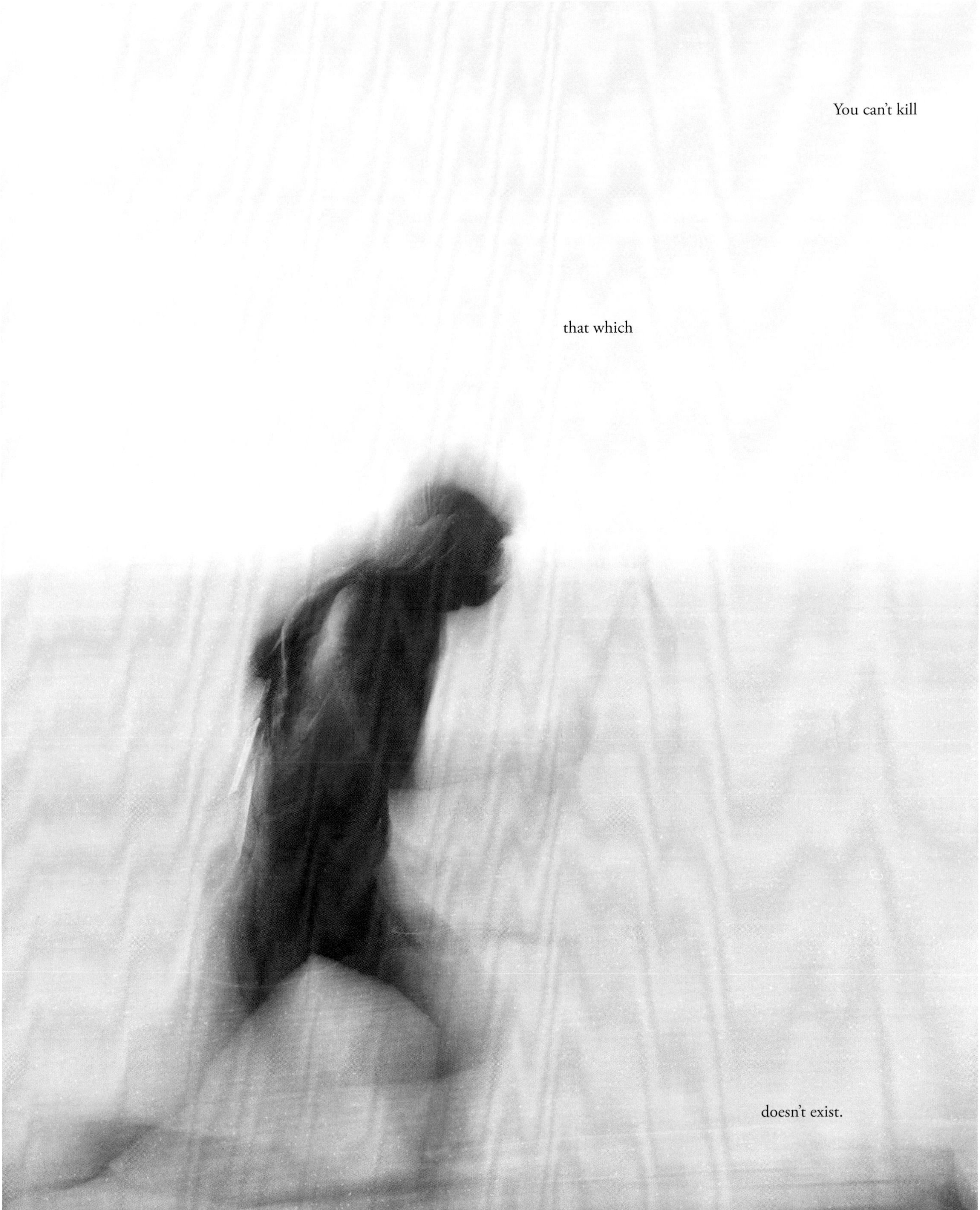

You can't kill

that which

doesn't exist.

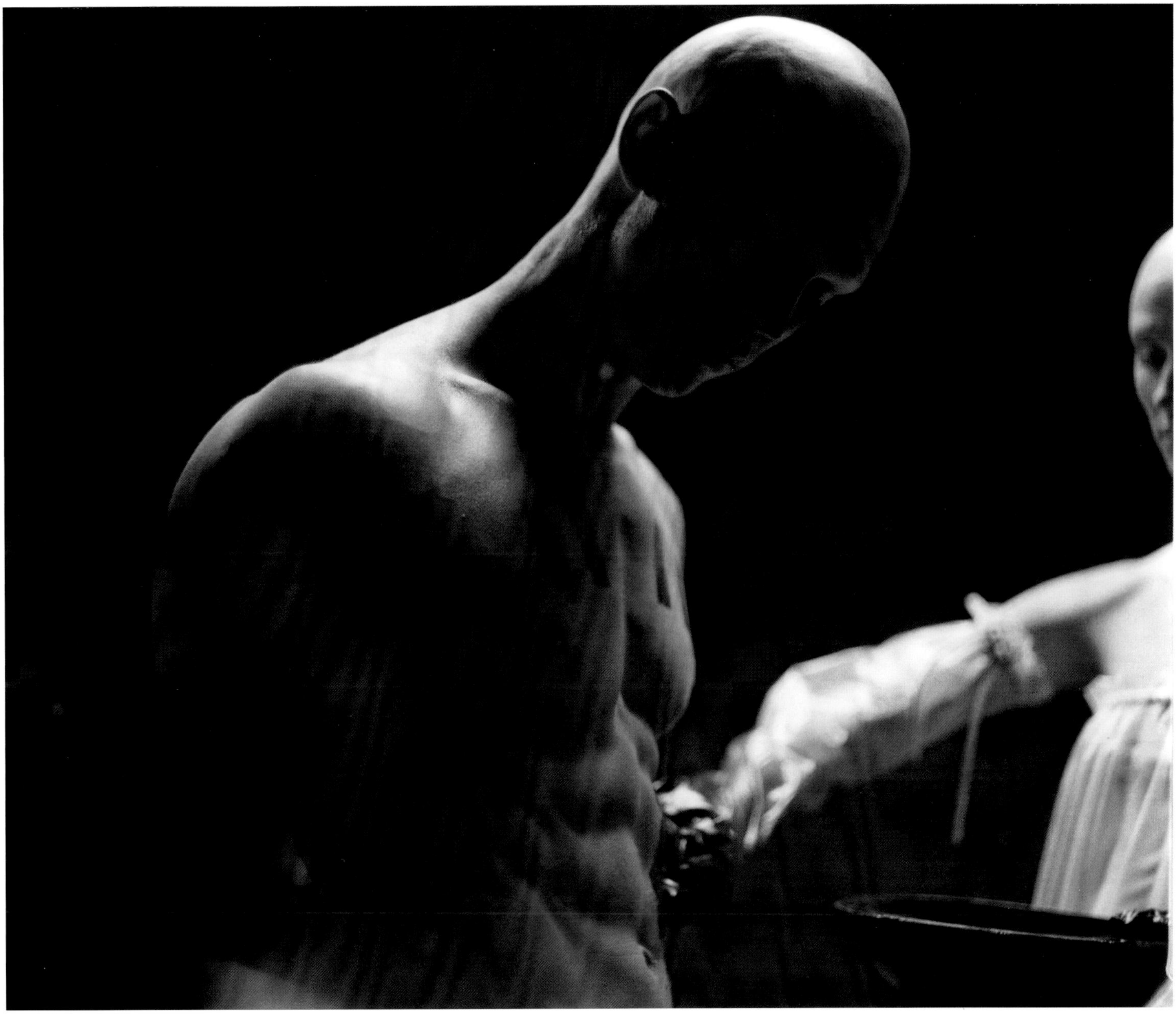

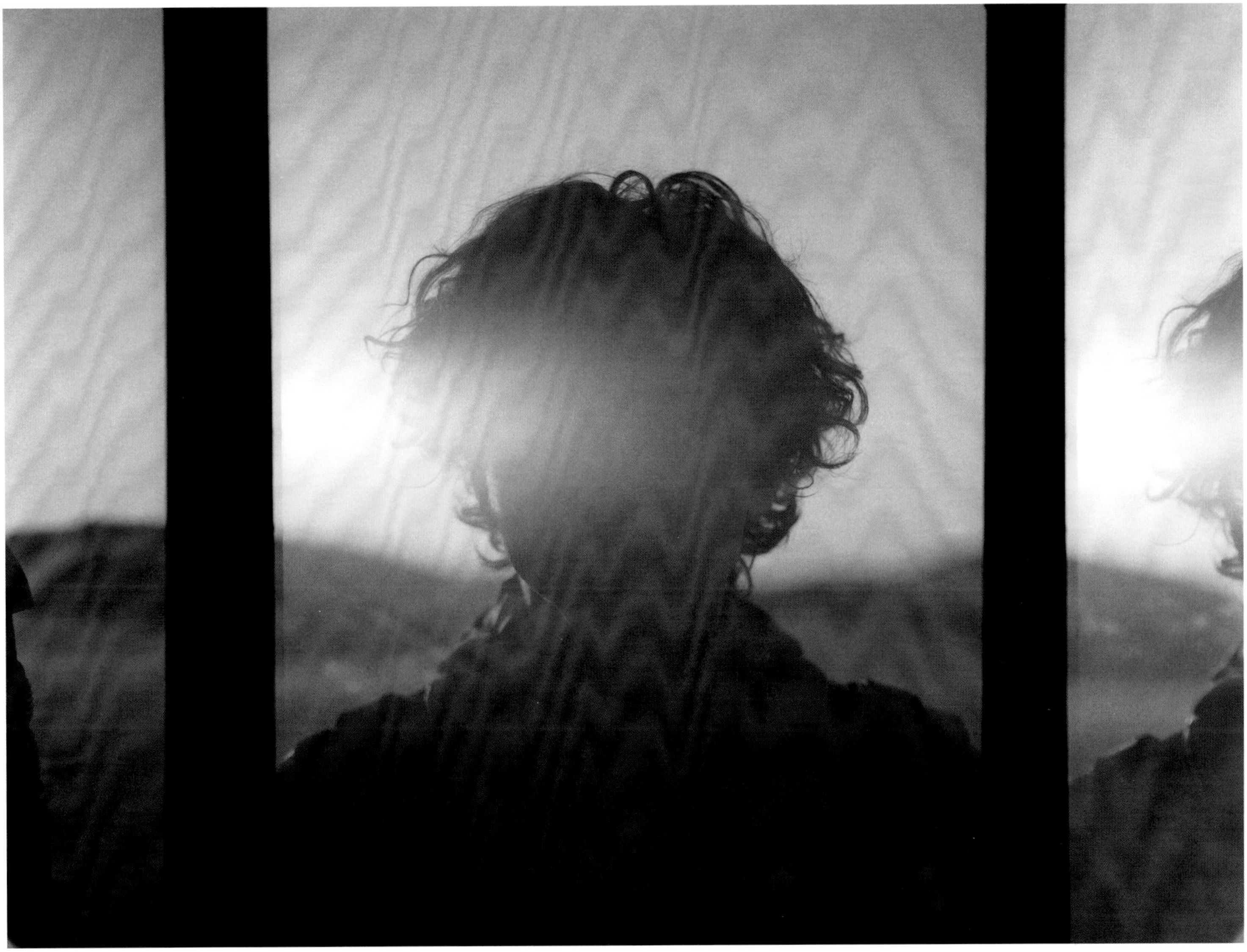

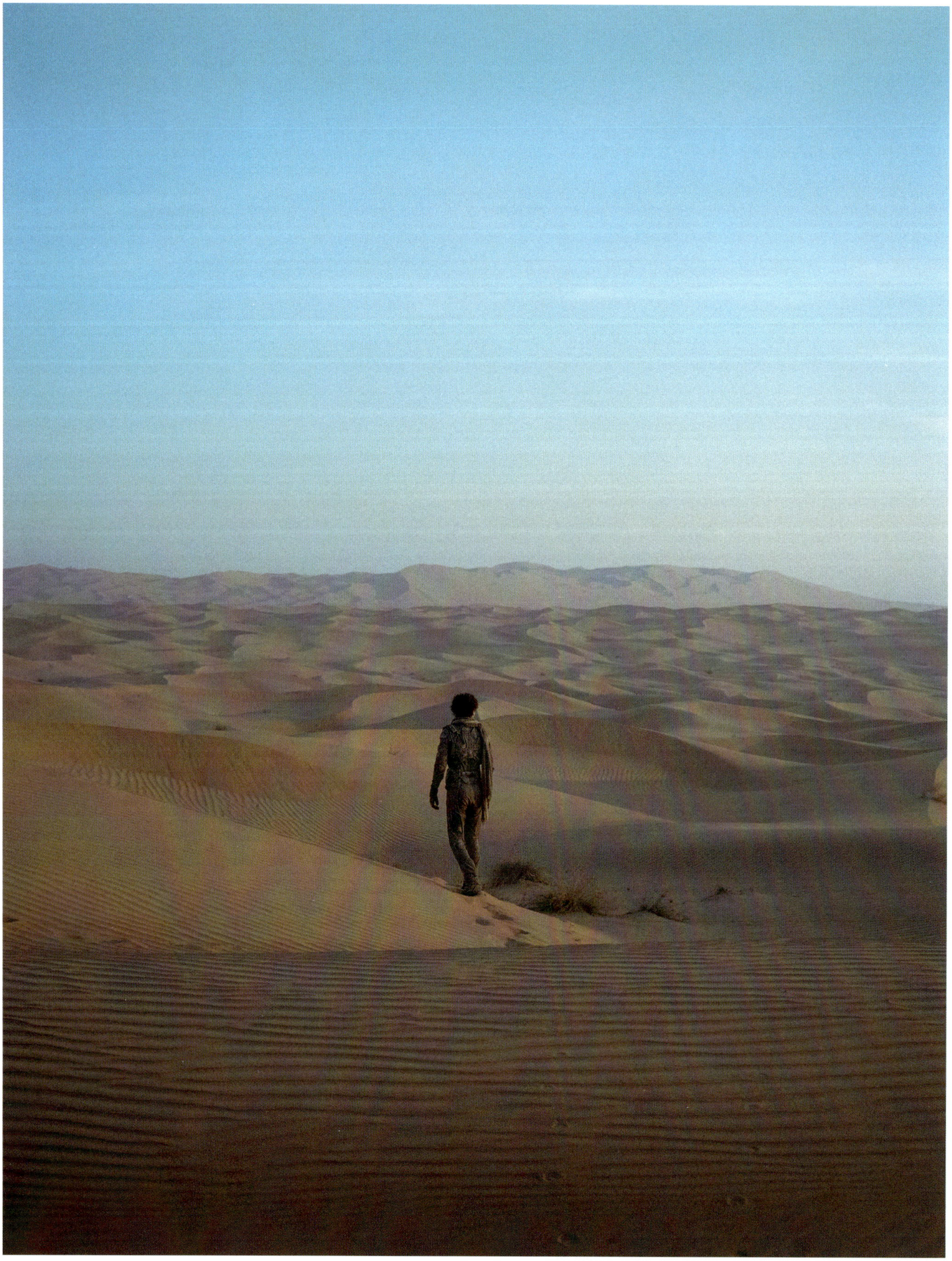

Crystalline fields of

Sand like oceans, rise & fall

Our egos defunct

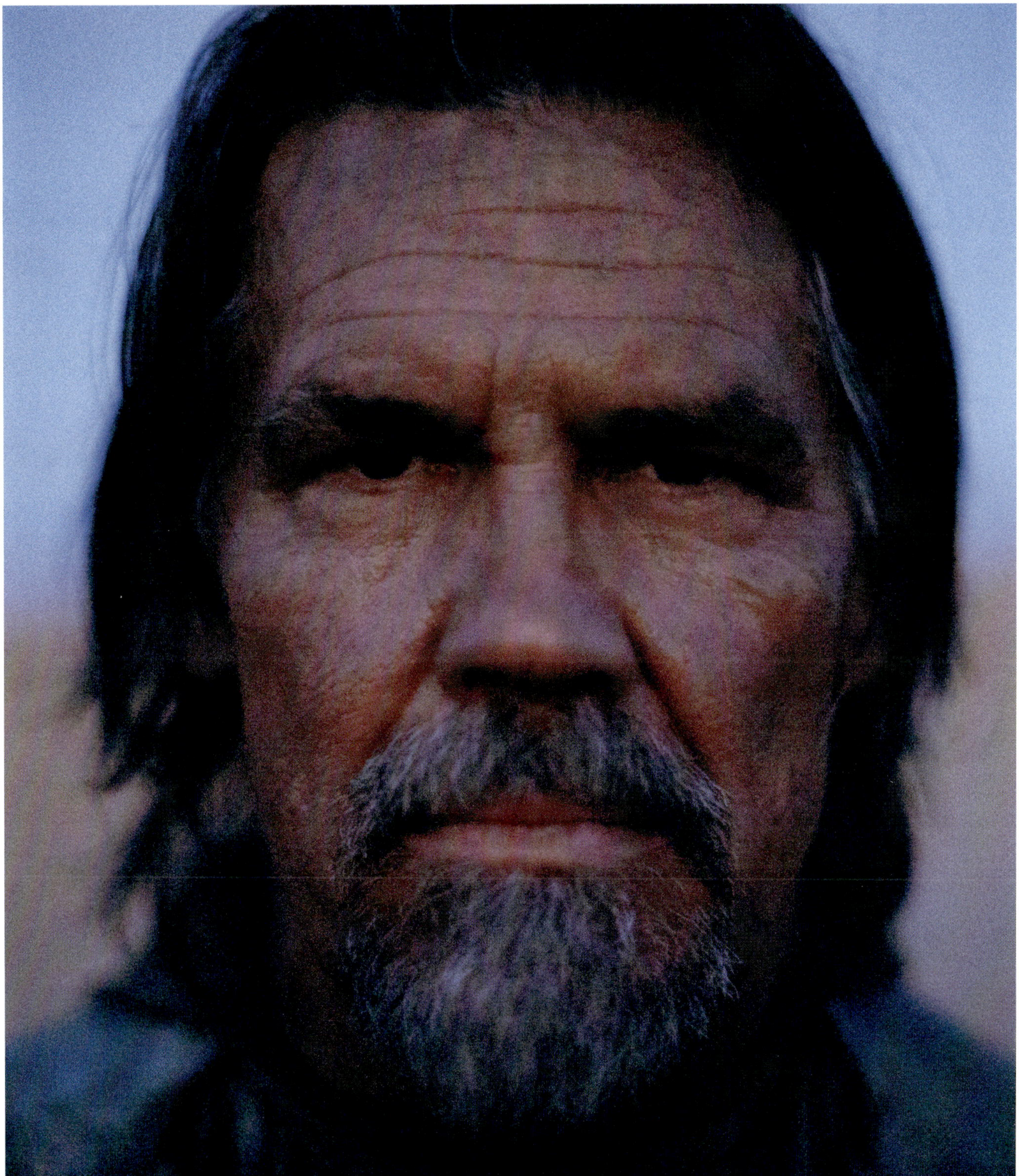

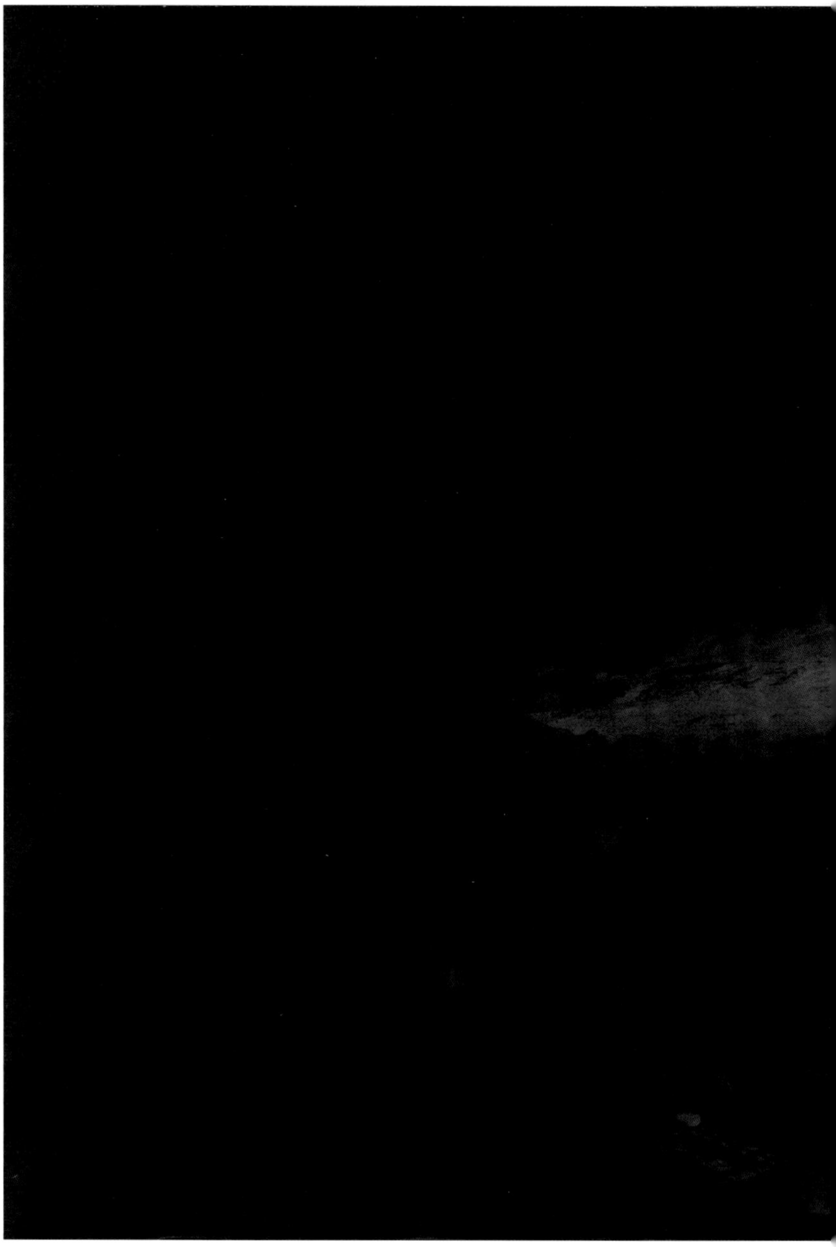

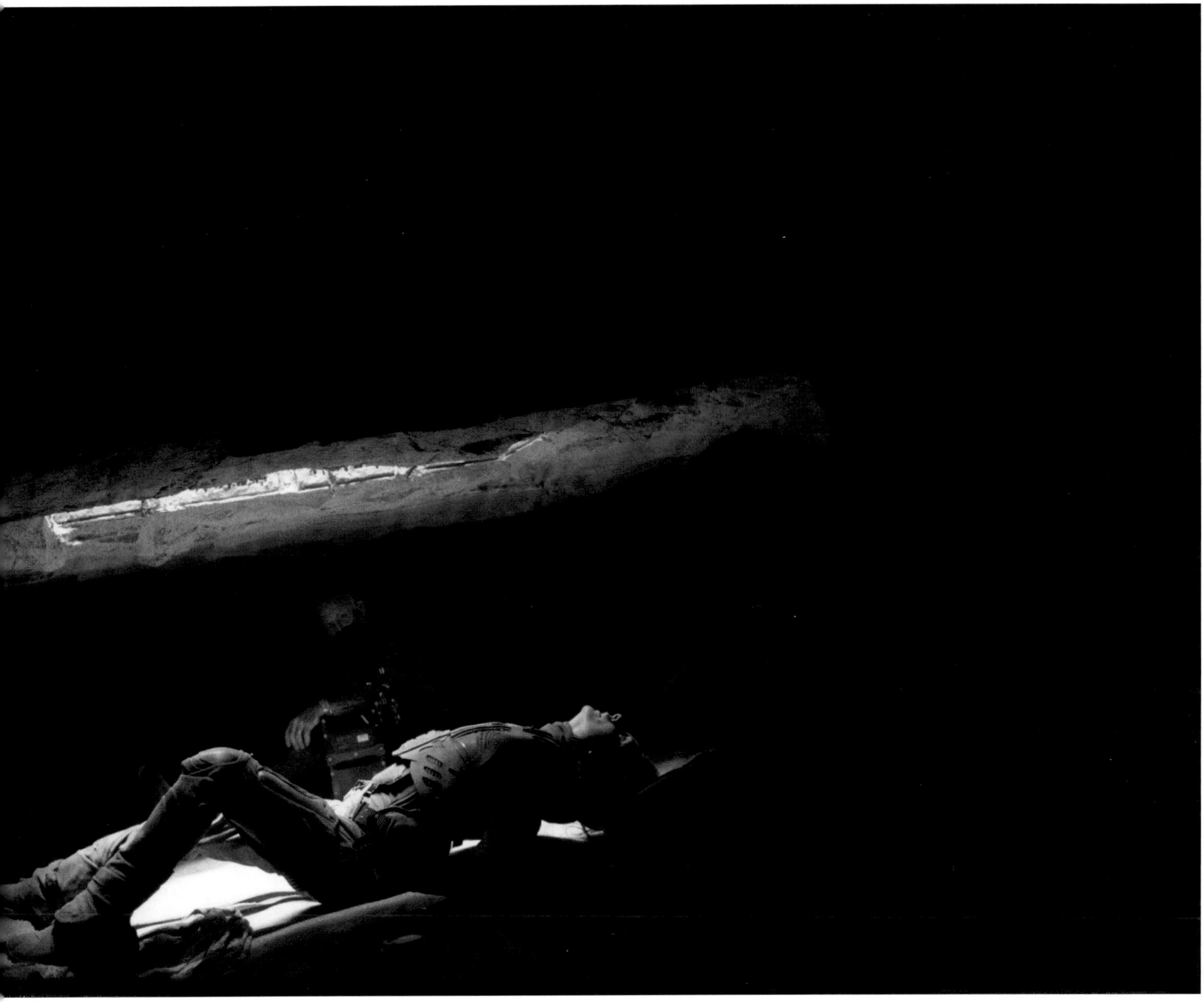

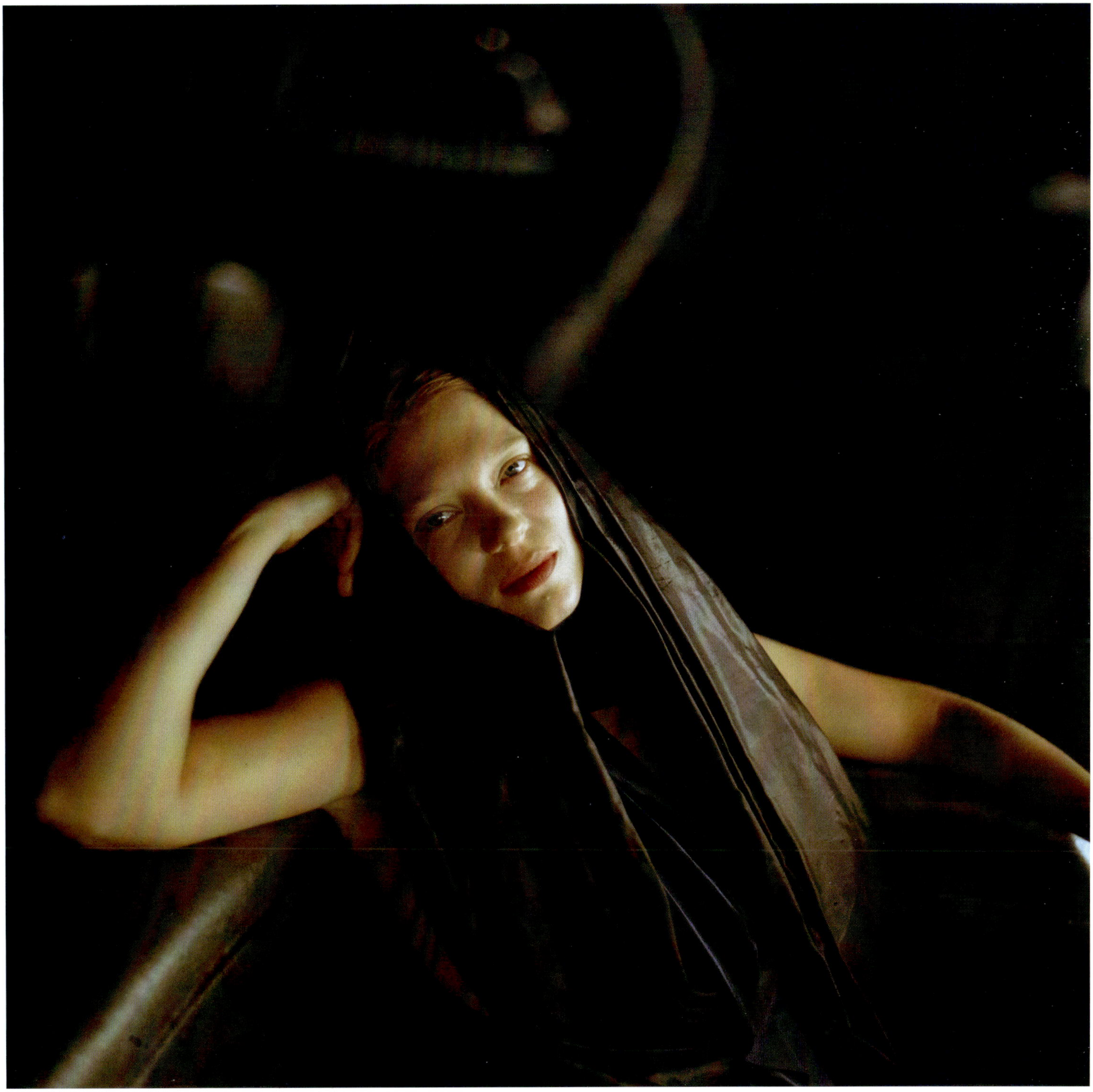

Madam
She is art
Thin words escape
Her imagination

You're a science experiment that foiled,
and the failure of it is
the consequence of your denial.
We all need a random wild to run us through when
we least expect it:
a love that tornados through you;
laughter that

breaks

bones;
silences which can only be heard
by a thirst that

hurts.

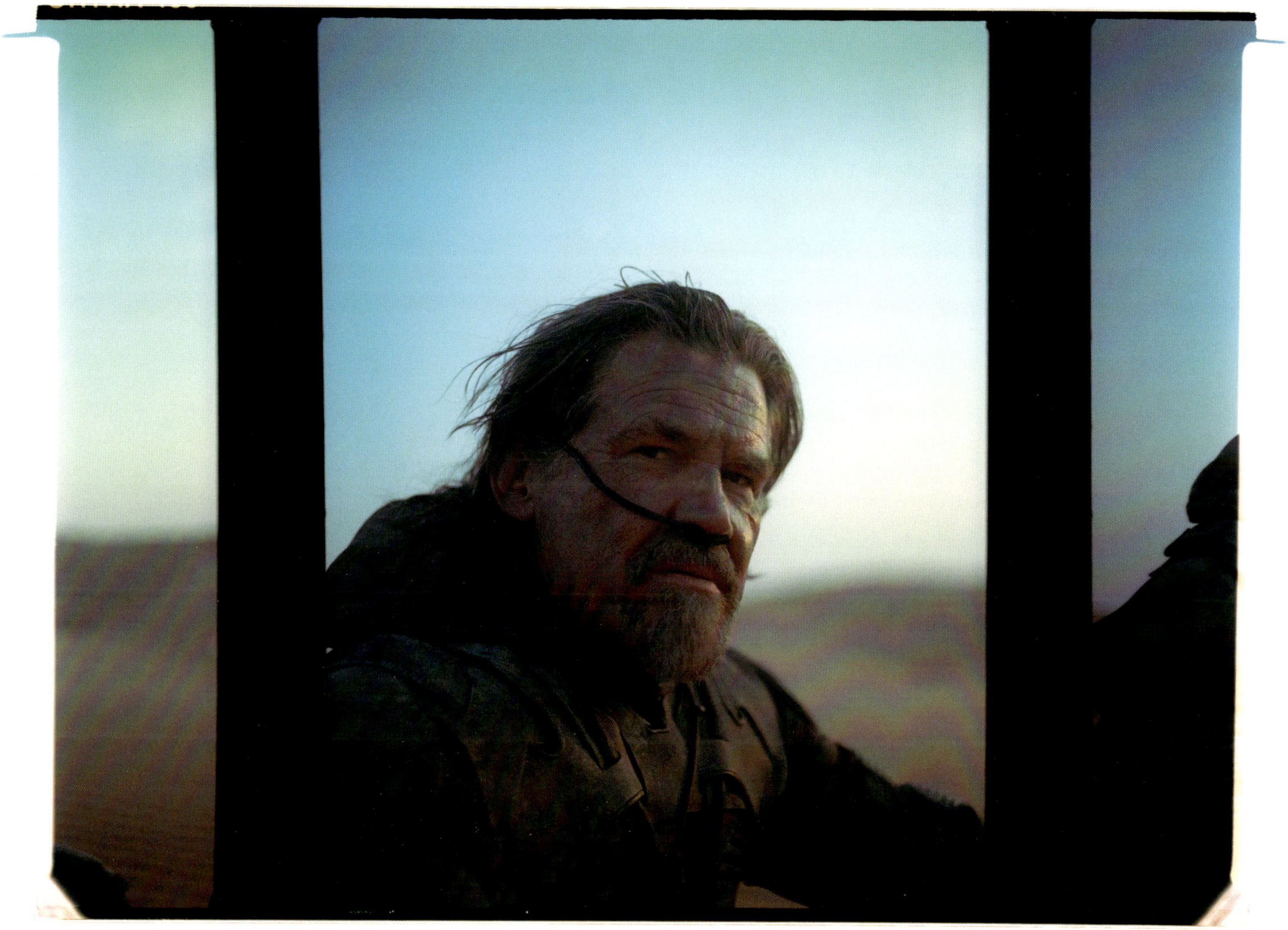

This day will soon dim
as the sculpted sand exhales
softly into night

Hold your knife in the air for all to victory. It is you
we have relied on. It is you, young pup, who has scaled
the sandy walls to the painful glory of self-assessment.
Denial does not become you. Into the fire you leap and
in that fire that burns away the forced paradigm that
so many of us cling to: the imprisoned life of an adolescent
feigning as adult without the painful transition of what
it is to develop character. But you are free, free to feel and
free to care for a bubble bigger than the one made around
the idea of your own safety. You are free to smile and
embrace a wider landscape whose music sings a more violet
tune. It's in your eyes that sweet colors surpass me,
and into that sky you go — me looking upwardly; me
gazing toward something we can all look forward to.

There are deserts to bake in,
deserts to lose your direction within.
There are sands to pick you up
when you are low and lift you
to the top of its World,
so you can view its horizons
and see the vastness with
which it is holding y
o
u
.

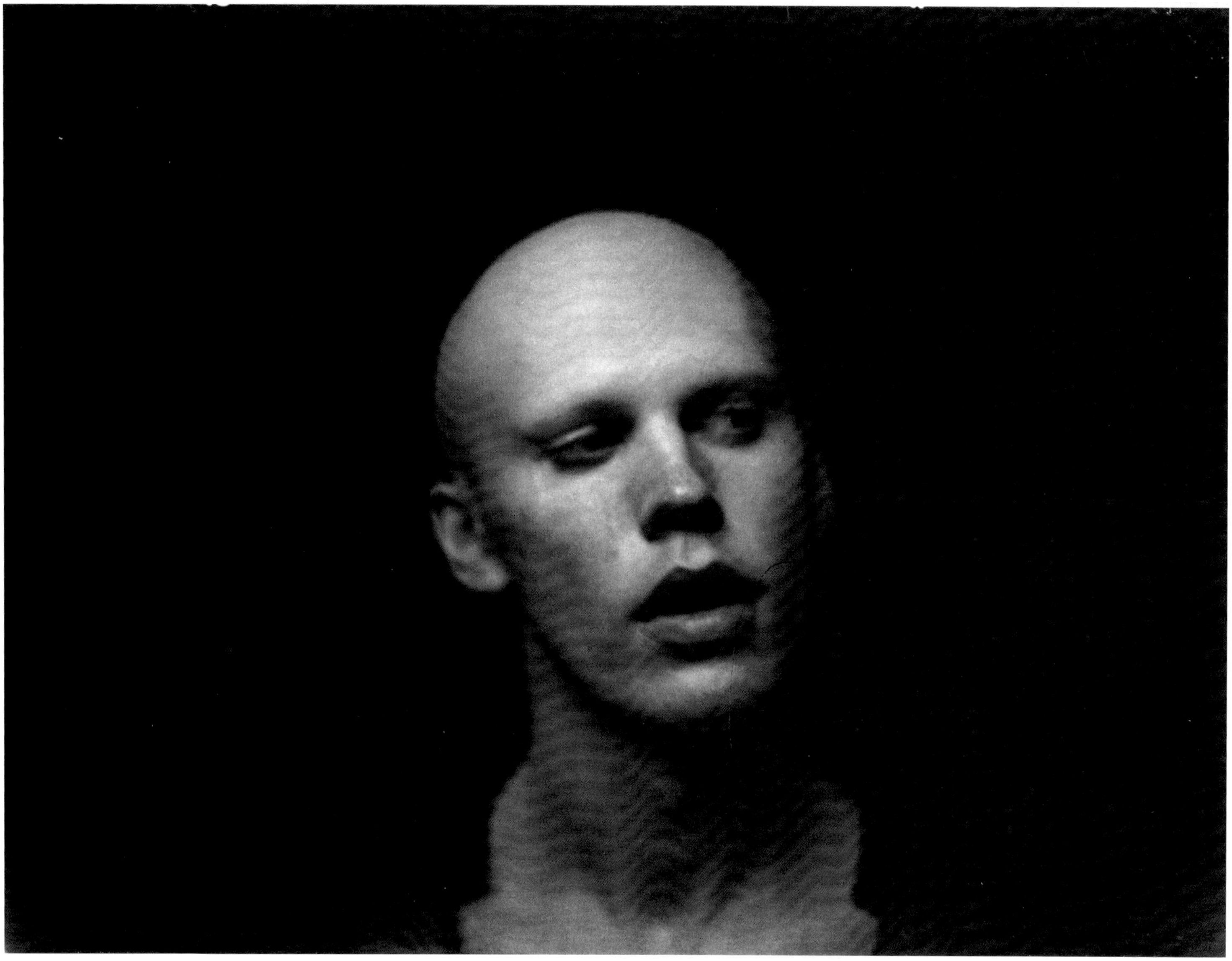

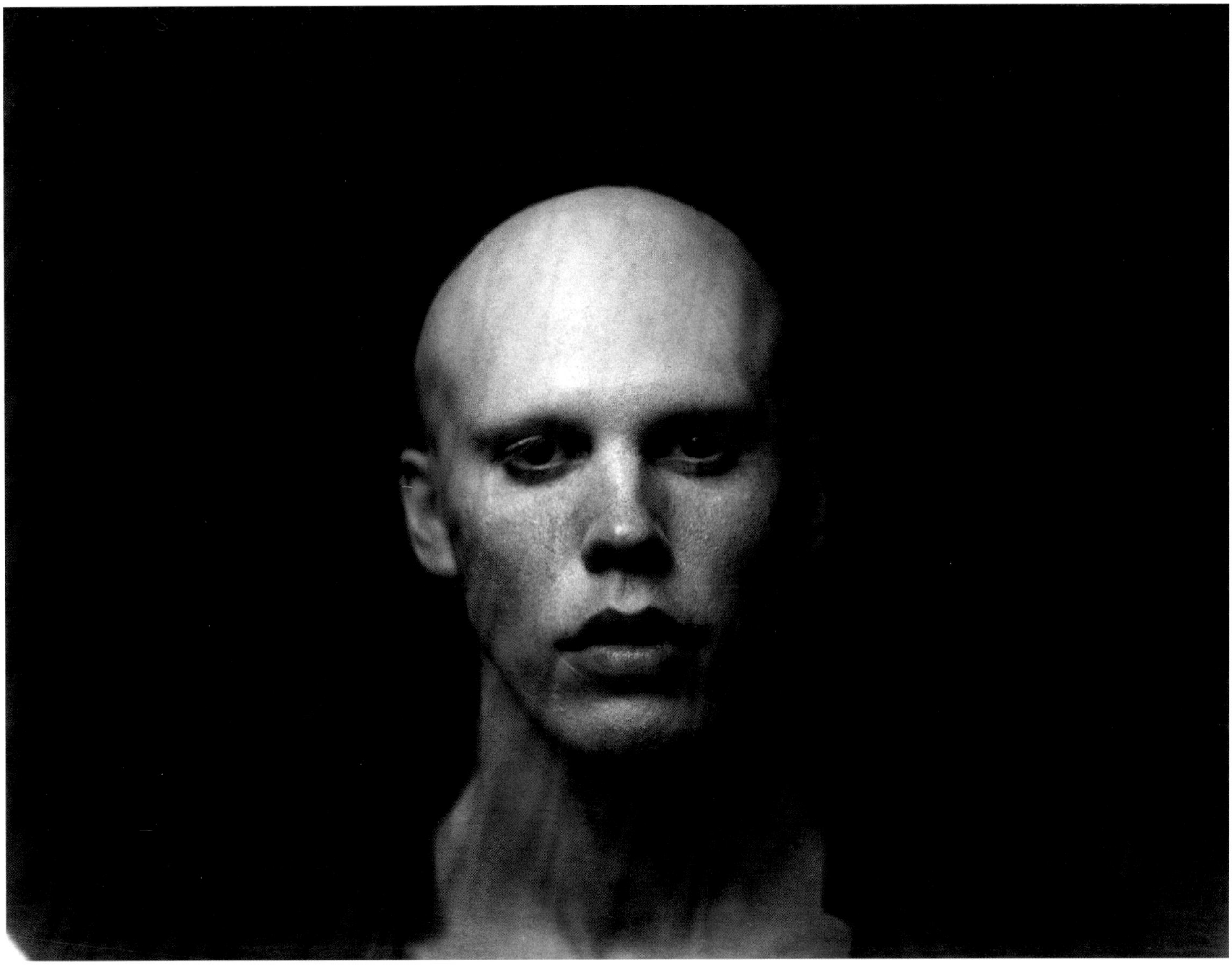

Umbrella shades a halo
black as the talent
that breathes under all the
would-be colors
in a rainbow

and while you
lick the electric palette of your skills
in order to find a truth
the crew looks on
silhouetted against
that sun
that melts

any ego
that might have traveled here
innocently
with great sculpted
visage
now rendered
feral

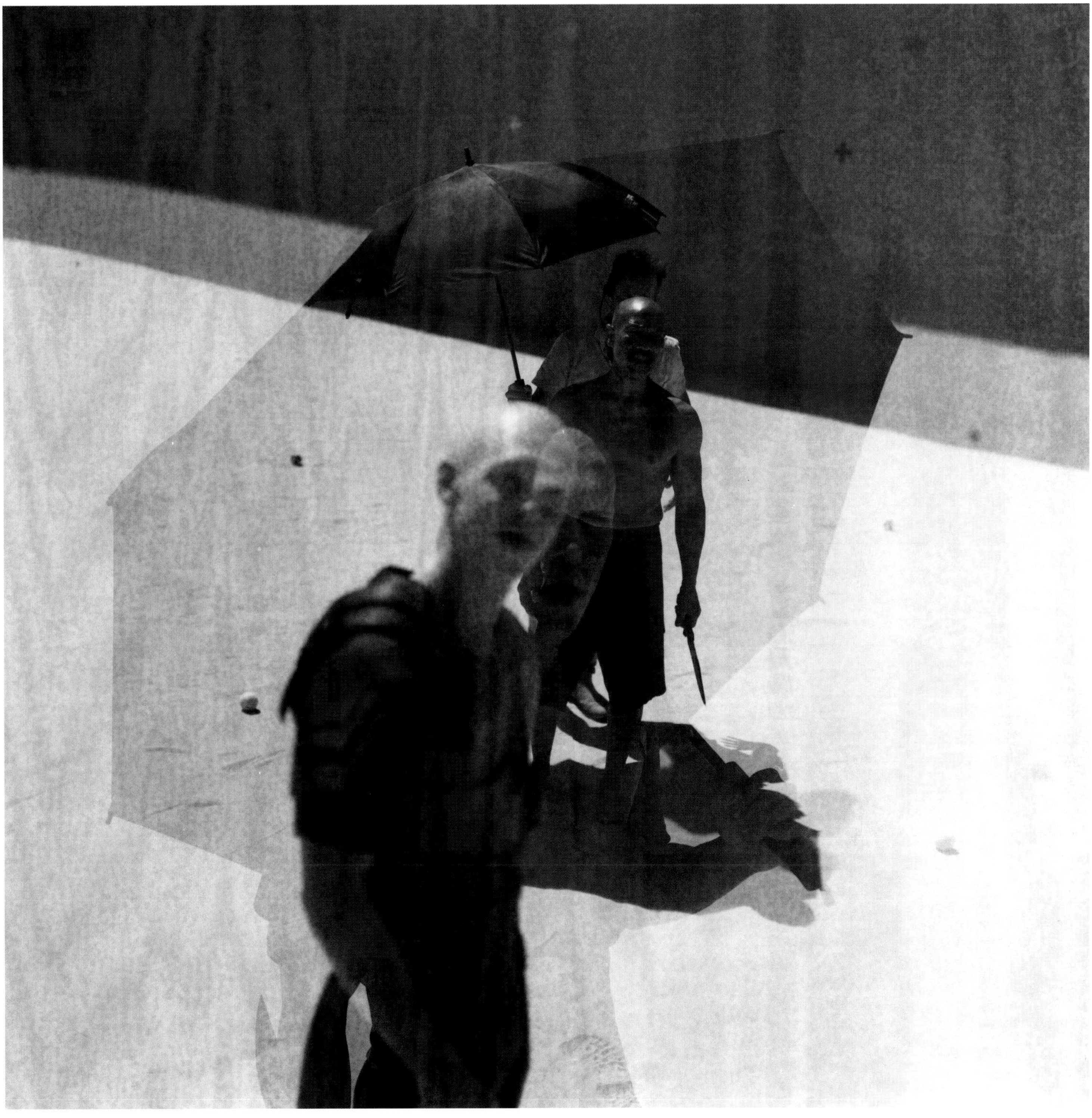

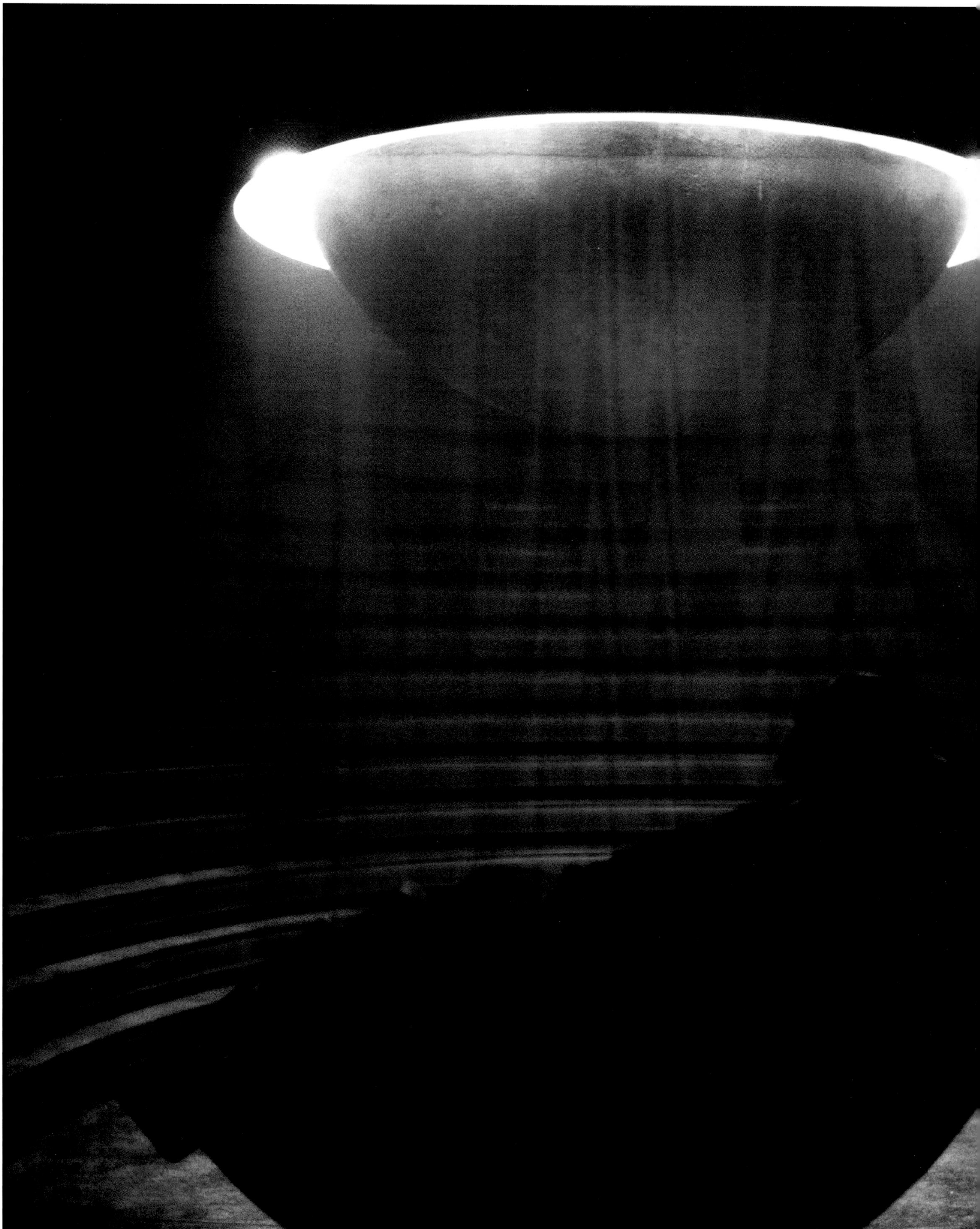

As the old finds my hand I gather myself closer to what resonates for me during this time. It's a more labored presence, this job. My solace seems to ignite with an older generation, those voices that speak a language foreign to me yet smile the smiles of the antiquity that I inhale within a hug, barely of this time. We sit in the sand and wait to be told where to walk, what to do. I am writing in my head constantly, predetermining my access so to be affected in ways that are enlivening and deeply human. The more time we spend in the sand out in the middle of nowhere, the more I understand our most basic needs: water, companionship, loyalty, honor, grit.

There will be a time when I am home that I will miss those leathery hands cupping mine. There will be a time when I get home to my pool and my paintings and the daily calls with the agent that I will desperately want to put it all down and drive to the farthest peak or desert, take off most of what covers me, and pretend that I'm back in those ancient sands next to people whose gestures speak volumes over what successes we are otherwise constantly trying to convince ourselves the value of.

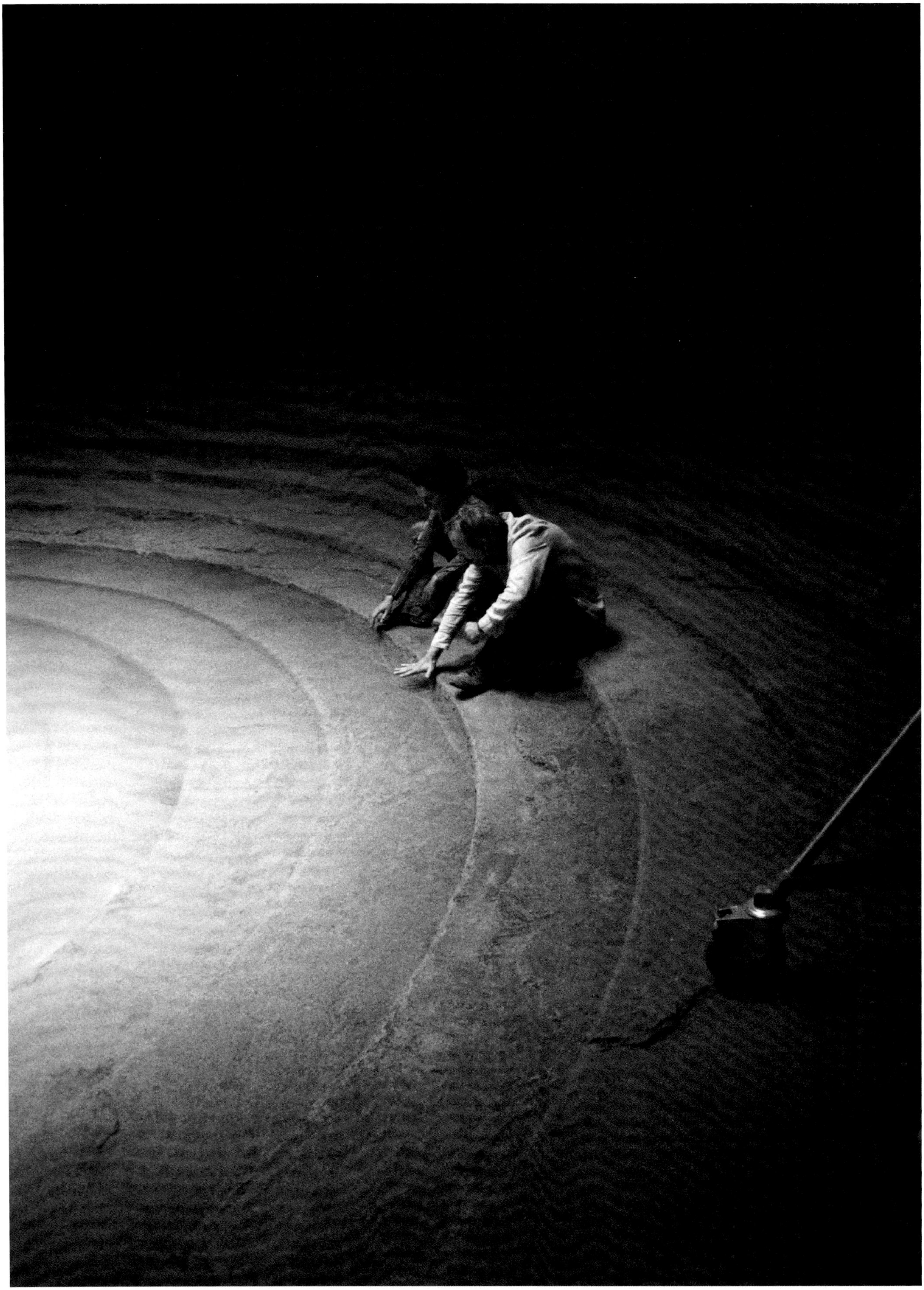

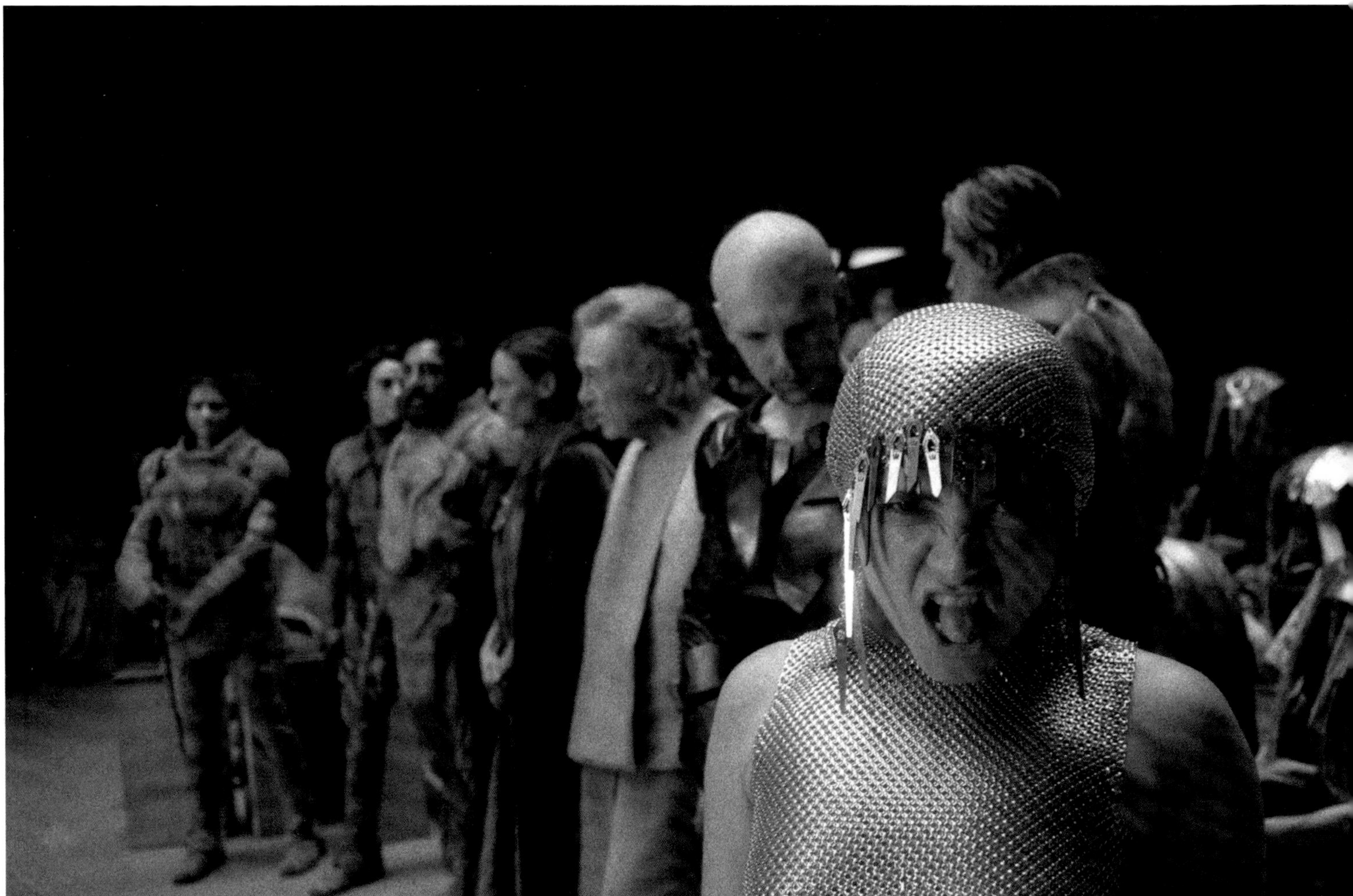

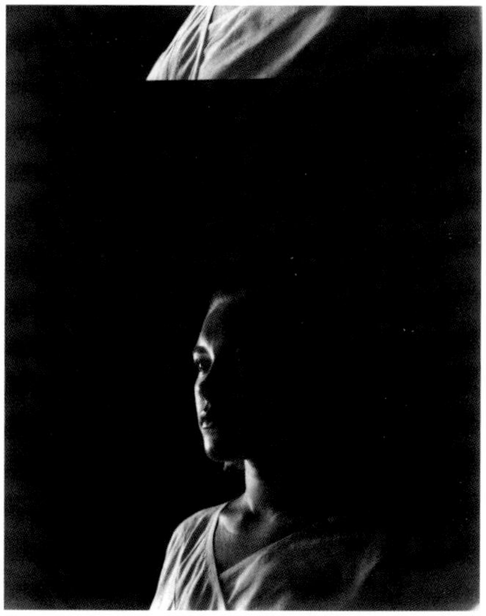

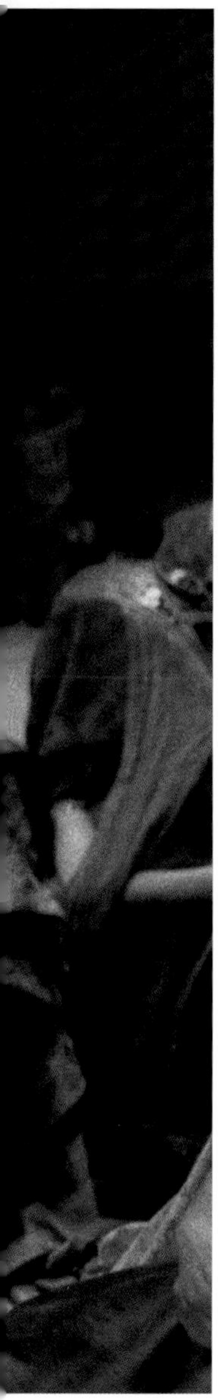

Where she looks matters. Even with a sparkling veil over her face, her eyes shine a mischief that's hidden by her soft orange laugh; always a laugh at the ready. A sun rises by a man lifting it over his head behind her, and her shimmer on this stage becomes its own performance, though she is unaware.

When Marilyn Monroe comes onto the silver screen for the first time you know immediately that she will rise like this sun on this stage until someone or something calls for it to stop. Like Marilyn, and even surrounded by the star-studded cast of *Dune*, you can feel her cells preparing for a thinner air, a higher ground: her talent becomes her.

She lies down between shots, splayed in her princess regalia. We are all tired, but she lies there without worry and her composure is one of easy royalty. I think with this character either rubbing off or being incarnate already, she's destined to a lava that nobody, eventually, will even dare approach.

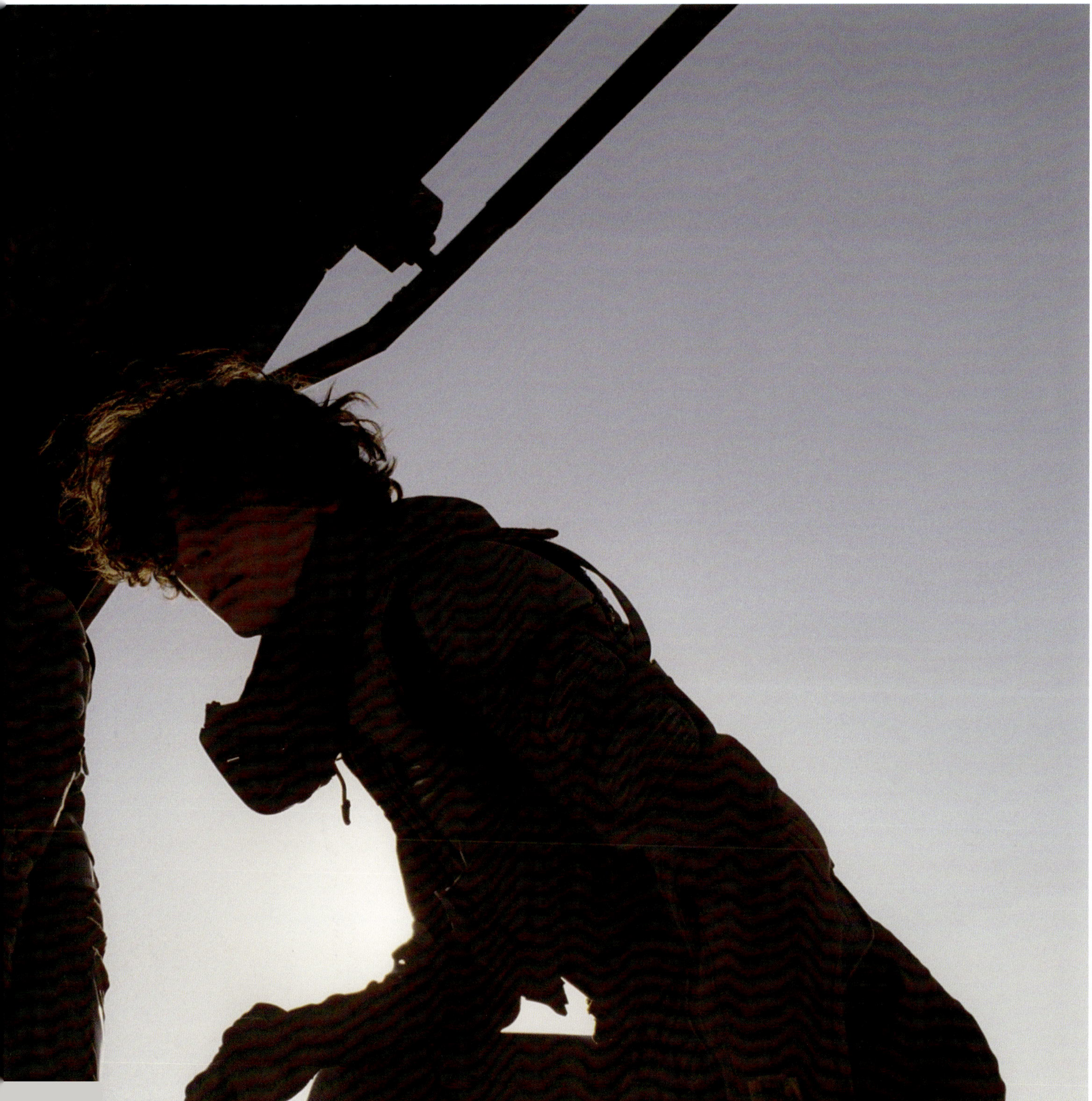

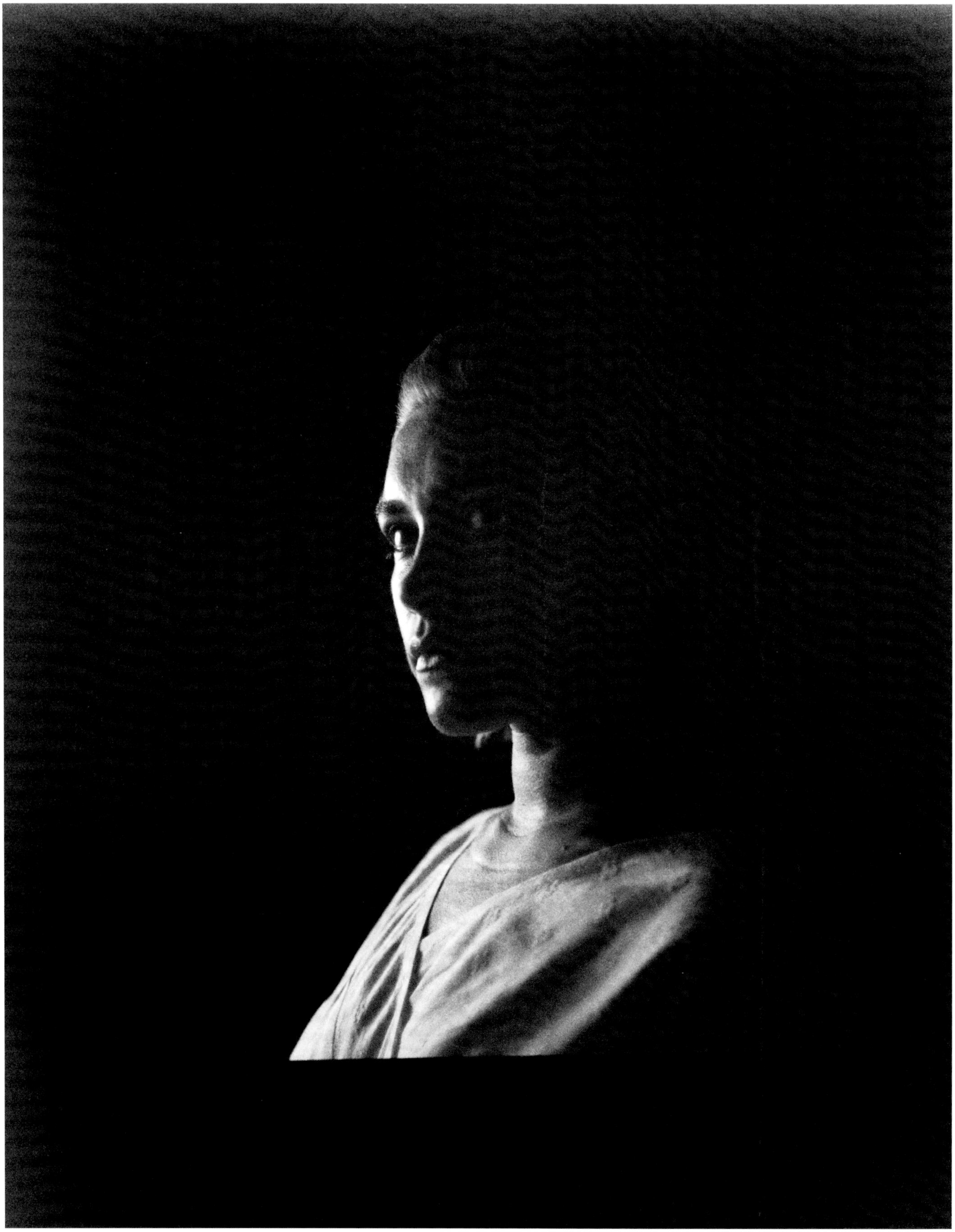

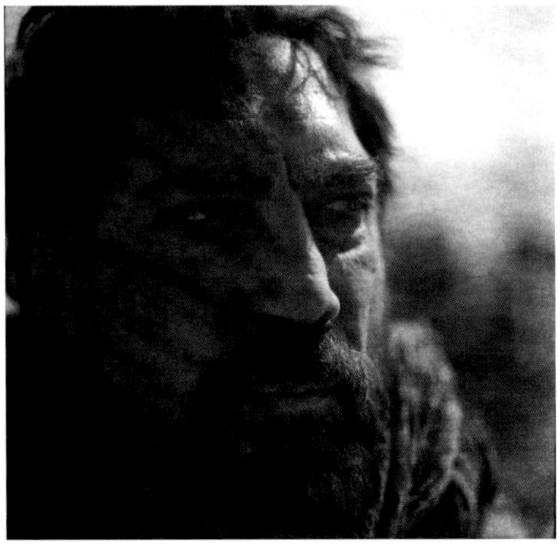
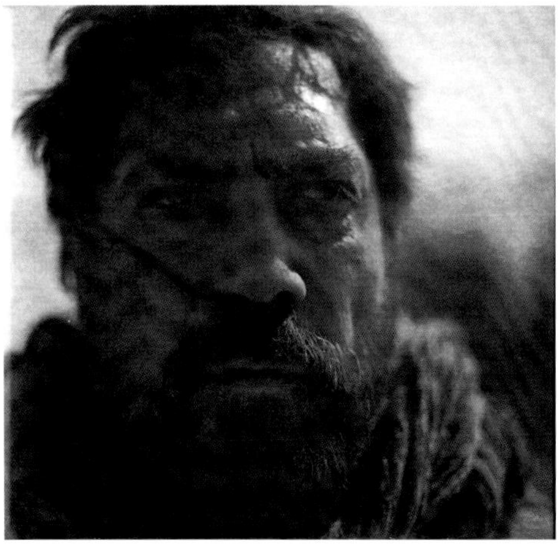
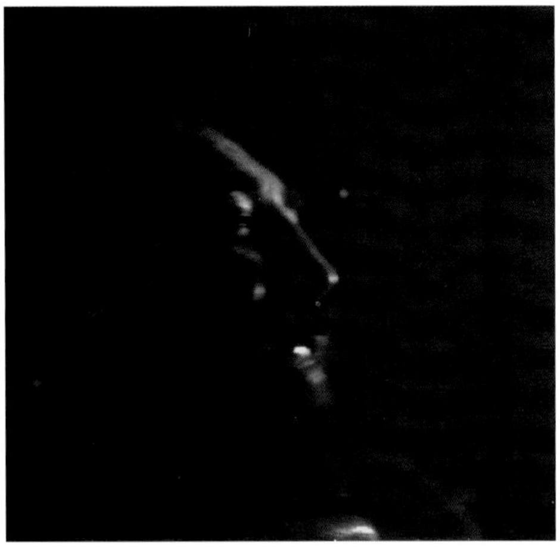
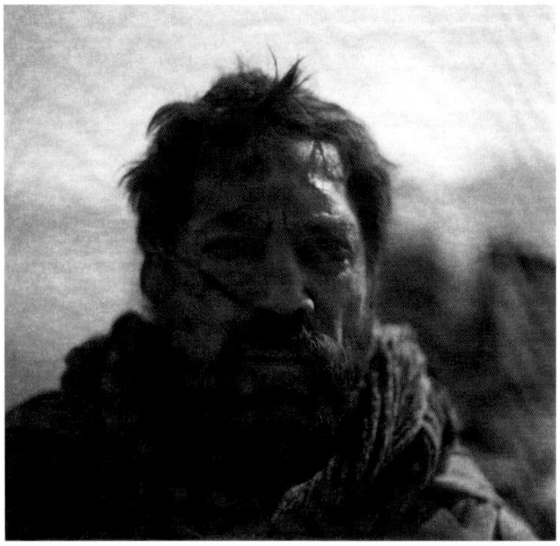
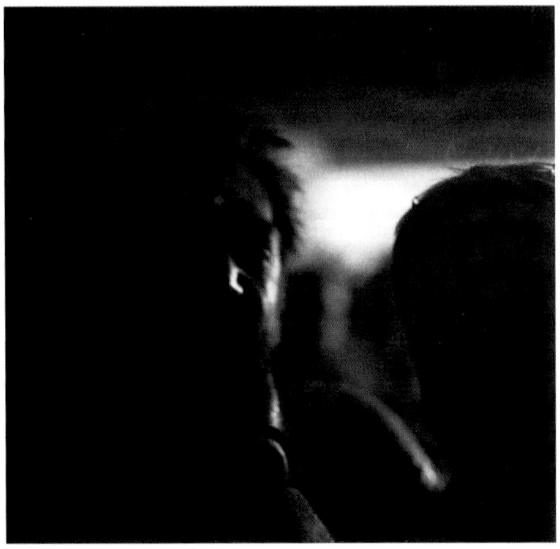
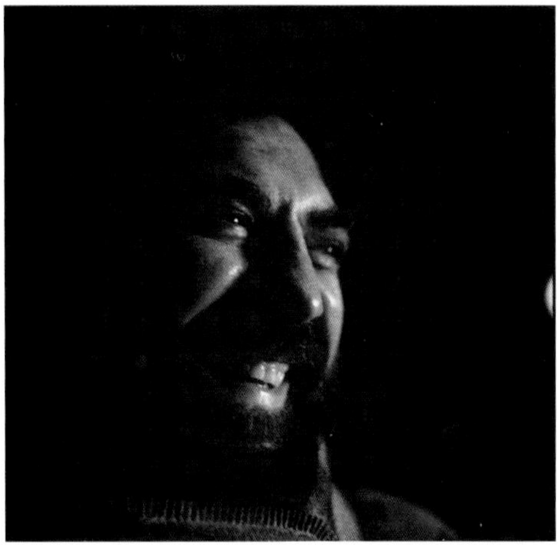

We play as resolve
dances between our laughter
of fragile living

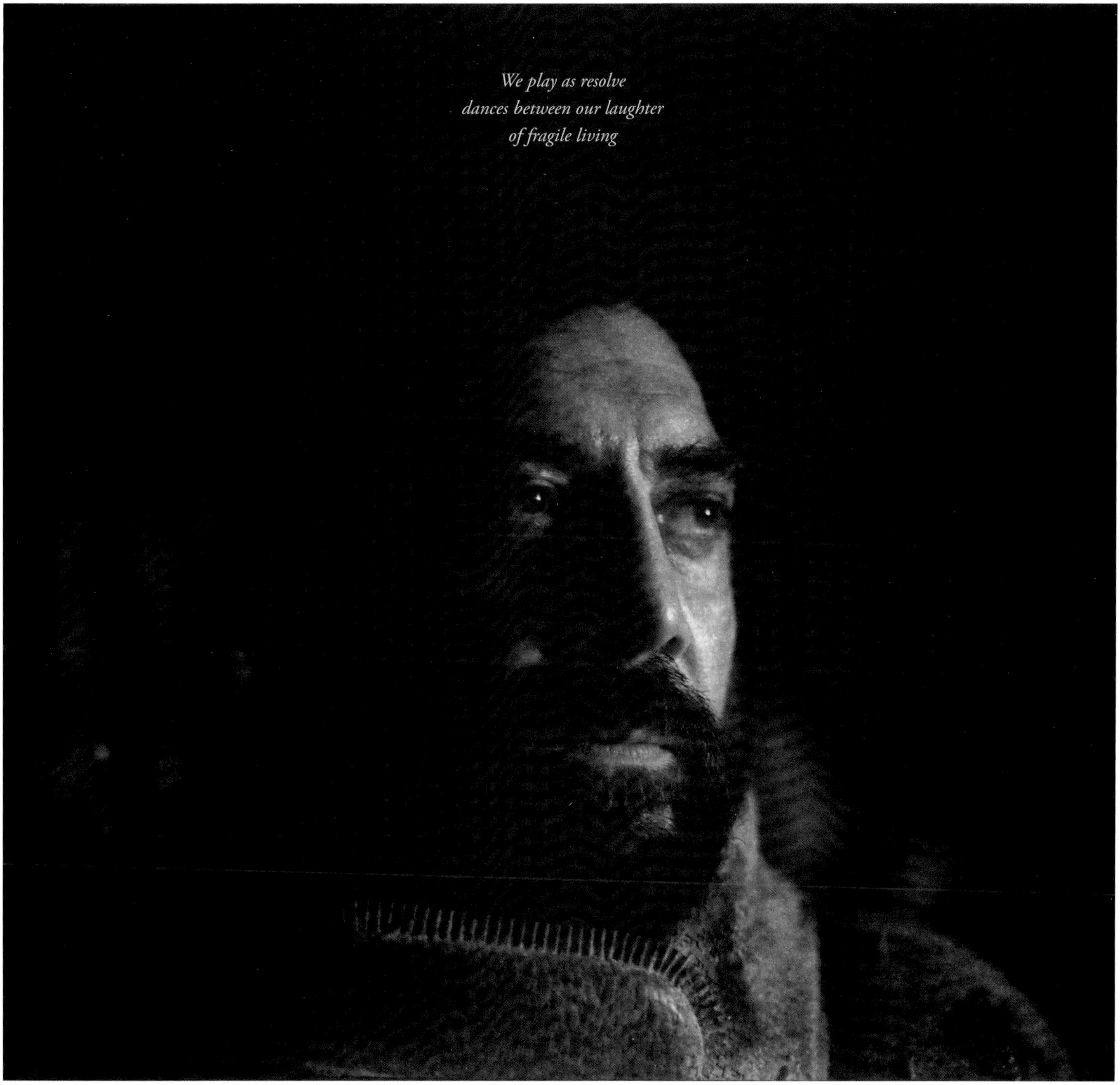

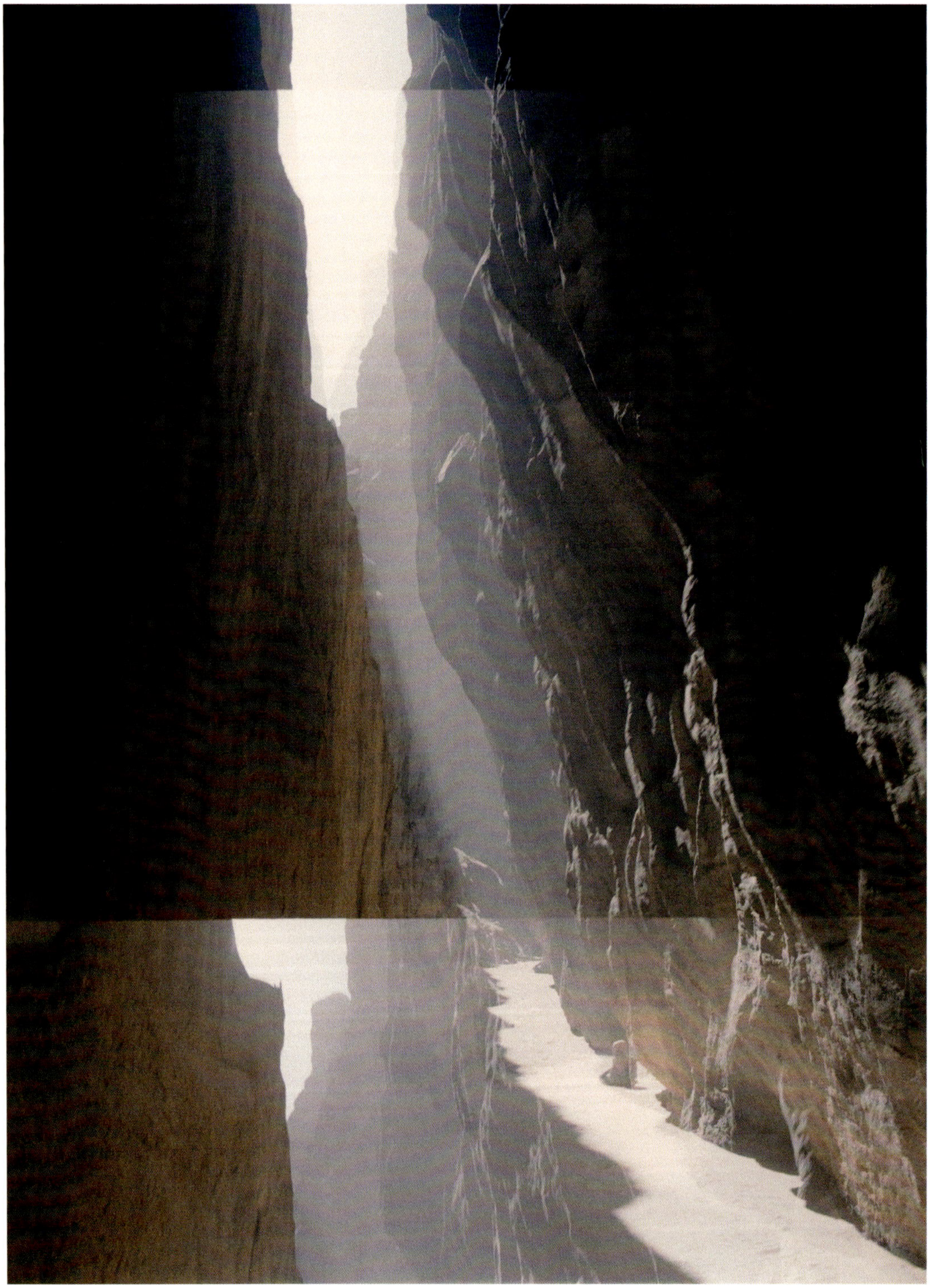

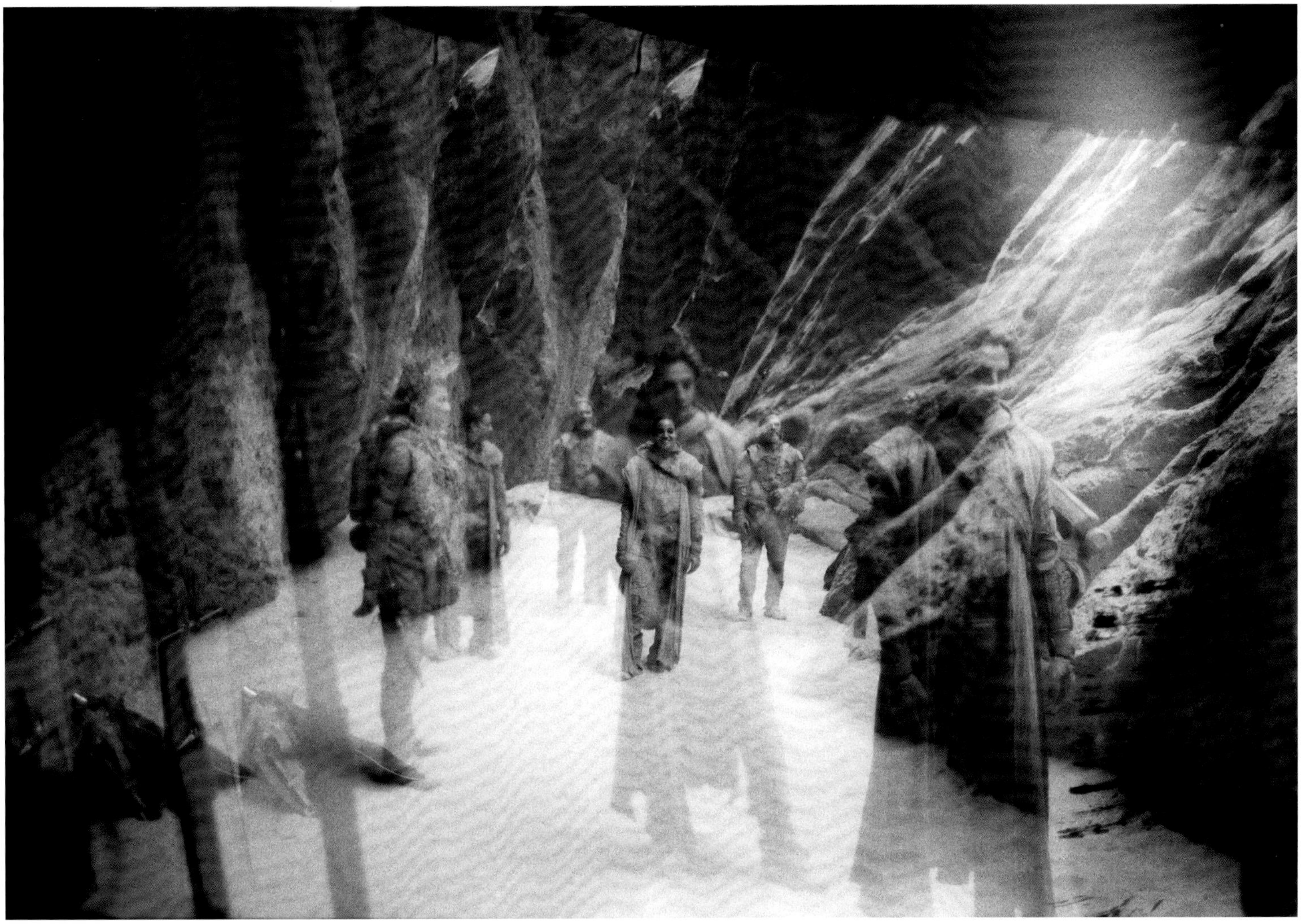

The progressives regress
into a safer prison
while they feel through thoughts
that now run through them
like vertical zoetropes
strobing images
that might never
know the random wild
of a kiss
planted firmly
if not

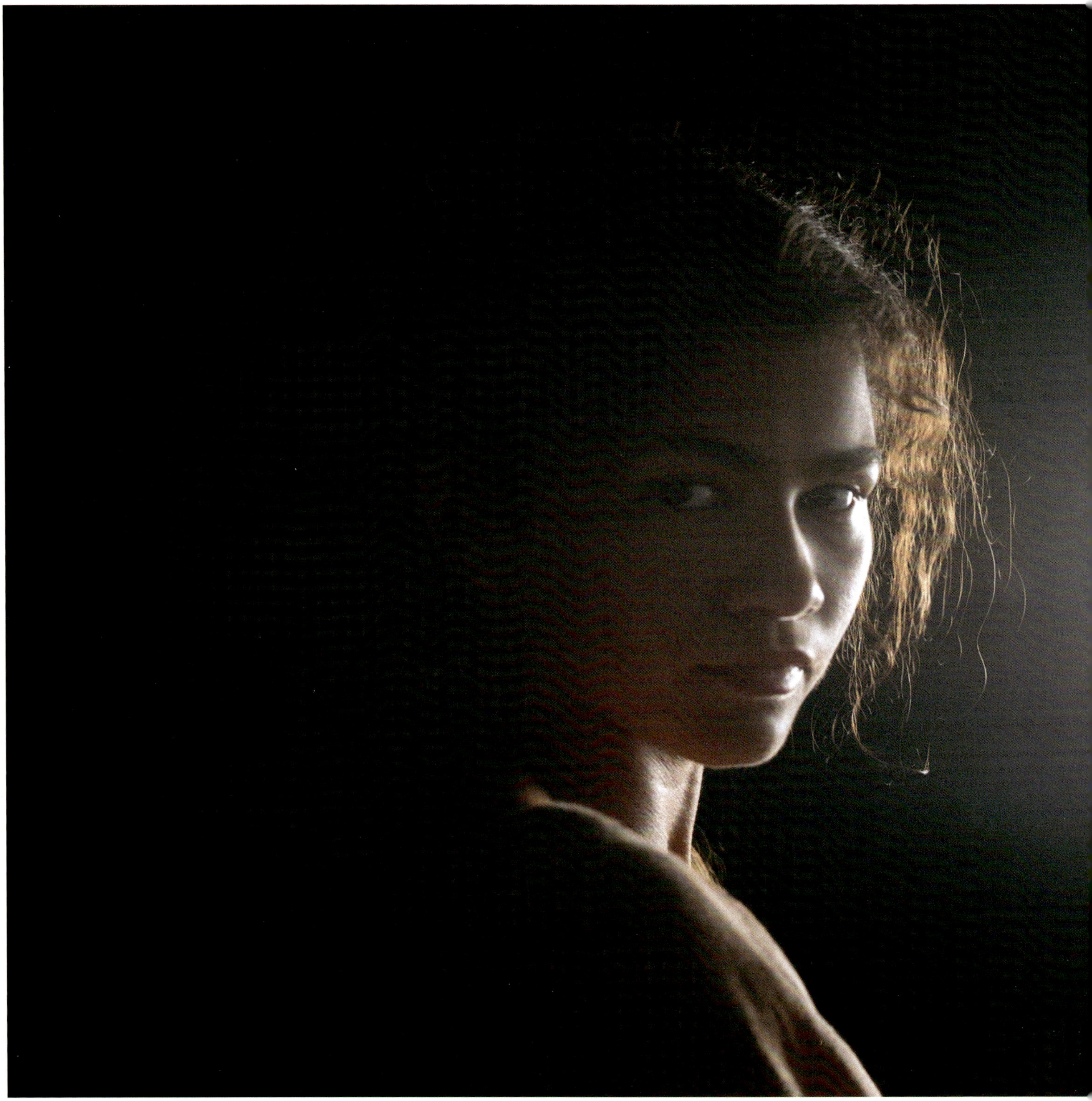

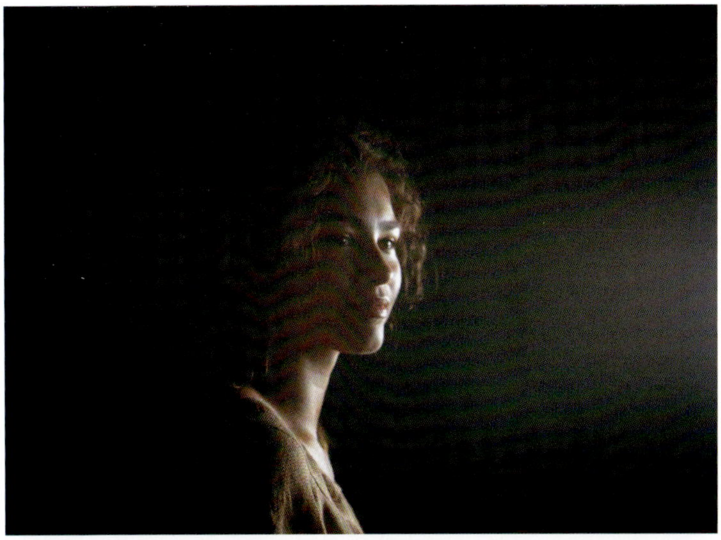

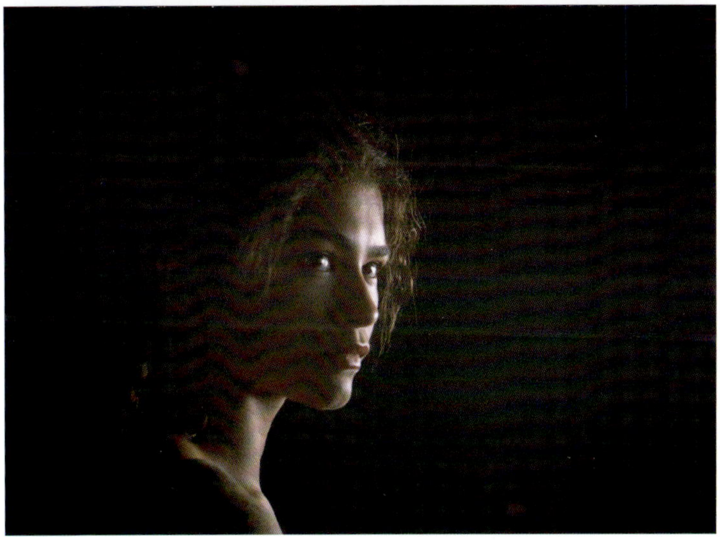

Electricity
has found residence inside
the whites of your eyes

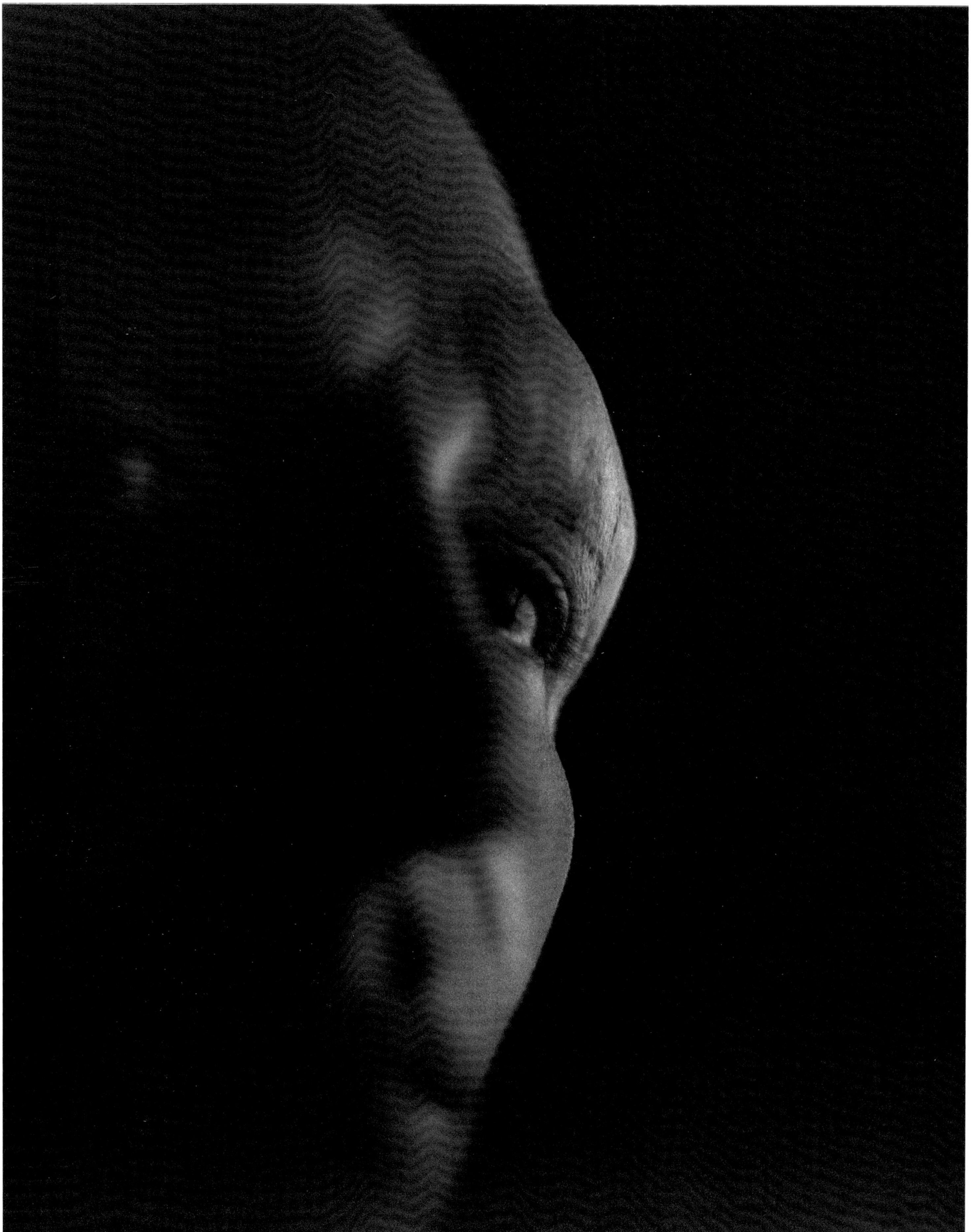

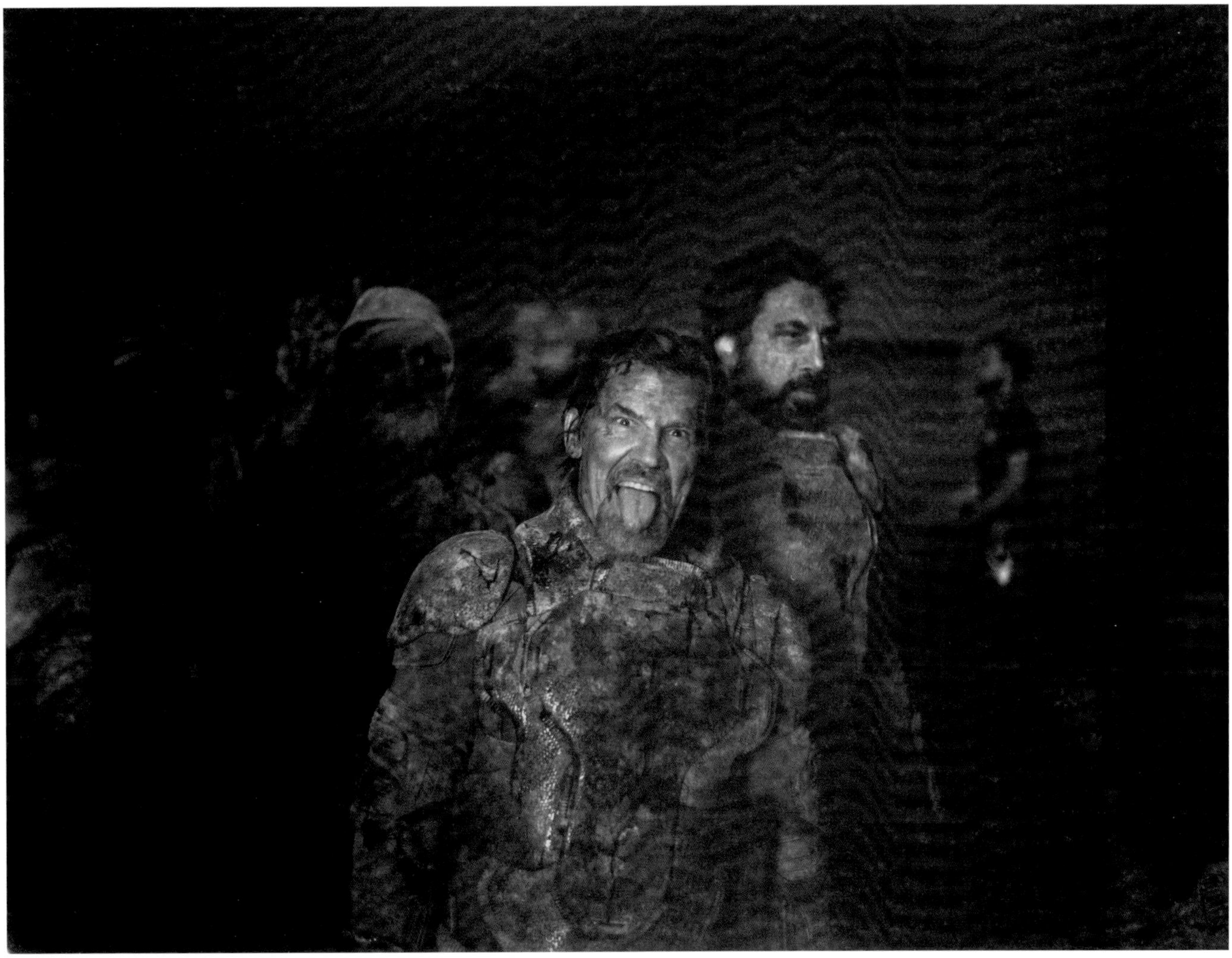

Dear Denis,

I have been trekking through the sand for months and I have lost at least four to five pounds of water weight each day. Can I sing my song now? The smuggling business is getting sharp and the sweat-drenched paper cuts are stinging wildly. I know you are shooting those things that need to be shot but if I might just sneak in for a bit, bellow or mumble a few verses I have been playing with along the cloudless red sun, my family in tow, my inspiration chafed and deadened with a sorrow that I miss the volley that is work—what is that volley that tosses and tosses until something pops in a tired, accomplished celebration of angel confetti.

Sincerely,

Gurney

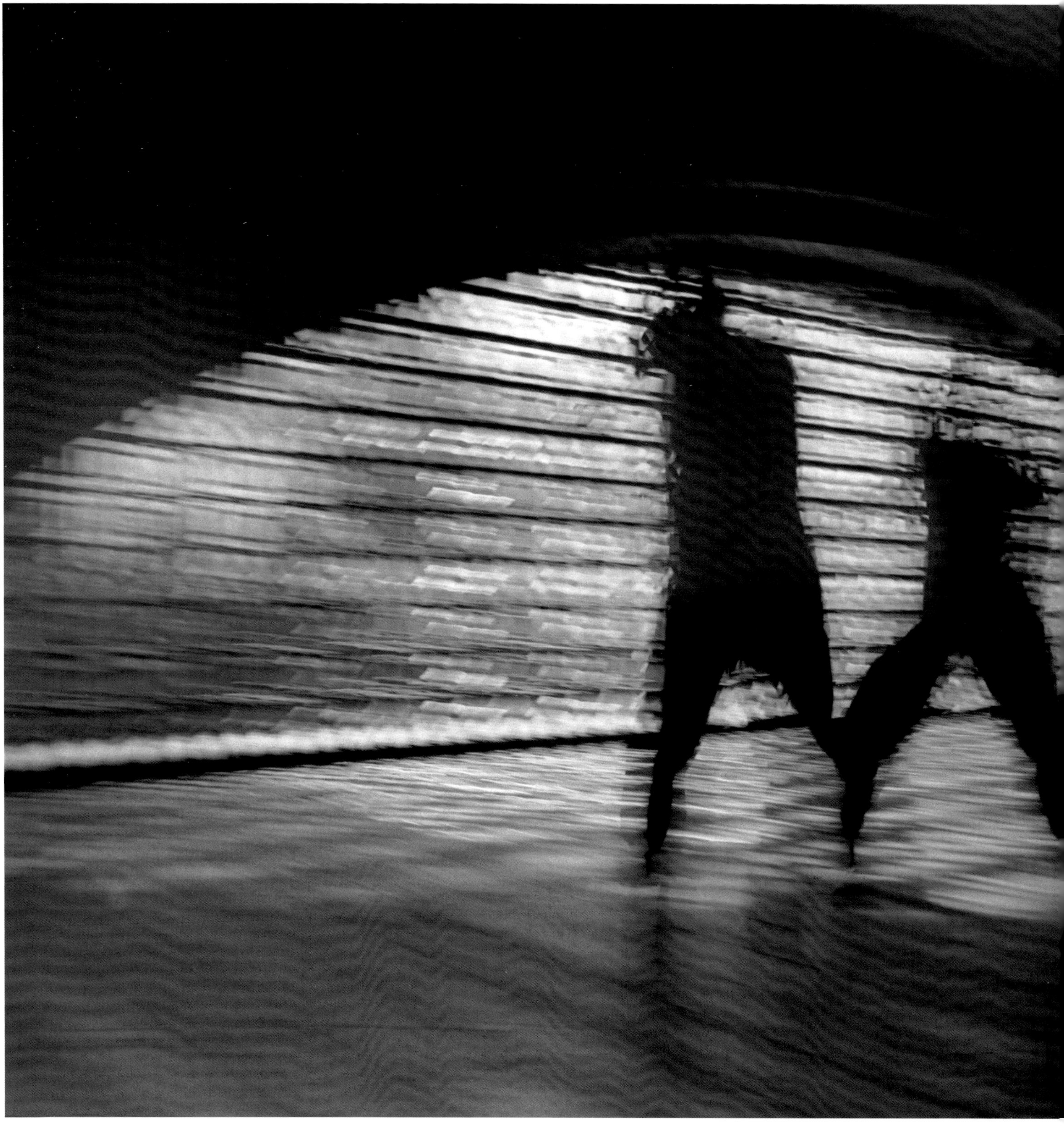

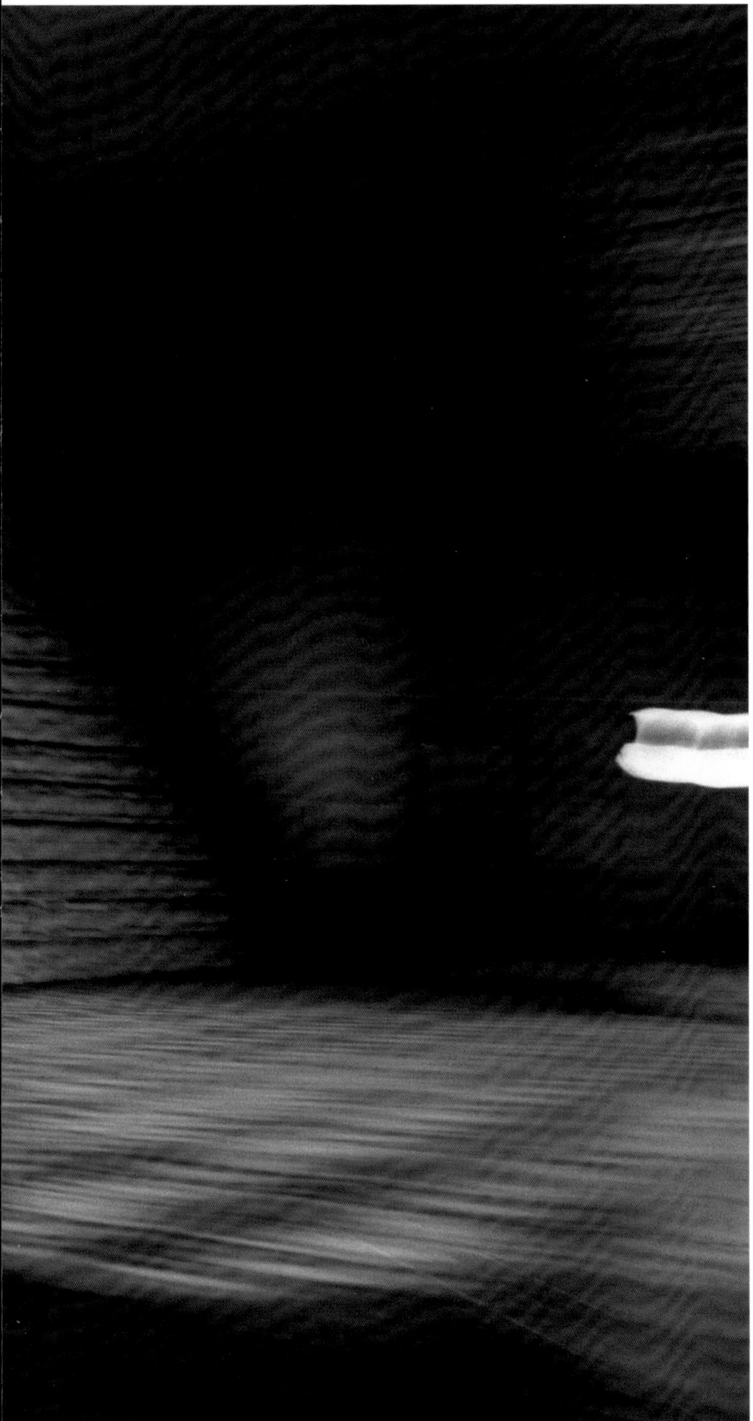

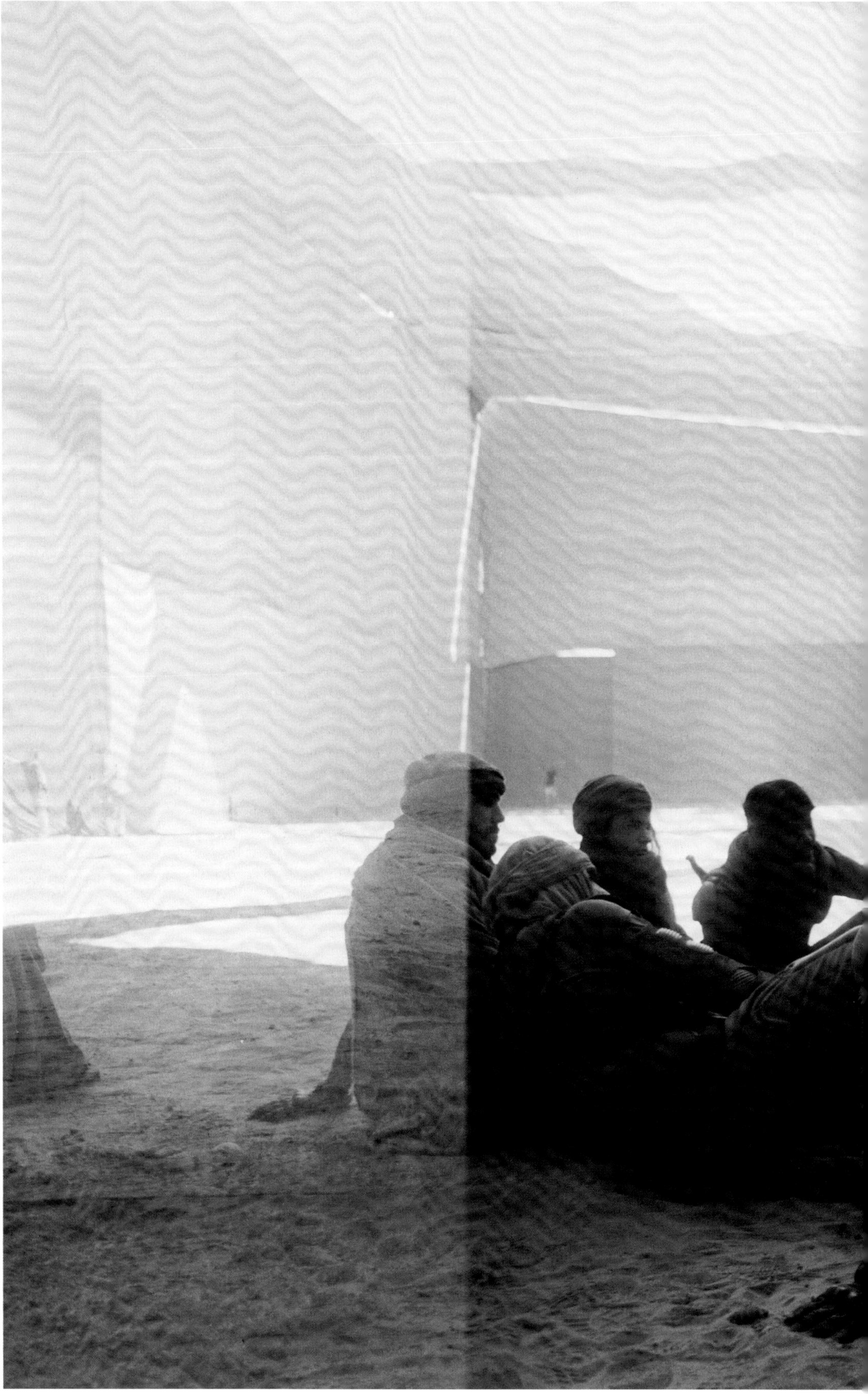

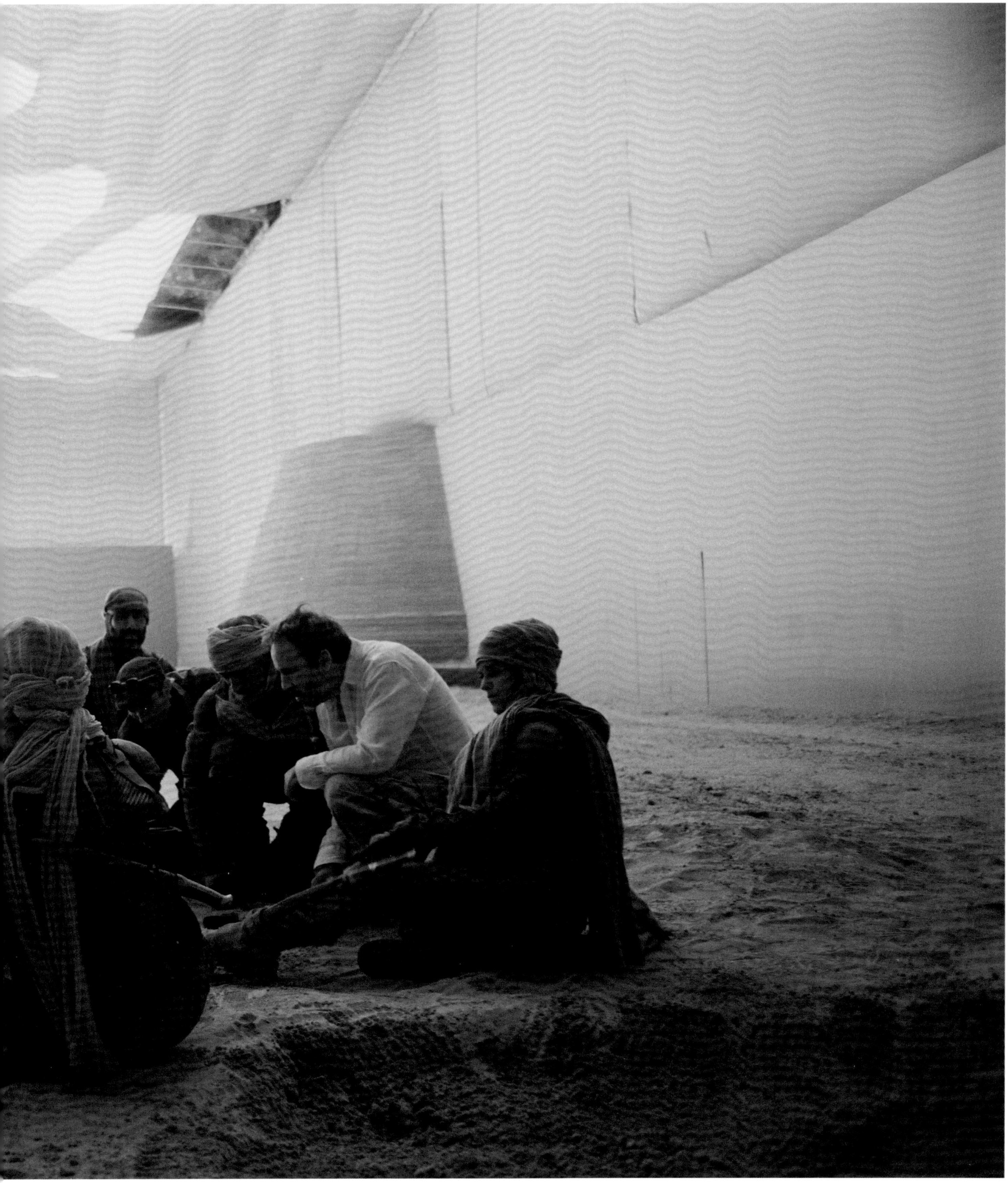

A set is like a war. You trained before you arrived, for the best and for the worst, but it's all played itself out in your mind, only in your mind, those synapses you relegate only to your imagination. Then you arrive and the electricity of reality sets in. You look at each other and start shooting words that have a foreign context because you've never met. People are staring in your face: makeup, script supervisor, DP, craft service asking if you'd like something to eat. The director waves you over and immediately walks into a dark corner of the stage so that he or she can have a private moment with you. You feel, always, as if you are in trouble or as if you are about to be sent on a mission that nobody else would agree to and you're the sucker who said you'd do it for the cause. Your nerves are exposed and raw. You're running 220 in a body that is comfortable at 120. You're a professional at acting as if every organ in your body is at ease, and that this is your greatest state of comfort. You sleep four or five hours a night, and run through dialogues in your head all day long, sometimes dialogues that are weeks away from being spoken, and it feels as if your brain is perpetually chapped and slightly bleeding.

If you drink you get obliterated in the foreign country you are filming in and the owner of the place protects you from being noticed or leaving at an ungodly hour in a blackout and getting in trouble. You wake up in the morning in someone's bed. She still has her wardrobe on from the day before: I think I remember she's playing someone who has something to do with spice, but I can't remember right now.

All this plays out in your mind (yes, you are back in your mind) as you exit the flight that flew you to the city that you'll be in for the next four months. You've been here before, you think. You get to your hotel and there is a manila envelope waiting on the small, plastic desk in your lavender-aerosoled room. You open it and look at the cast and crew list searching for anyone you might have worked with before, a name that might bring some comfort, but the minute you recognize the name you wish you didn't have to see them. There's no reason for it. It just is.

You lie on your bed and you pretend like you've always lived there and that this is just another day. You order a drink and an ice cream from room service. By the time morning hits, you've gone through the whole mini refrigerator of alcohol. The phone rings. You lean to pick it up, clearing your throat before you do. You say hello in a sexy whisper, a slight rasp. And on the other end of the line is an automated message telling you about the Continental breakfast that is for free from 7 a.m. until 10 a.m. every day that you'll be staying here. Every single day.

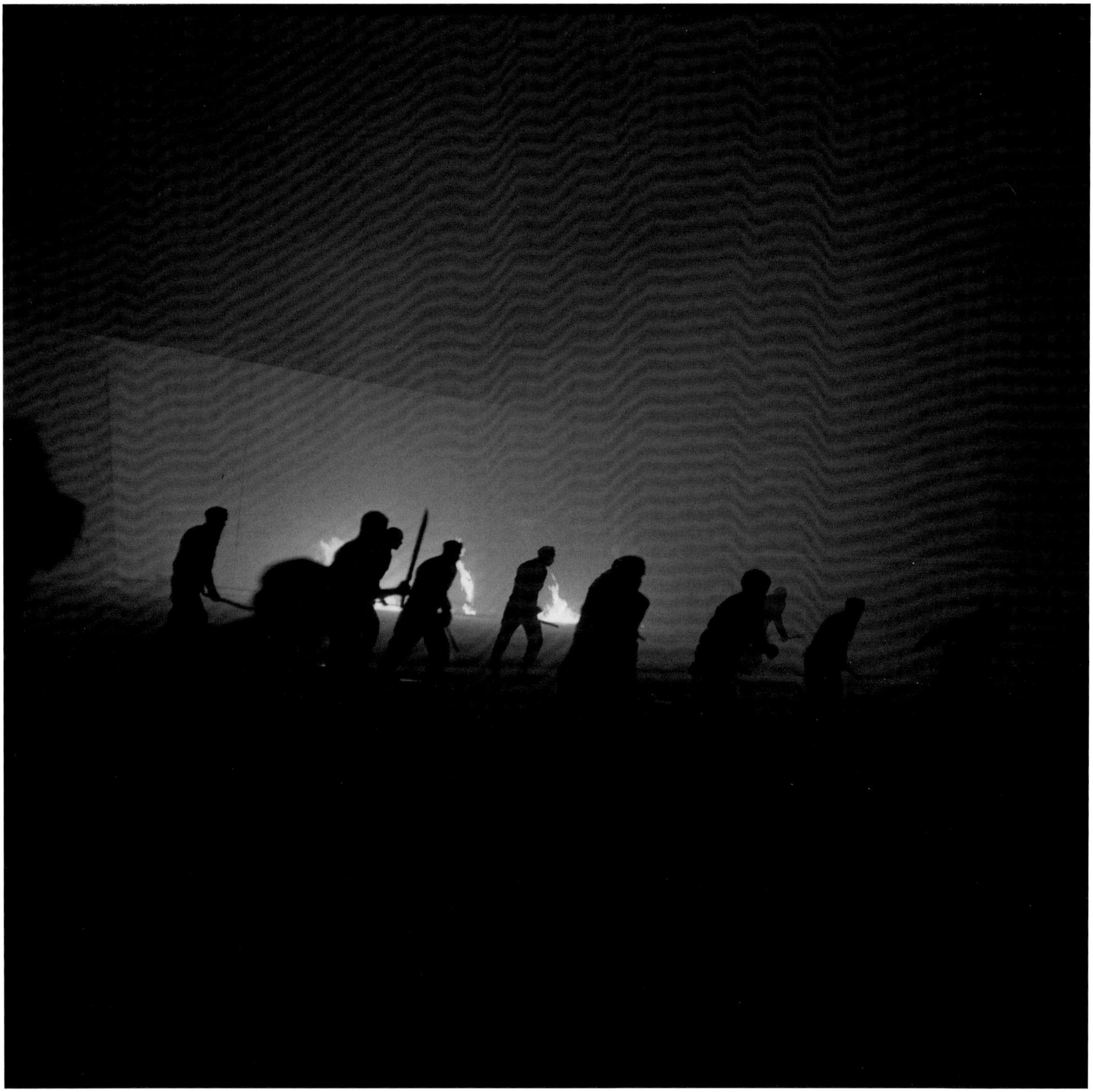

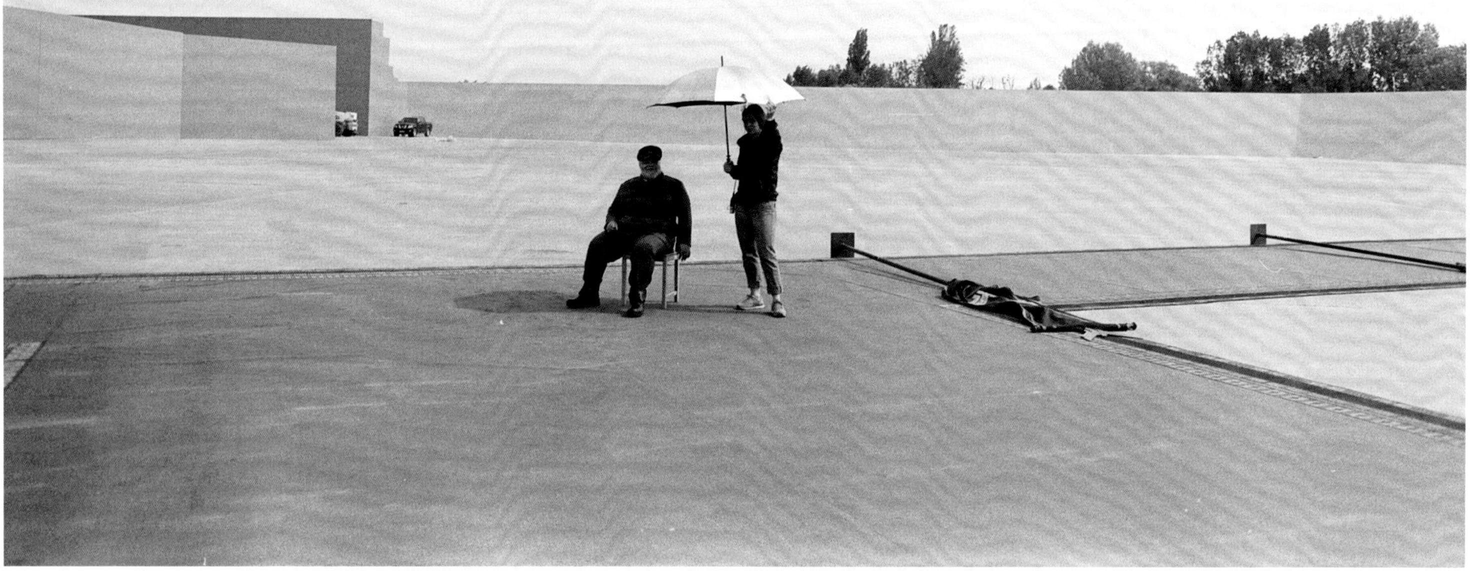

The few clouds in the sky aren't part of the set dressing. Neither is the sweat that comes free with the job. Shade can only be found by finding rock, and rock doesn't exist out here. Once in a while an umbrella shows up with someone holding it, but the shade of the umbrella ends up on the person holding it. They can't help it. It's survival of the fittest.

There are men buried in the sand. You can't see them, for they lie in a hole that was dug for them. They linger in those holes longer than anyone alive should. I will walk the sand as difficultly as it might be to walk on the moon and eventually will reach those buried men and women.

They will suddenly grow out of the sand as if they are being born on a time lapse, and they will run toward me with swords at the ready, covered with the sweat that is theirs. I will forget there is a camera behind me, and I will fight within the choreography I have learned, but that too I will forget about at some point, and for a moment I will be fighting on a planet that I was placed on against my will, as I travel with miscreants in a harvester that's much bigger than the Dodge truck I have at home. There will be a moment when all the red or beige runners laid under the flashing bulbs and bulbous protruding microphone heads will free-fall into an oblivion, and I will be fighting the fight of my life. Just for a moment, it will be real, all this silliness, and I will be eight years old headlong into a book that is transporting me into a world that I will find my feet on, as if I am really there: a different man, a different cellular development, on a sabbatical from my life with these parents, these chores, and the bully at school who never lets up.

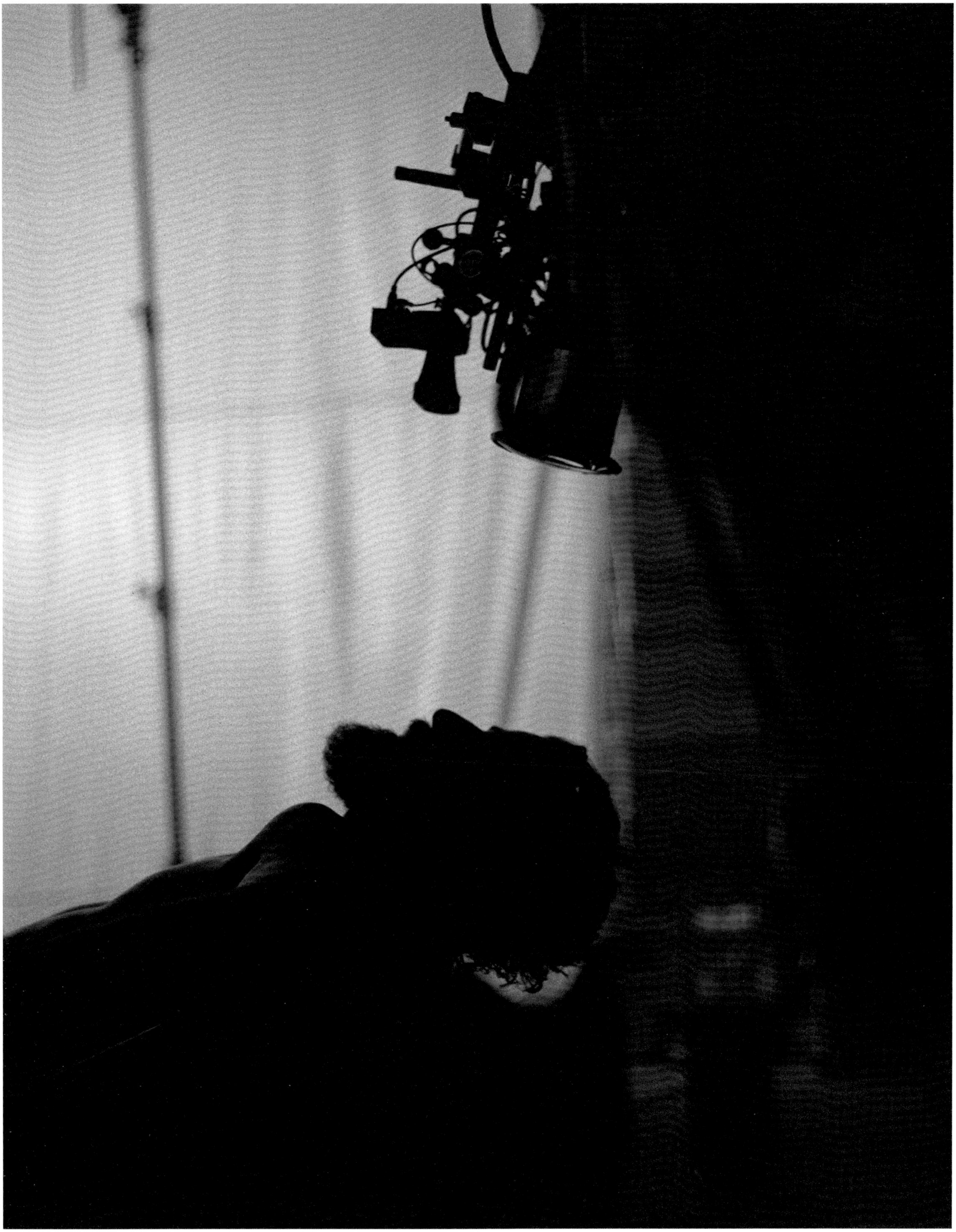

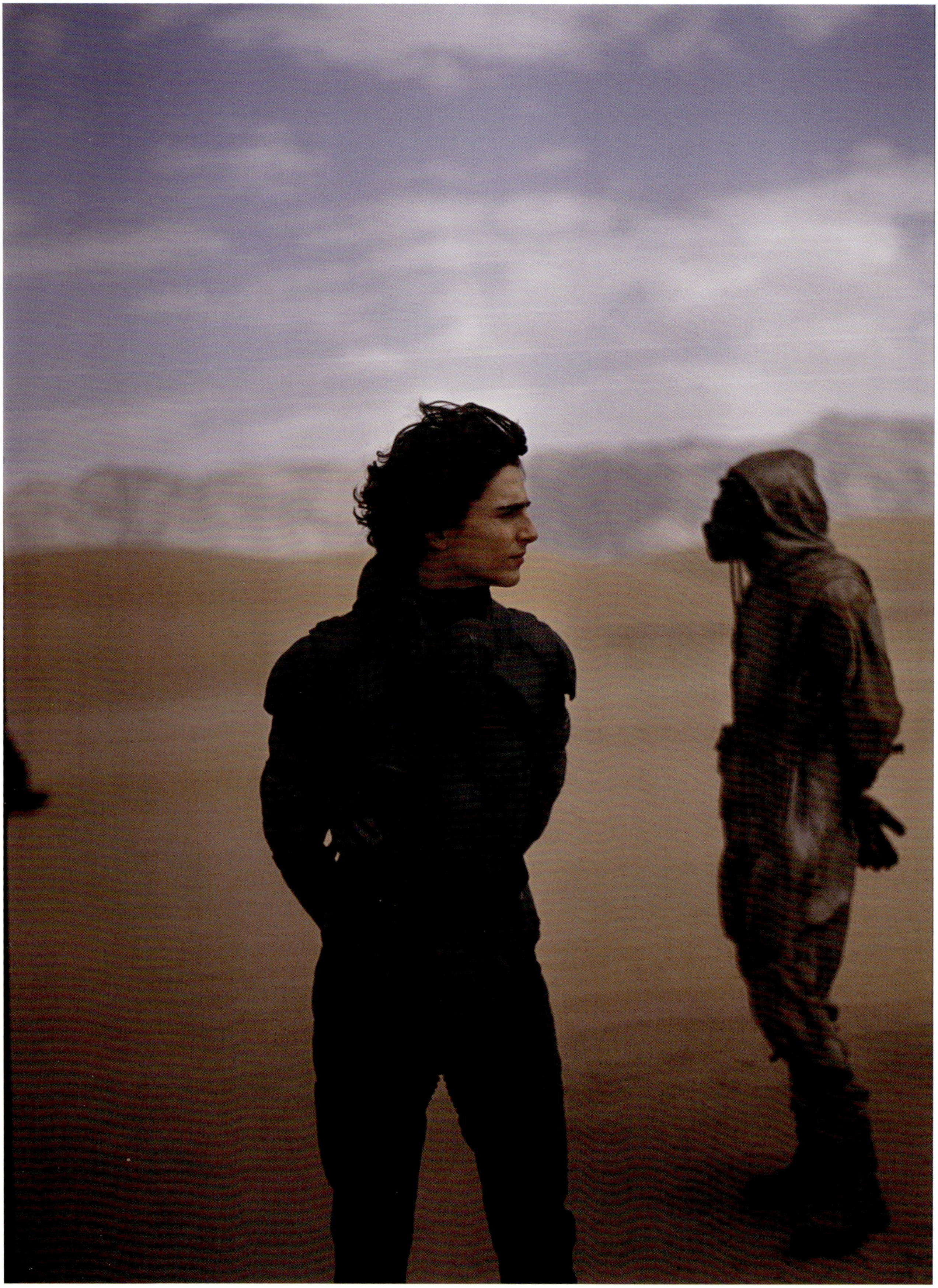

There is a wind today.
It's coming from the west.

Winter's last and spring surprises
but the wind suggests a warning
for something later, something
that might need to be prepared for:
an ominous air whispers to be heard.

Things will be falling, it's trying
to say; either that or trickling.

There will be people struggling
and there will be laughter,
but only from children, playfully
high-pitched.

And it will be far off,
so with the wind, you might be
able to hear it: the faint laughter
of children with what might be
rain falling on them.

The sounds of anything else
will most probably be muffled by the
struggle of other things that have
nothing to do with children
or wind or, especially, laughter
and/or rain.

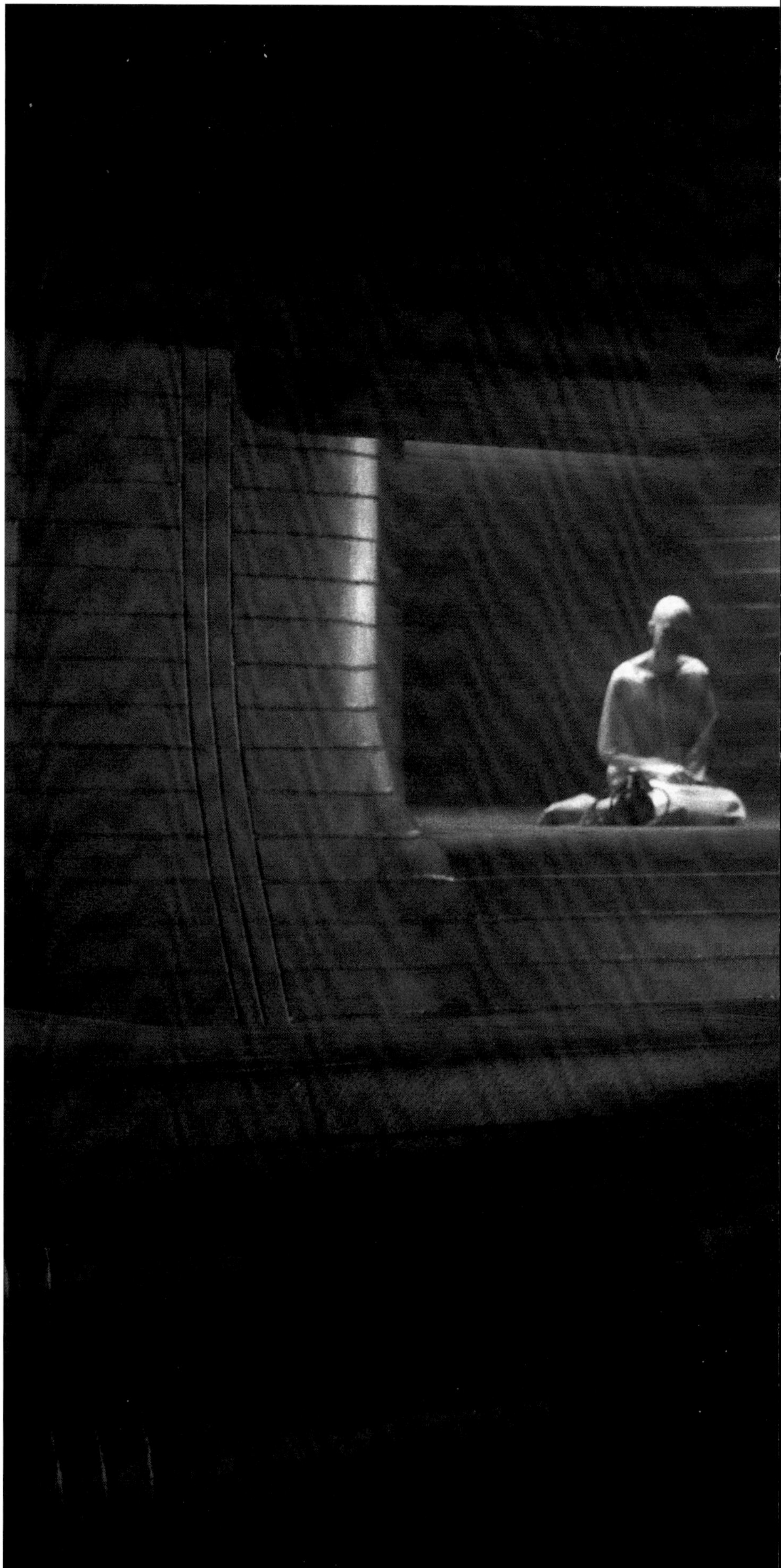

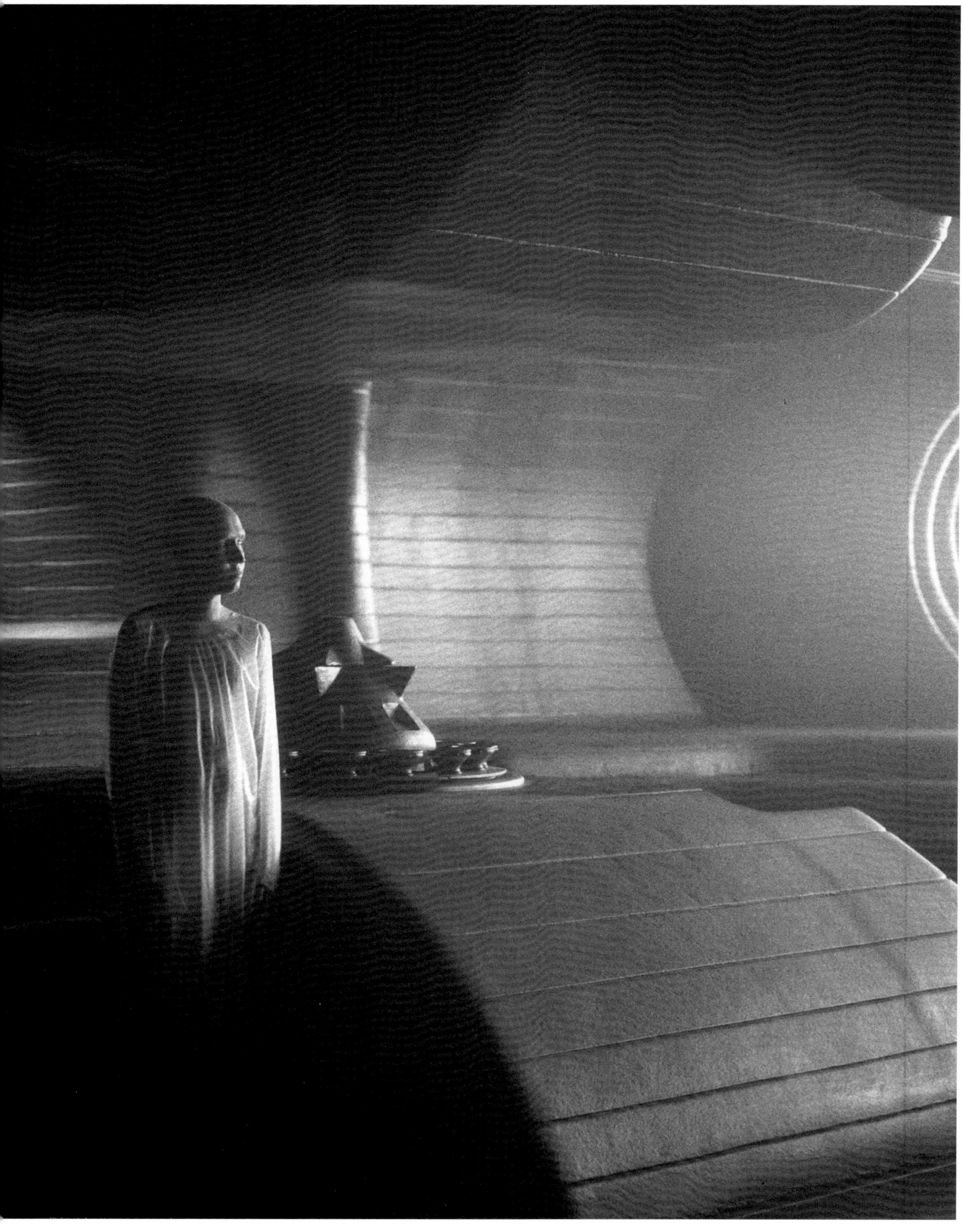

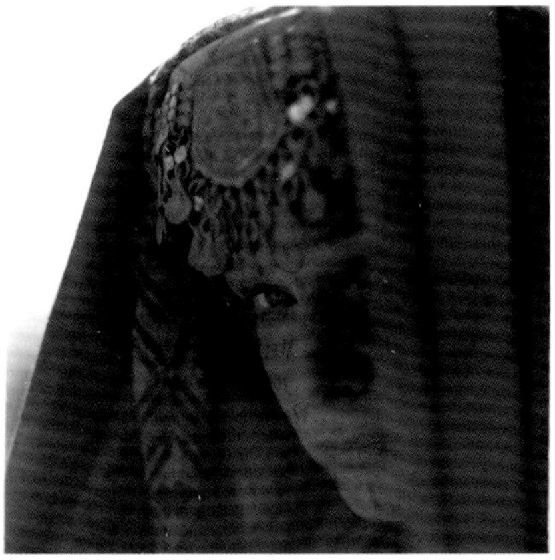

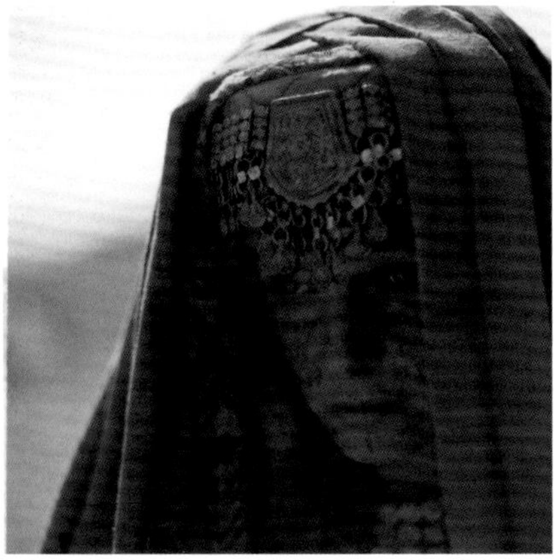
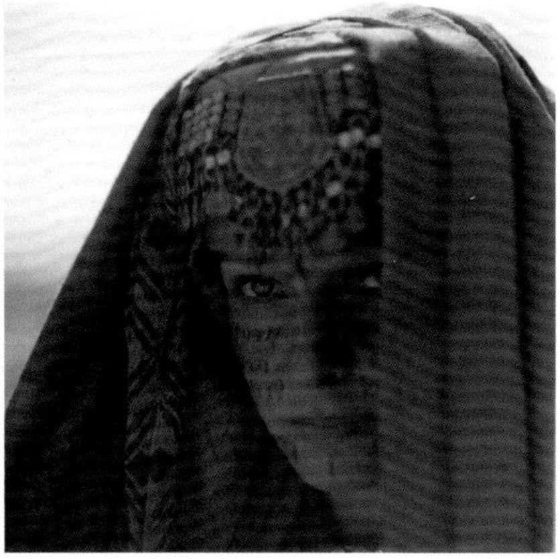

Paint me with the blackest ink. Turn my albino skin
into a mythology. Tell my story for generations to come,
if we, indeed, dare to arrive there. Sit down with your
grandchildren and illustrate for them the tale of those
swathed in bible—night black; the one who reached for the
moon and attained it. The glory sought and the glory won.
Touch me with your minion claws and mix my blood
with sand with ink with spit and rub it hard into my skin
until it becomes me. I have arrived. For today is my day,
a day others will but collapse into, devoted.

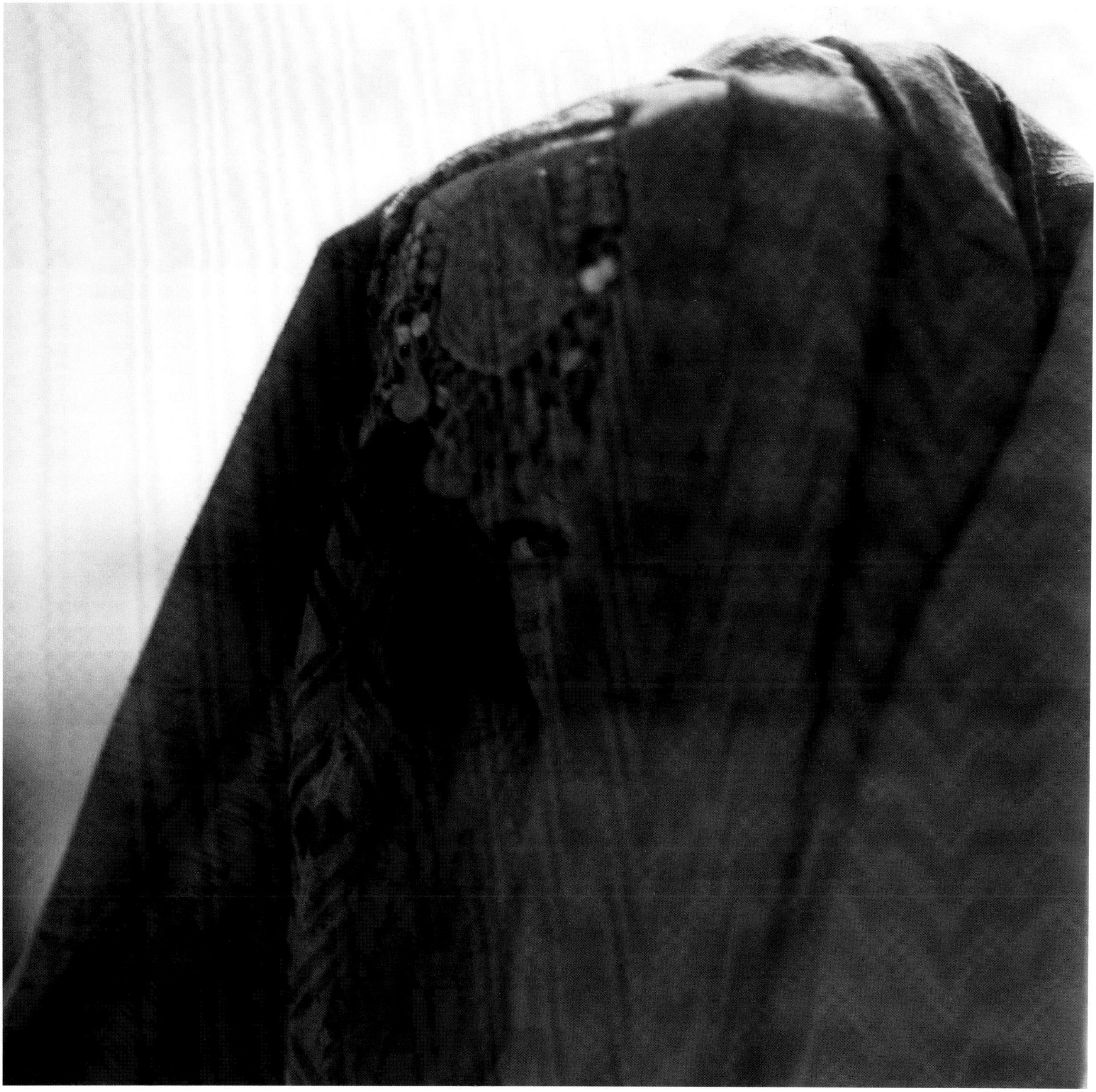

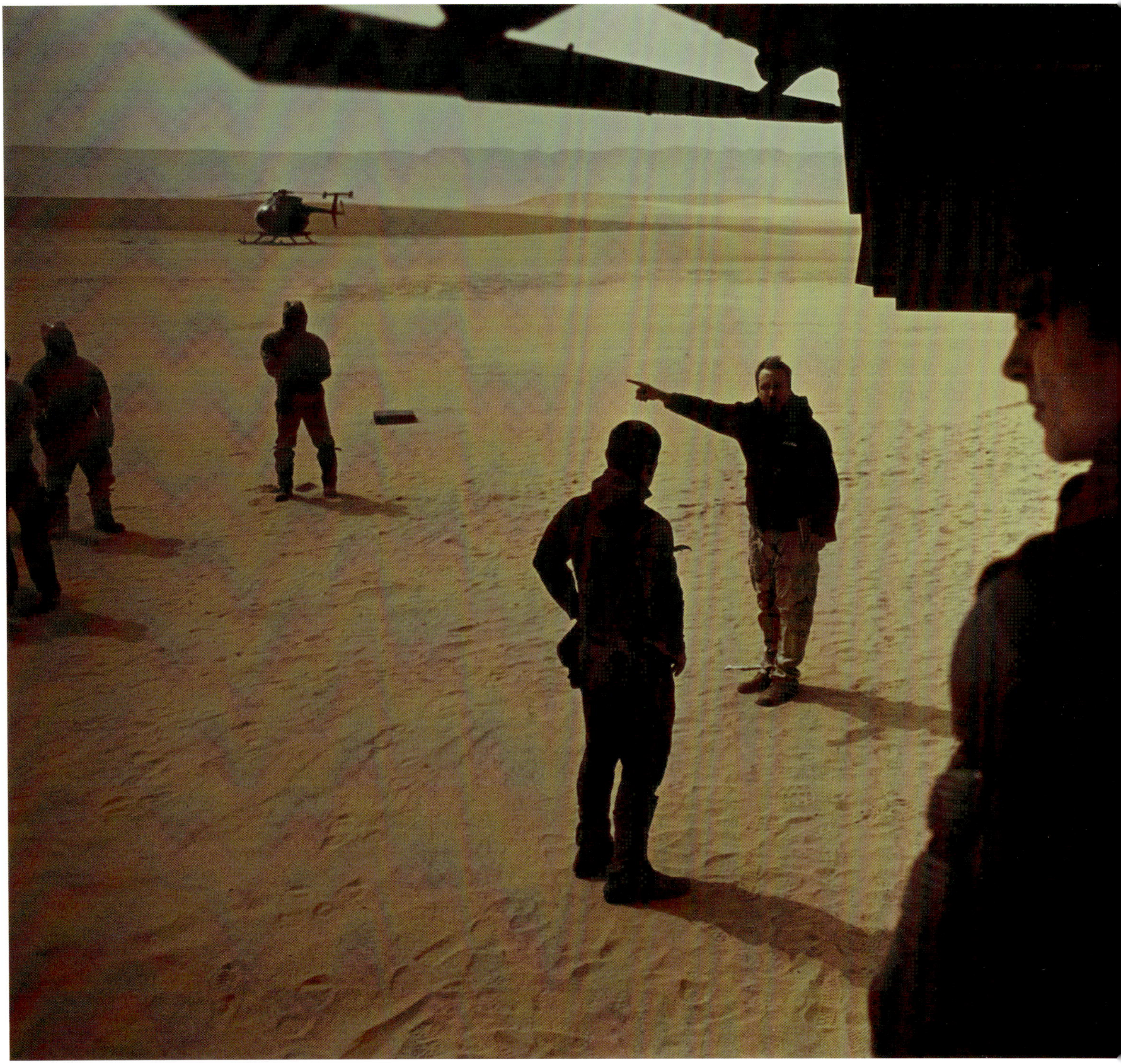

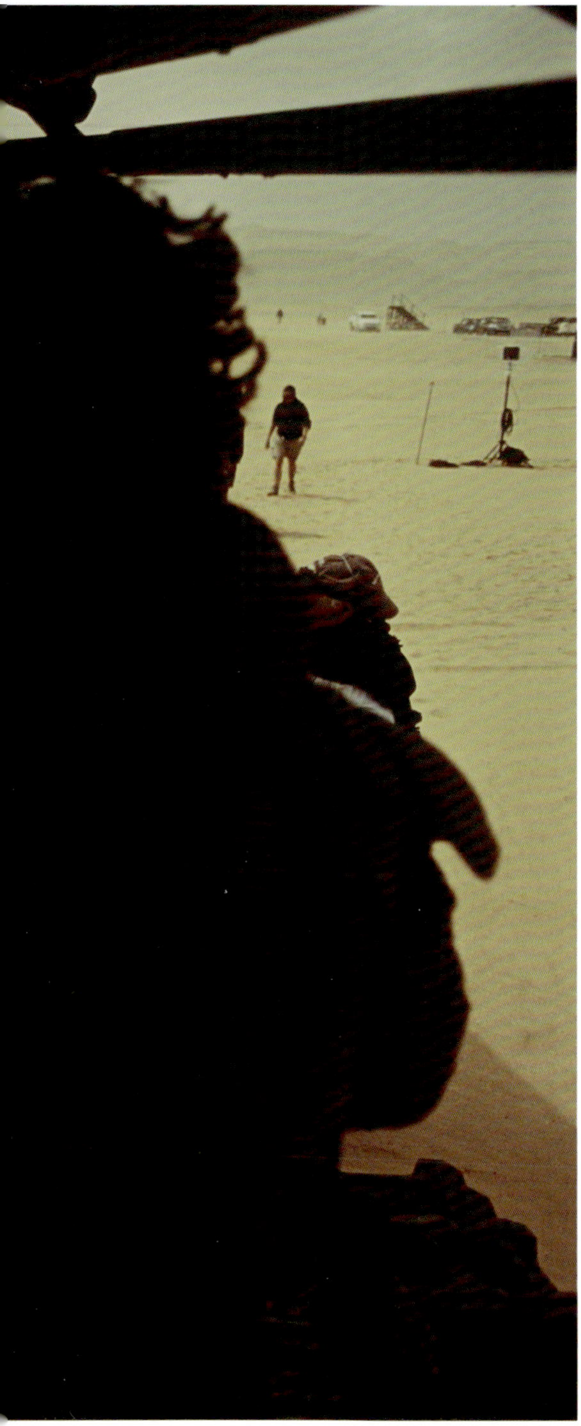

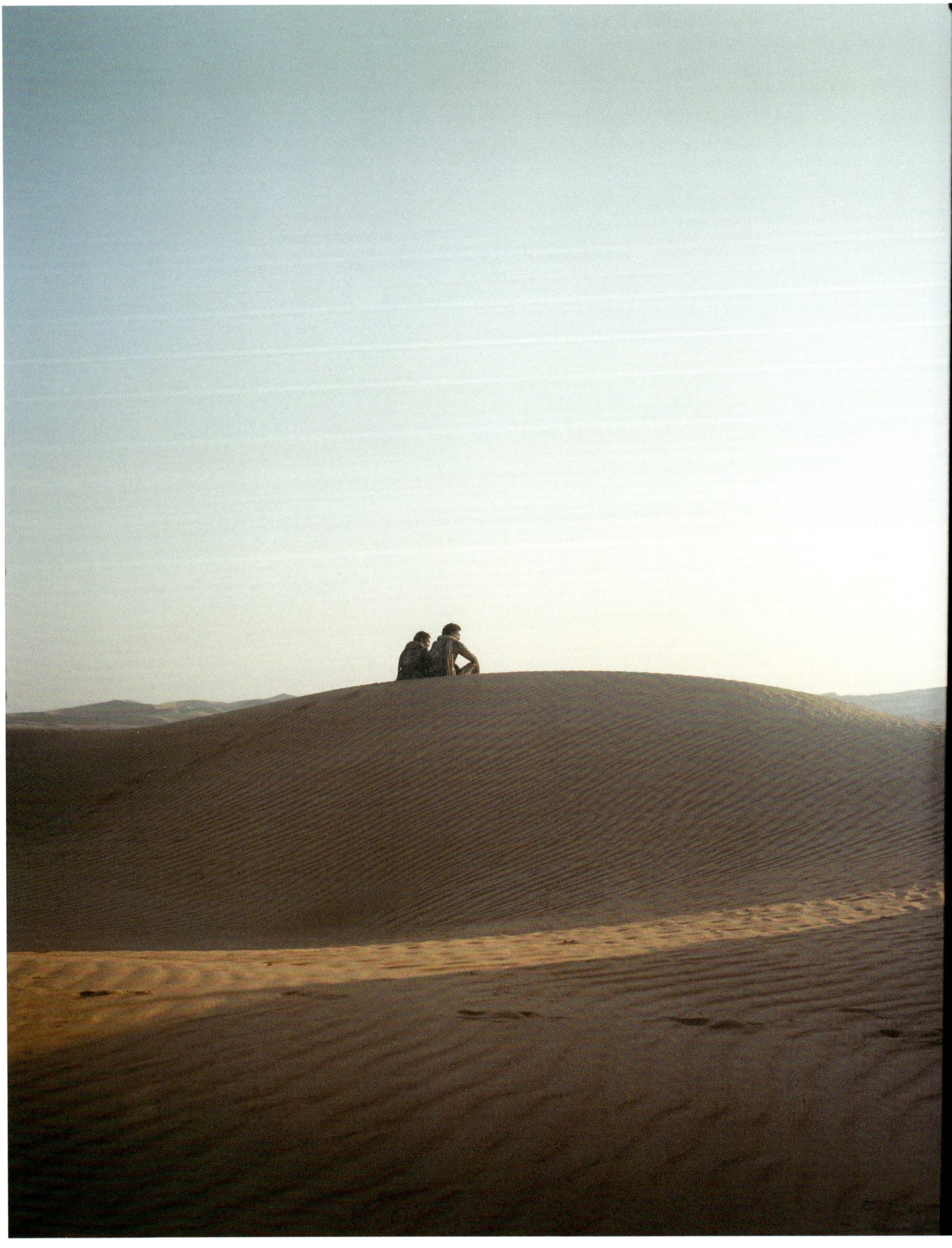

When you look into me
a mirage whispers
all the Royal you
want me to be

There's

nothing I've ever done
to accumulate
your wealth

So, as I fight through the
raging swells of
my convictions
and facades
there continues to live
the soft pressure
of your dark blue
infinity

untouched

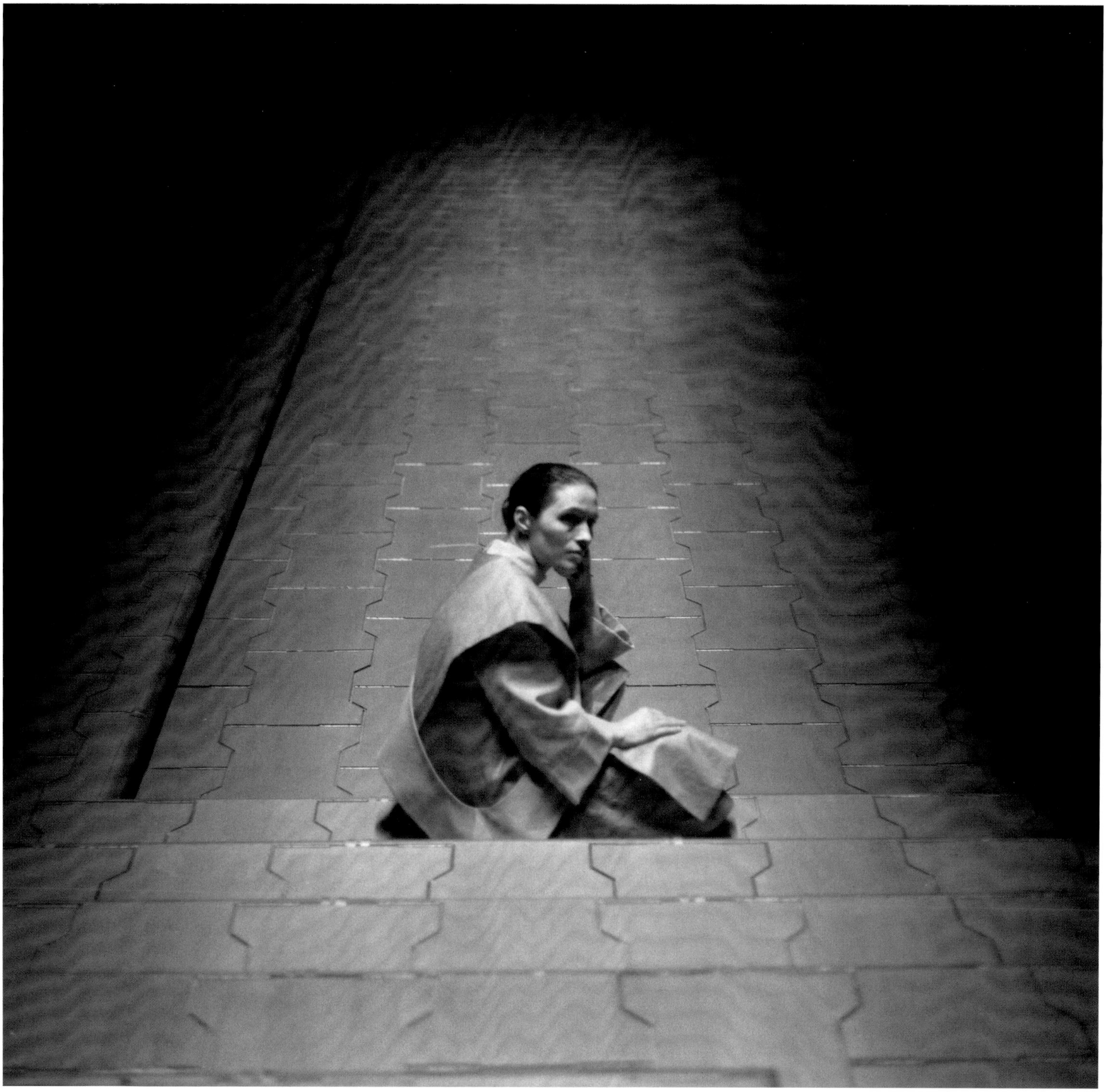

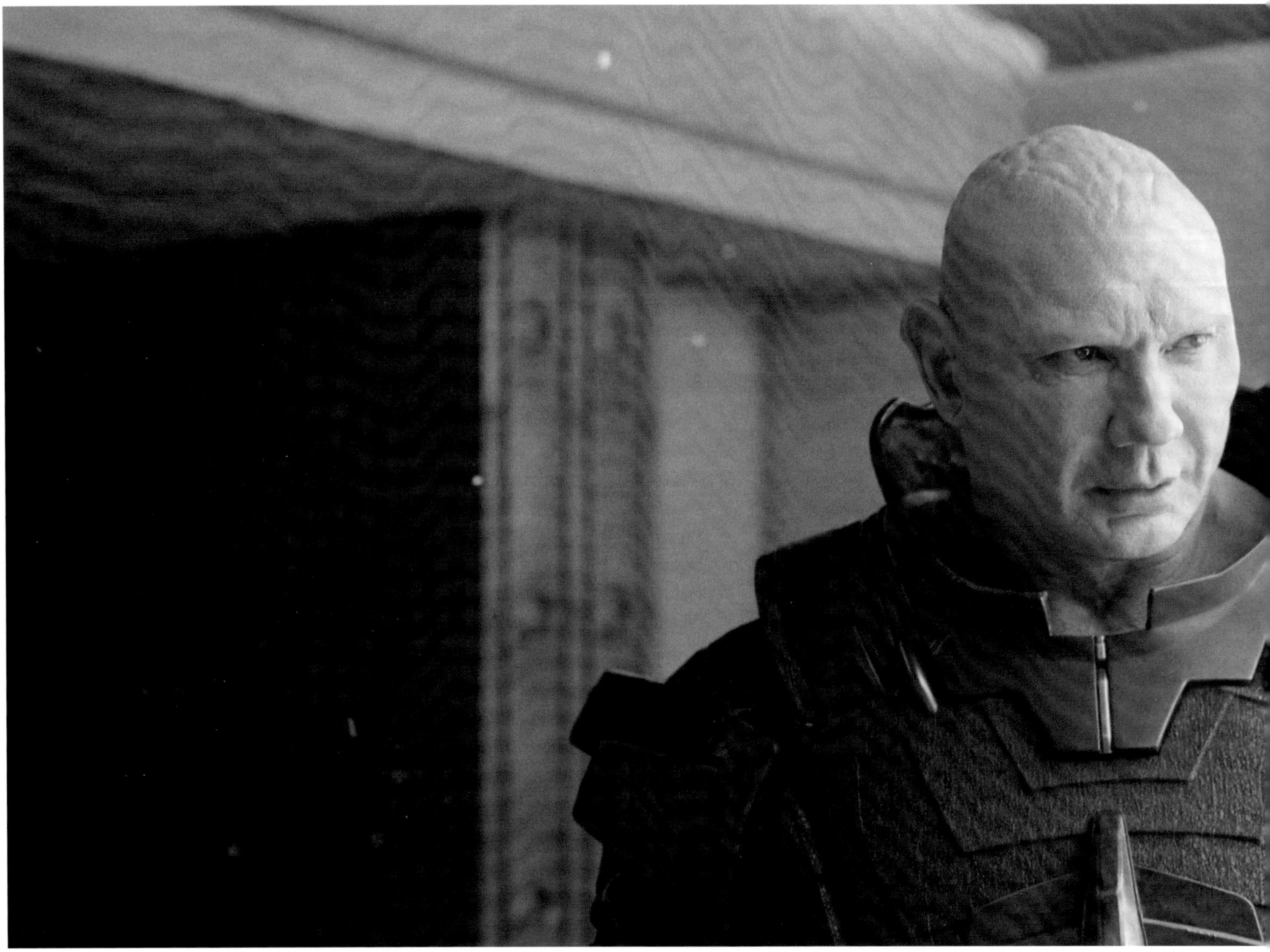

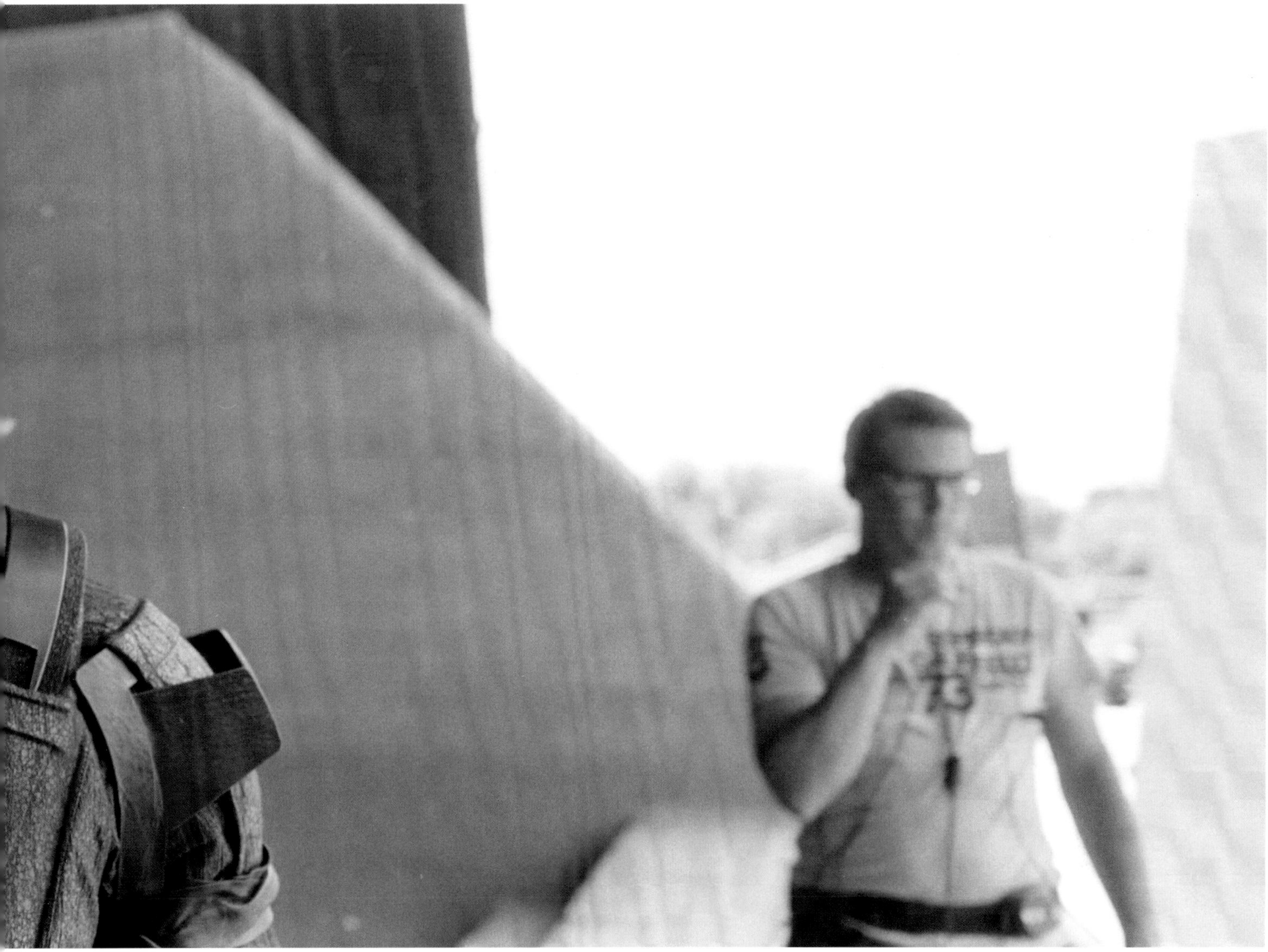

I never got to see Bautista when he was there,
but I knew he was there because everybody knew he was there.

He's Bautista.

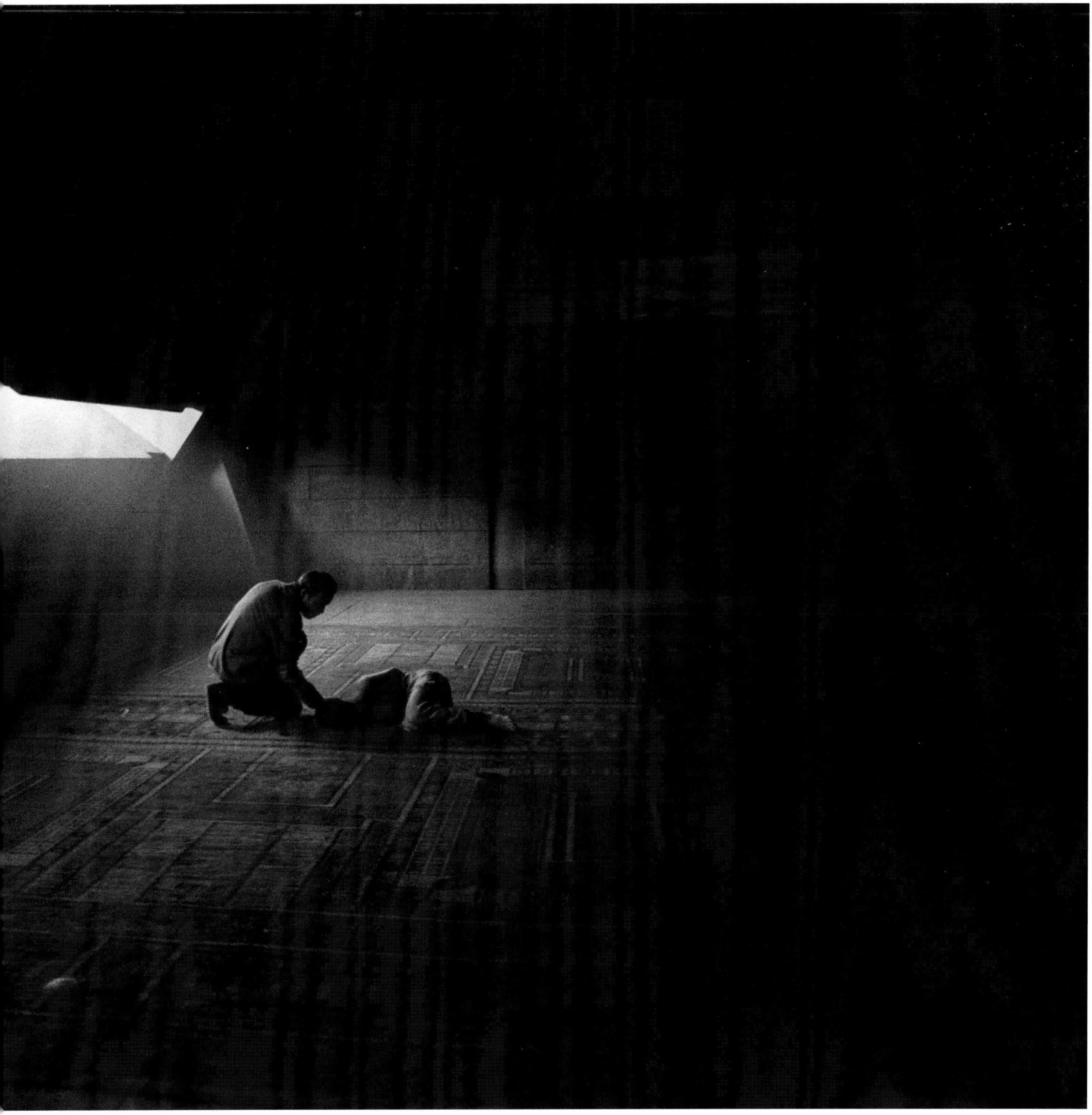

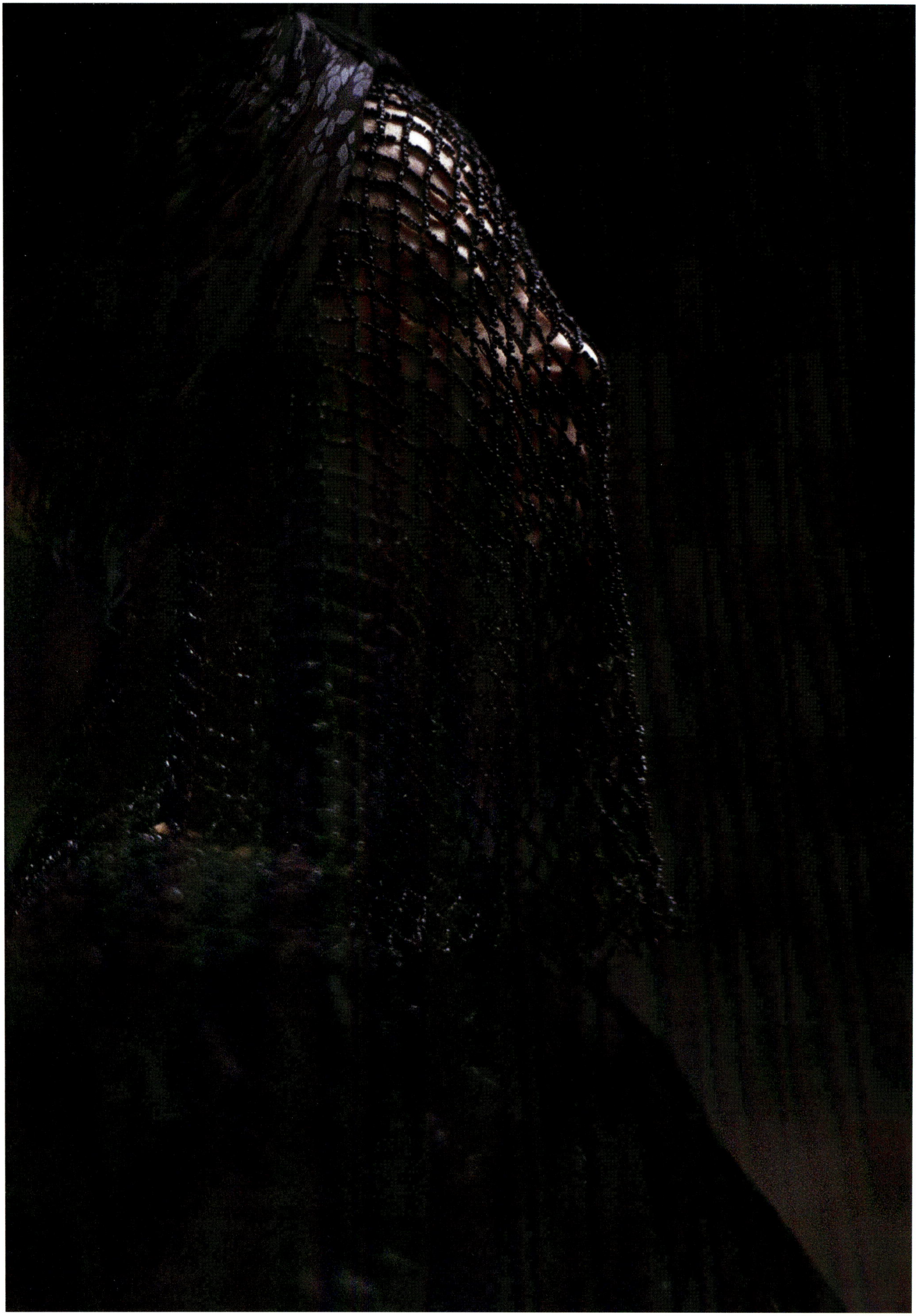

She is always pleasant
but will, I think,
forever hold a look of slight reprimand
toward

me.

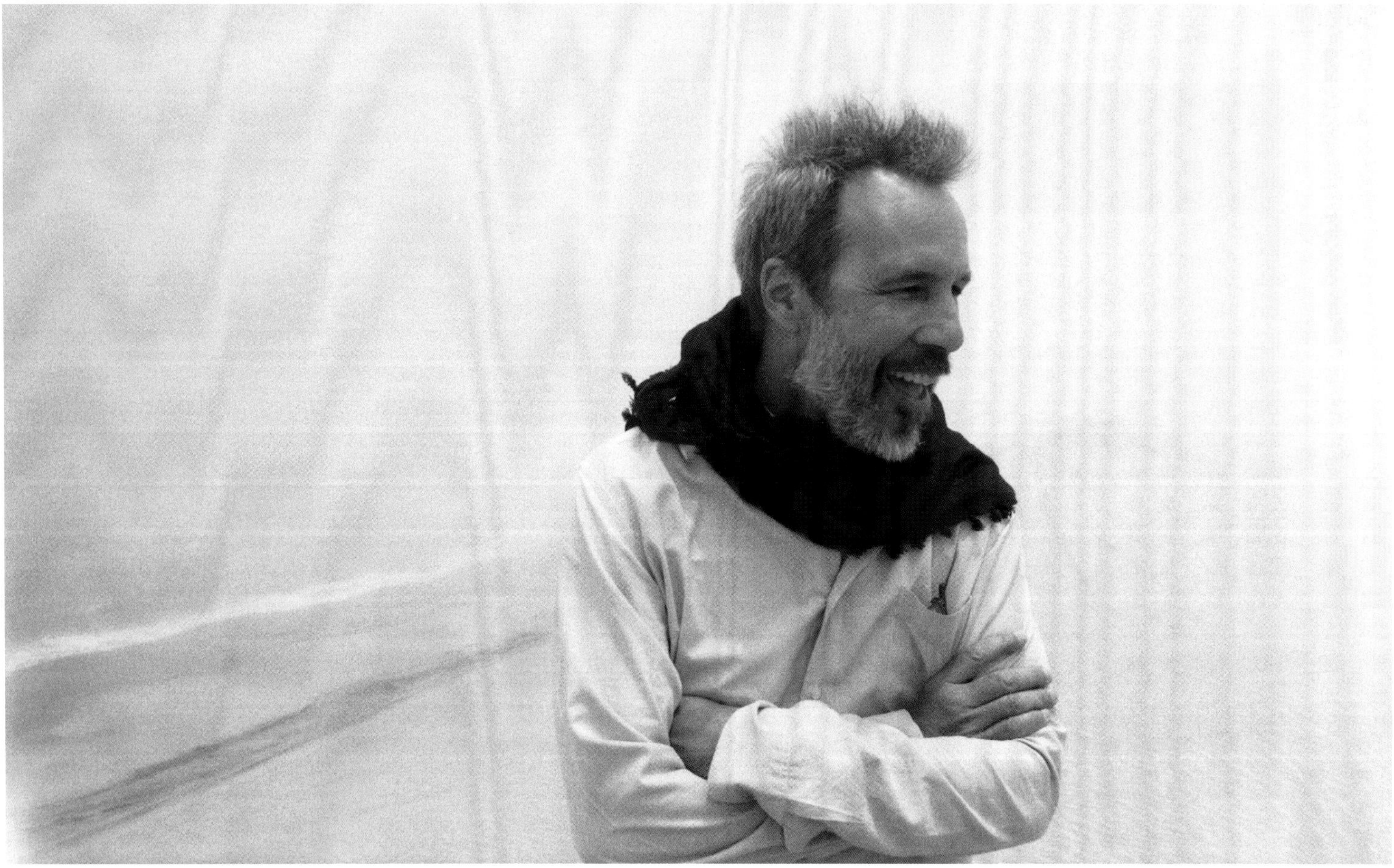

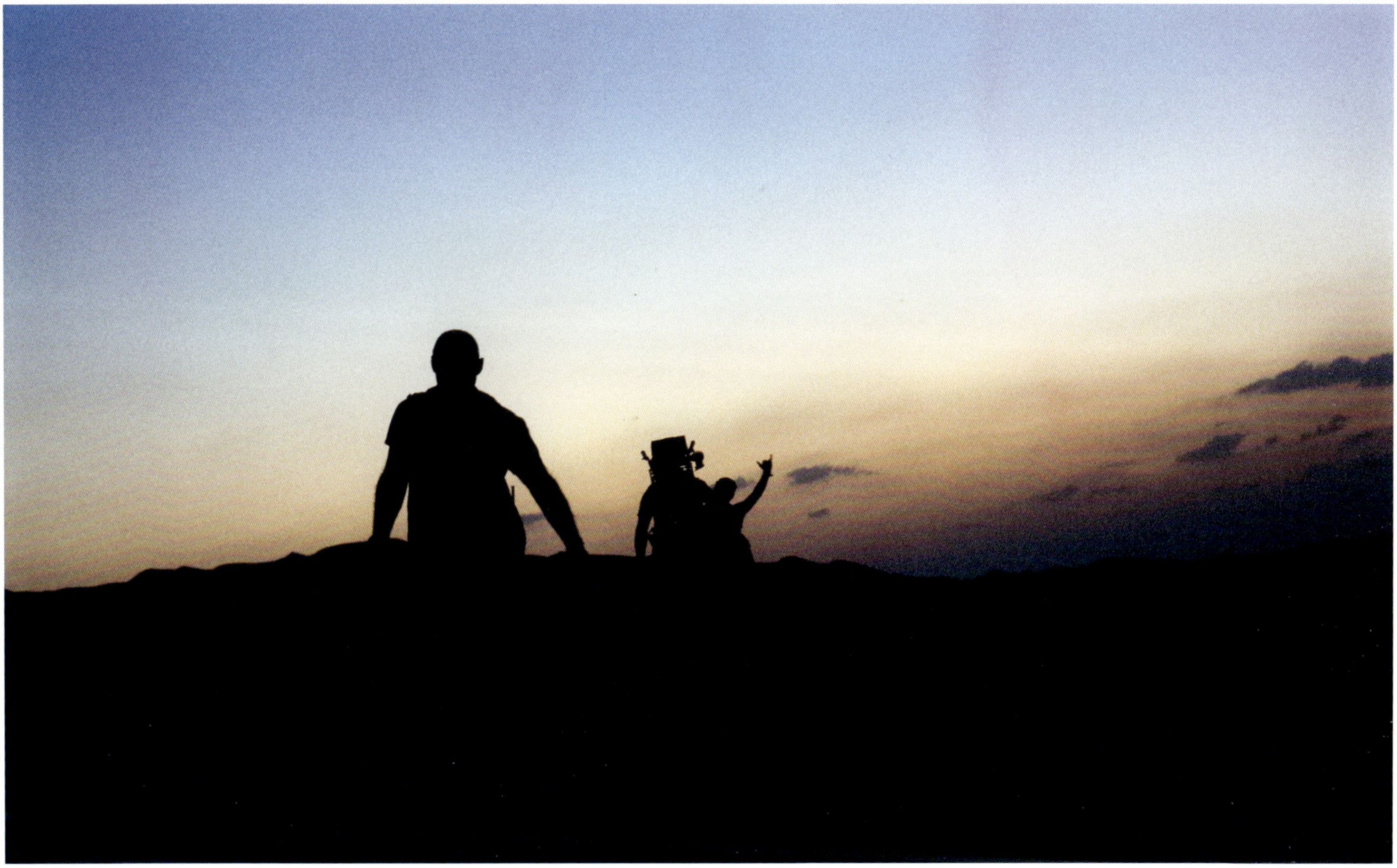

laughter from your thoughts
brush sunset with colored creams
only inhales churn

sunsets ignite you
where our deep laughter grabs hold
the night disappears

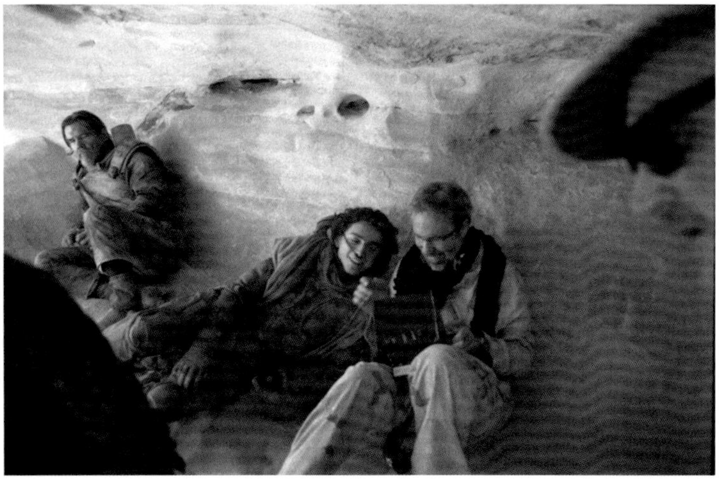

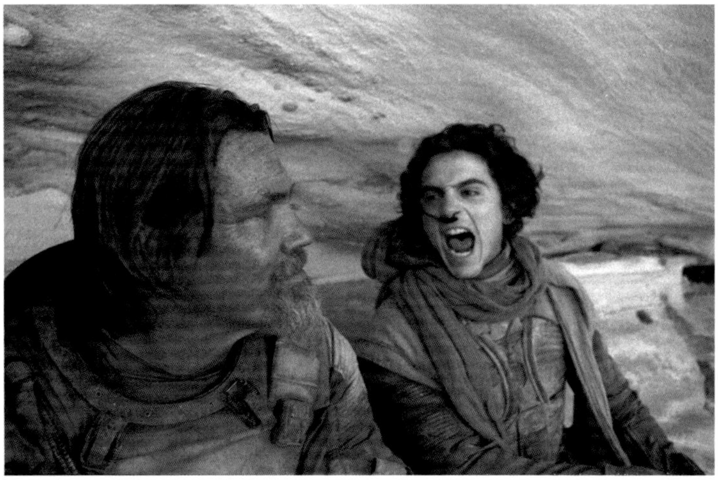

The younger generation is even younger today
than they were

yesterday.

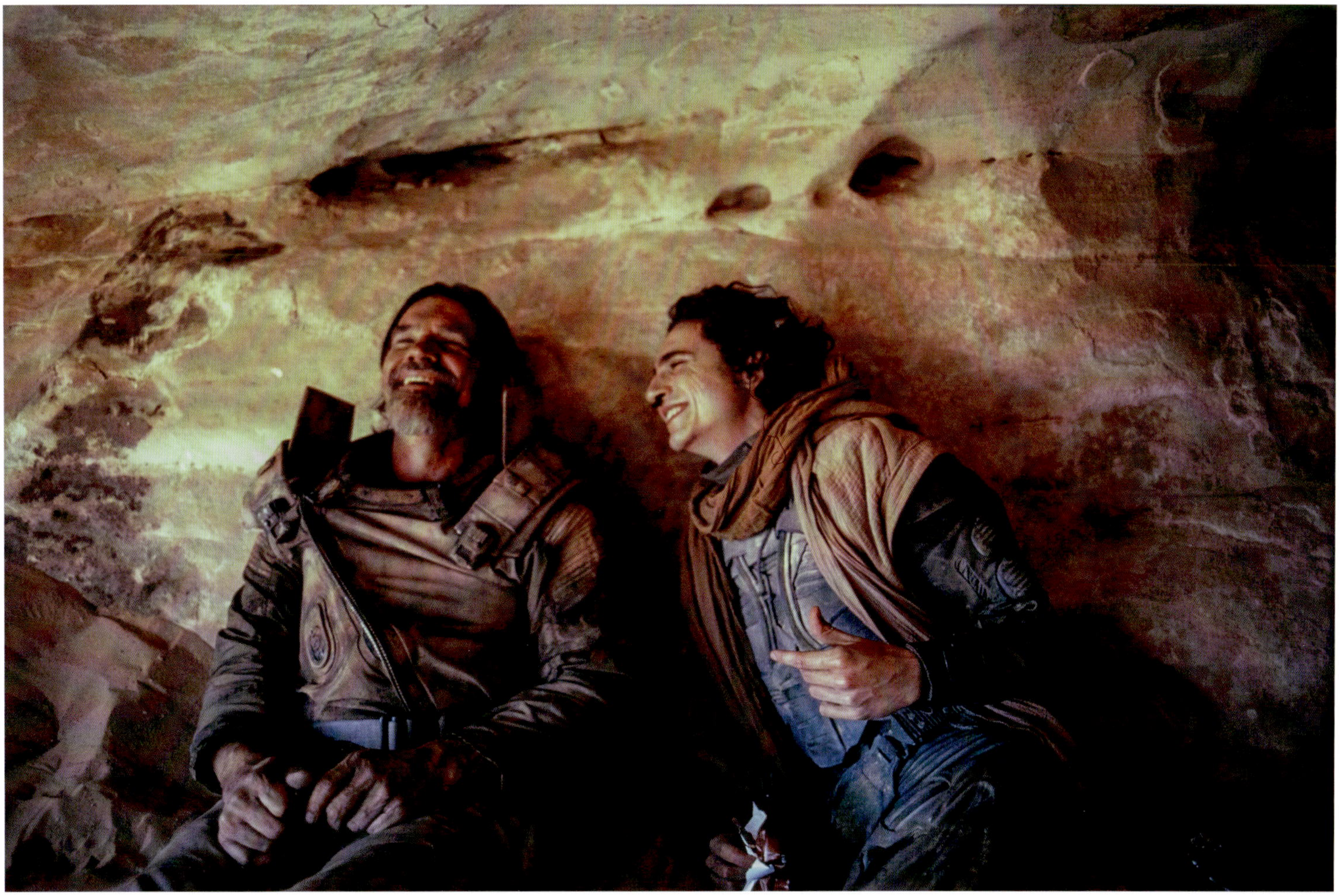

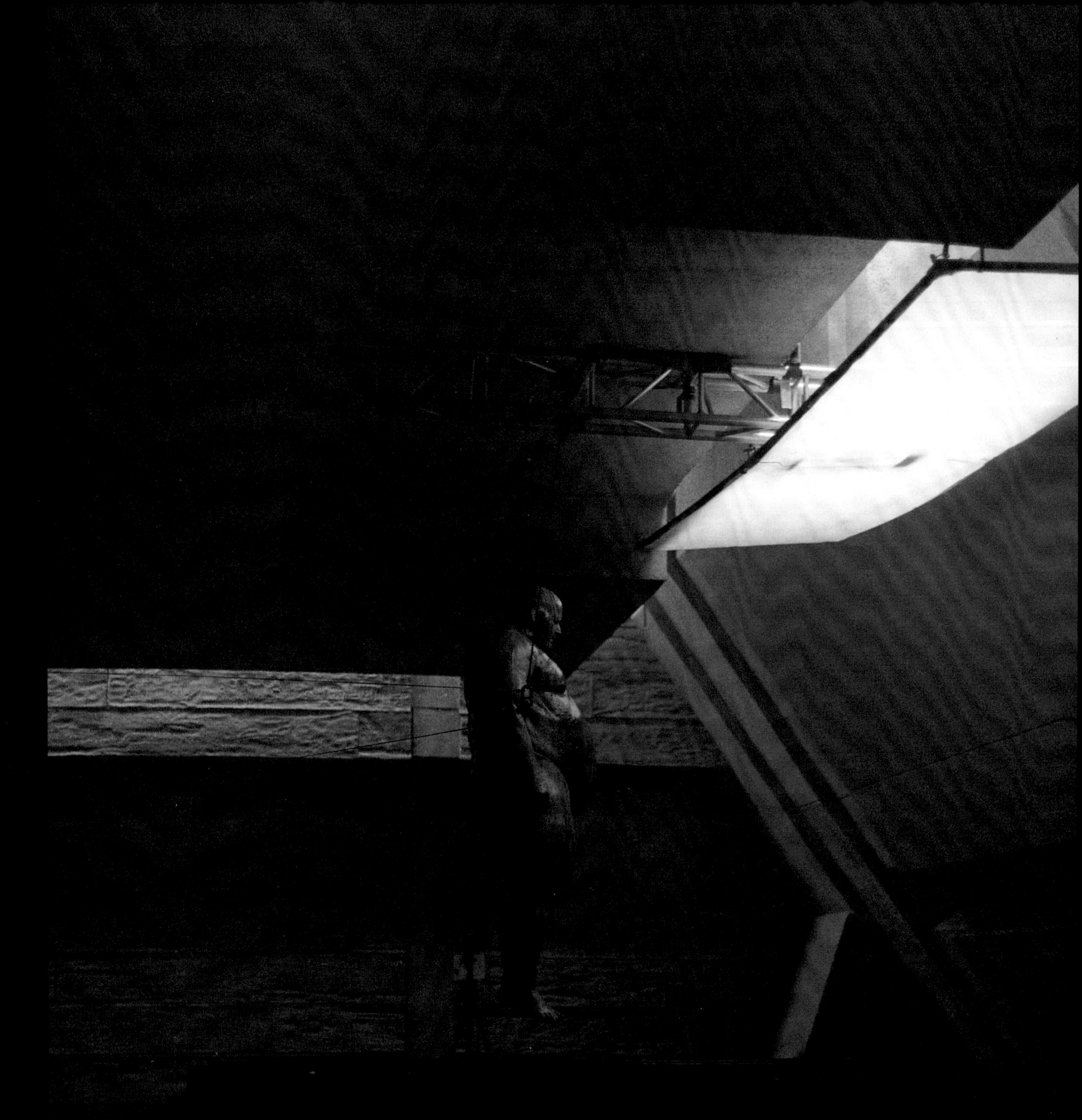

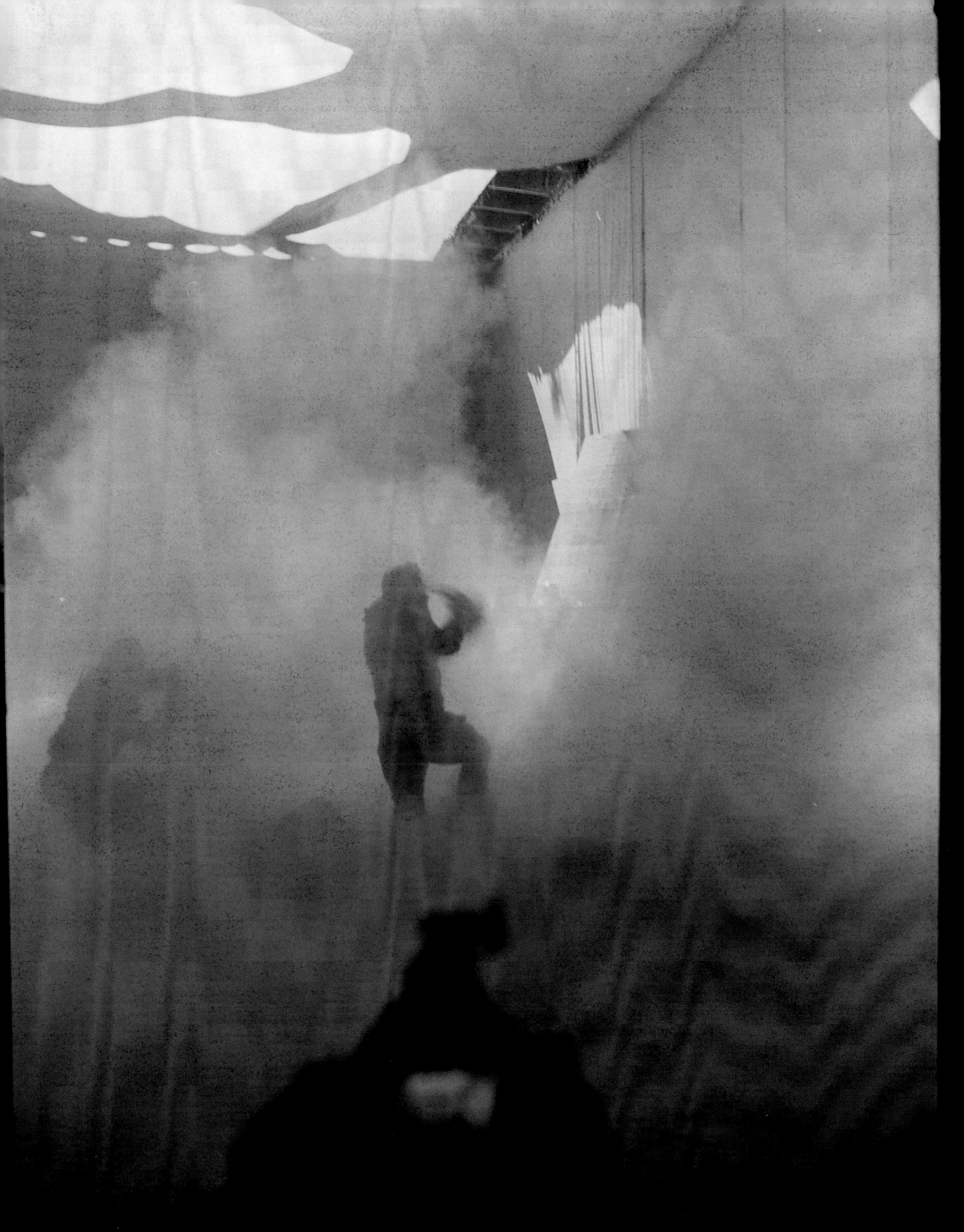

She can't wake up. Every time she opens her eyes she can see the sandstorm raging outside. It's still dark, but sheets of it slap against the glass as they pass like furious ghosts. Yesterday was rounding everyone up, making sure people were in the correct clothes, positions, hydrated, and corralled in wait in their proper places. It'll be another day of that: the cranes, the dolly tracks, the SUV transportation to and from, and the tents that have to be set up for when all the A-Team arrive. "Can I have a cappuccino, please. Less foam today?" Of course. Of course, you little shit. Let me run to Starbucks a thousand miles away. Let me milk a fucking camel for you and tell you that it's foamy oat milk. "Right away."

She lay there, and the slapping against the window continues. It's been 67 days of shooting and the seven-star pool still hasn't rippled once because of her. A drink. All she wants is a little laughter and a drink or two, then sink into the water, glass still in hand, blue rum billowing in and around her, to close her eyes and float in the amniotic fluid of imagined excess.

Relax into it. Relax.

The alarm triggers a Middle Eastern radio station spitting something incomprehensible to her. She's learned a few words, mostly greetings, but she misses the banter of a pub, the abandon of a Netflix binge. Yet, the sands continue to twist and swirl toward her. Today will be more difficult.

Today others will be irritated and on edge. The goal is to make the day, save money, keep everyone happy and feeling good about the foundation that is being held in place by her and a few others.

She lifts her body off the bed and her feet touch sand. She's still inside and the sand from outside has accumulated onto the floor of her hotel room, finding its way through small cracks in the construction. The light tries to find itself through the storm. Barely. There is someone sleeping on the couch. Save money. There is someone already in the shower. Save more money. There is someone knocking at her door. Coffee. Begin.

The sand burns as it blows
towards us in a gale of beige,
animal shapes that you can't fight off
but, instead, enter you under an iris blue sky
and with a heat that ruins how you justified
these dollars ~~you~~ you're to receive and
a celebrity that might come with it
that nobody will ever know you burned for.
What is it that makes us yearn
to catch the ego's sharp tail? As ~~yer~~ years rewind
I see myself scribbled on a cave's wall
and someone trying to decipher the meaning of me.
And as this story tethers momentum to shape
I am suspended somewhere between
the mouth of these sentences and the projection
of where this will ~~take~~ take us once it's over
and the sand settles and we fly home,
take the trash out, walk the recently coiffed dog
and say "yes" more often than I care to admit.

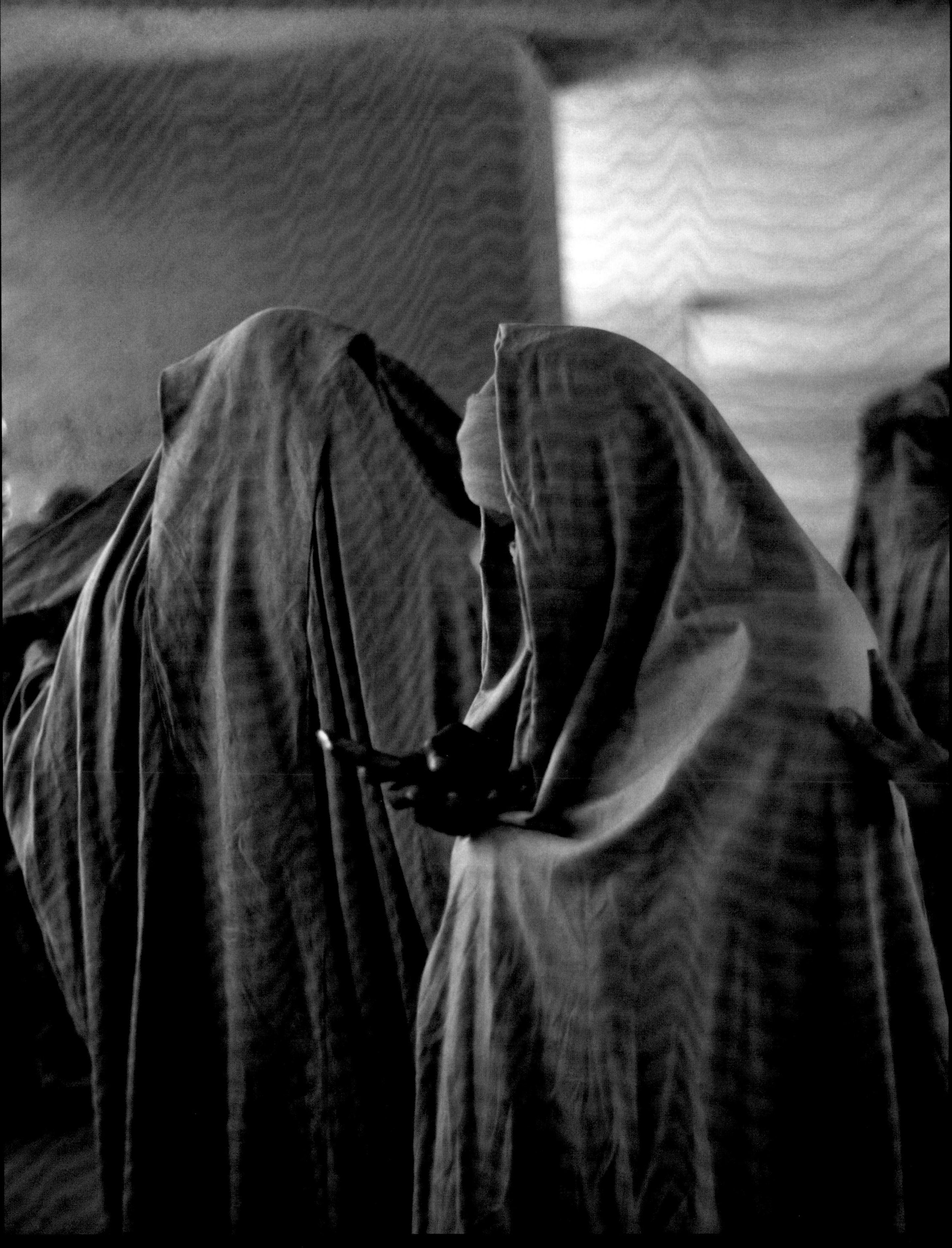

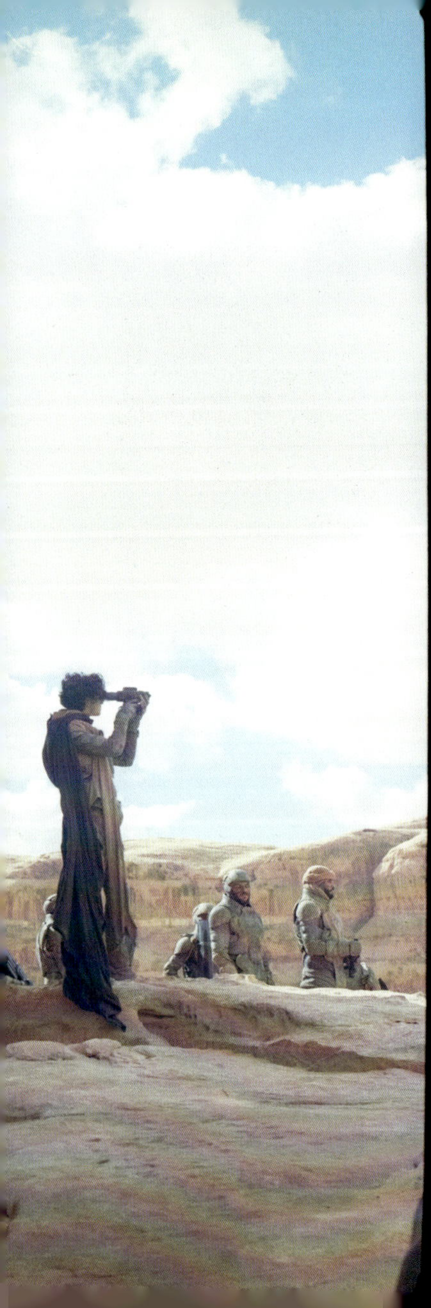
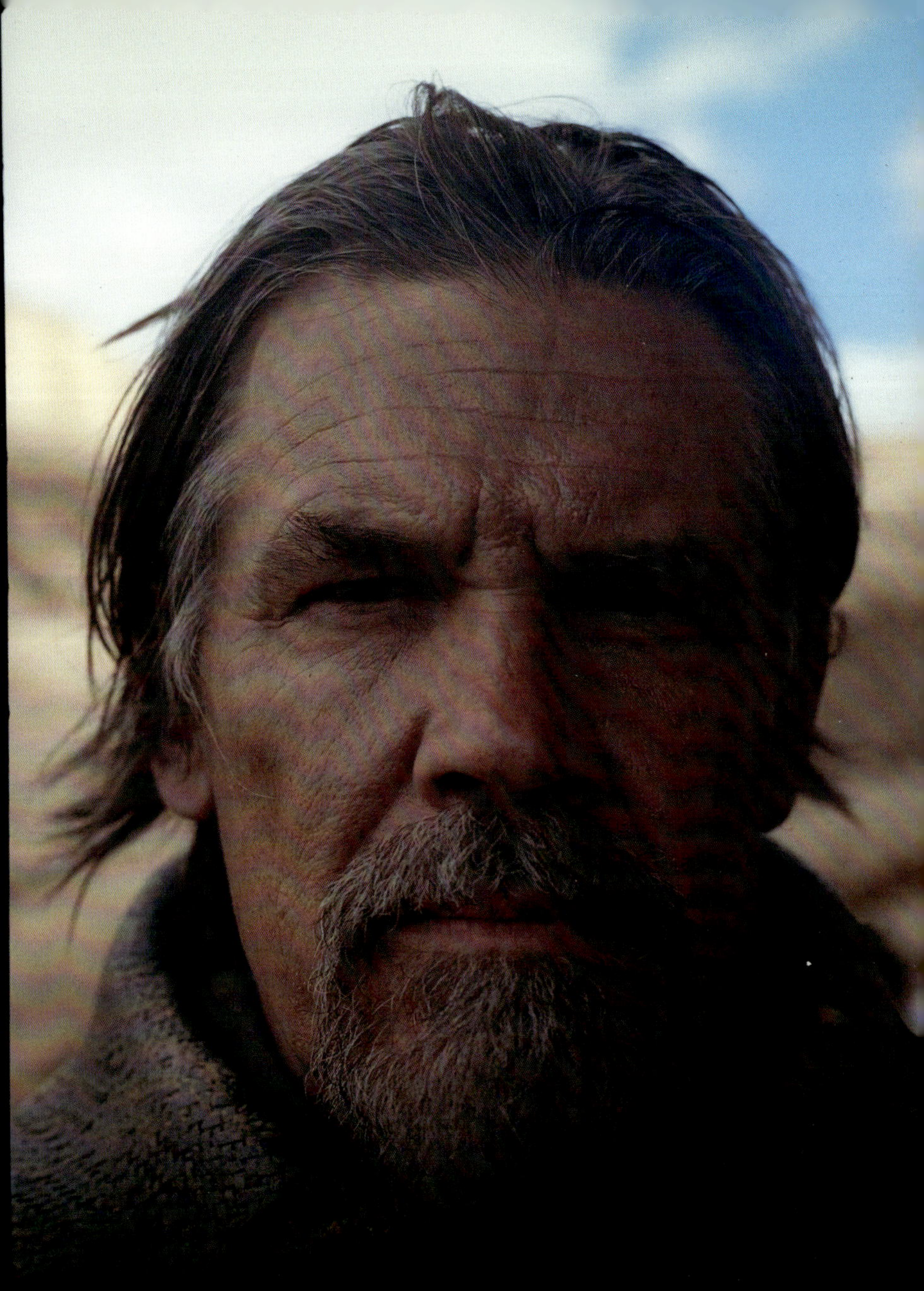

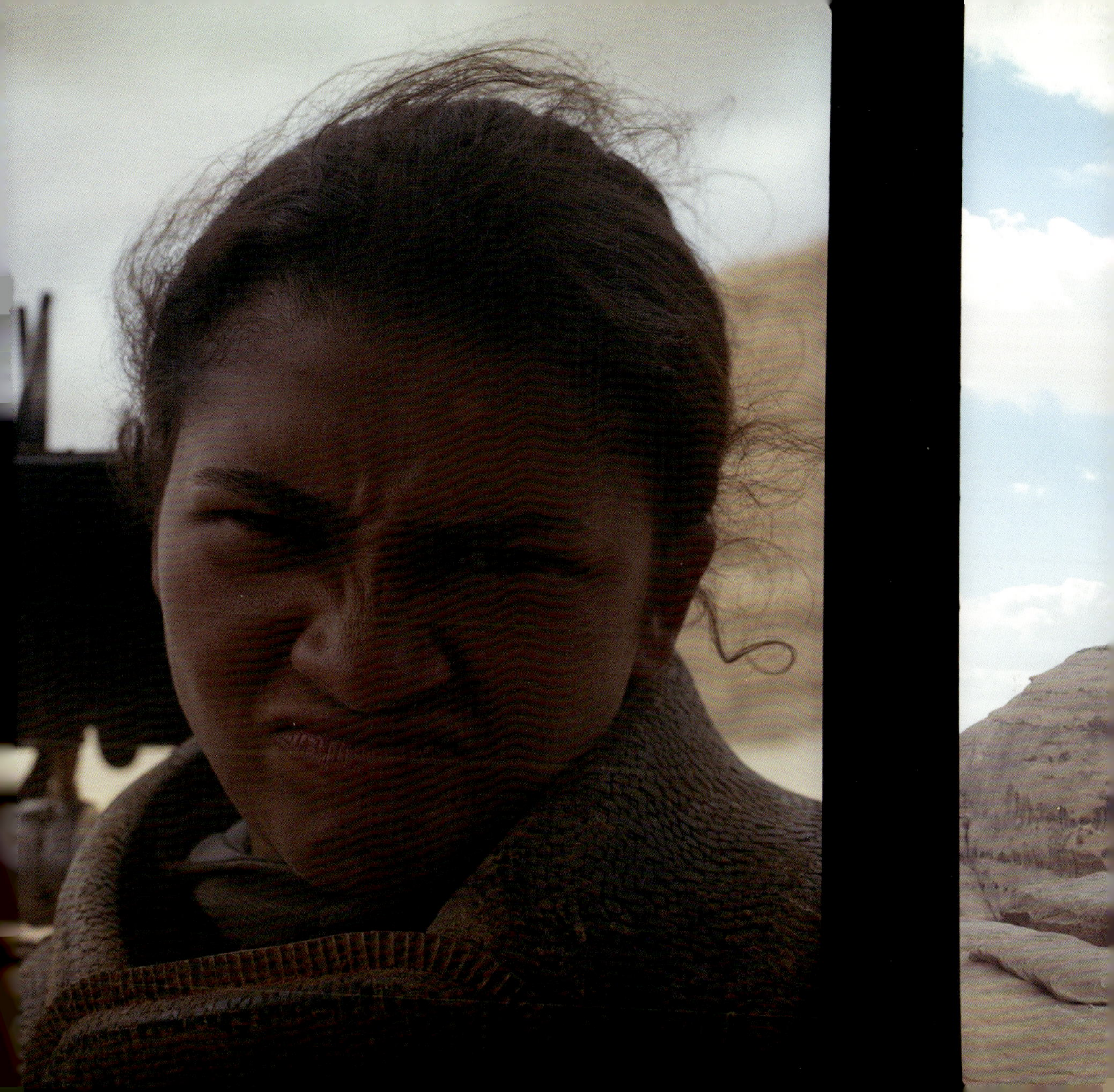

Your face is etched by
adolescence.

Your cheekbones jump toward
what are youth-laden eyes that slide down
a prominent nose and onto lips of a certain poetry.

And the way you hold my gaze
makes me fear my own age

because something in me tells me
you are going to offer me something and,
for now,
I'm not sure
it's going to be
something
I want anymore.

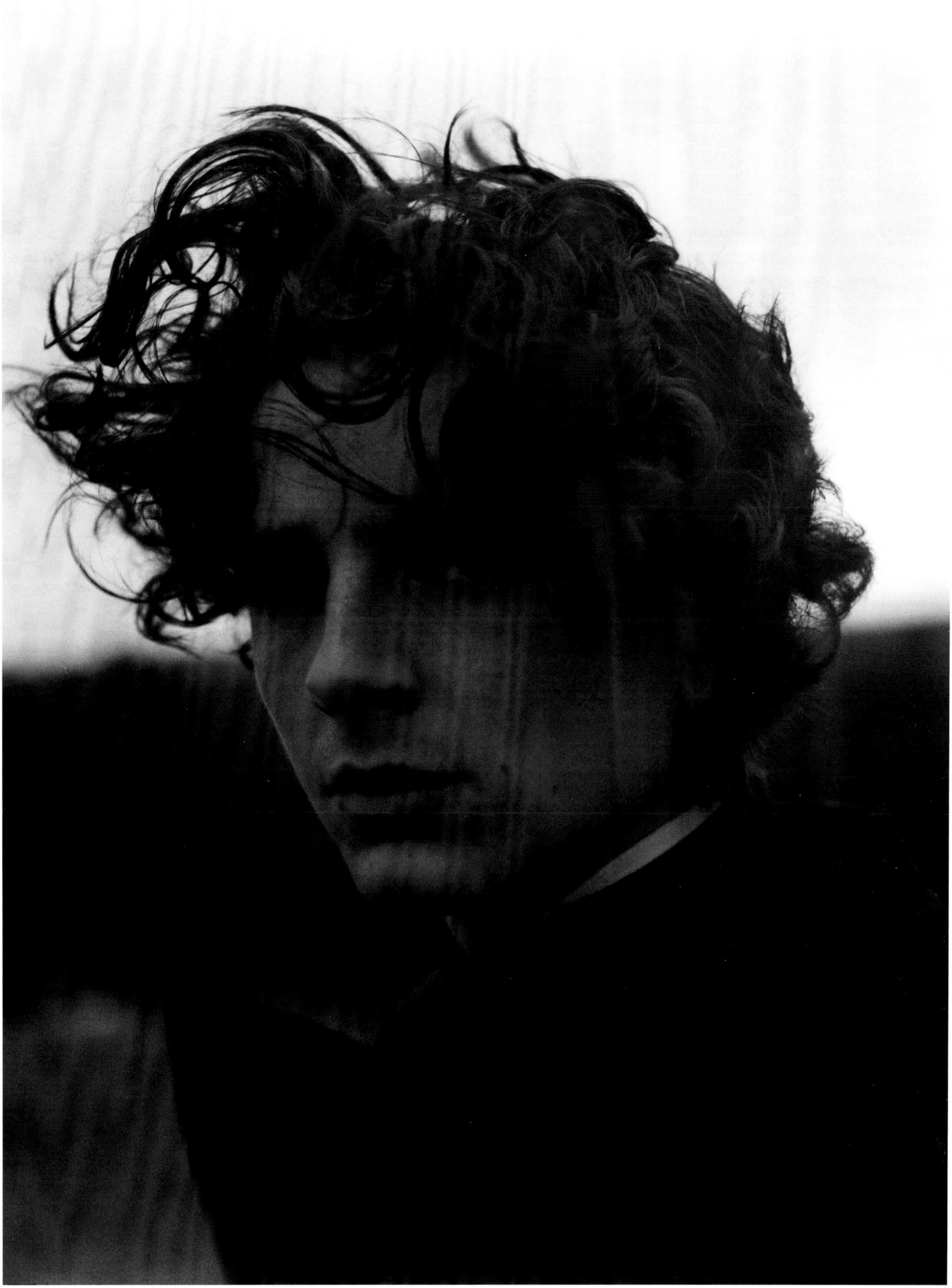

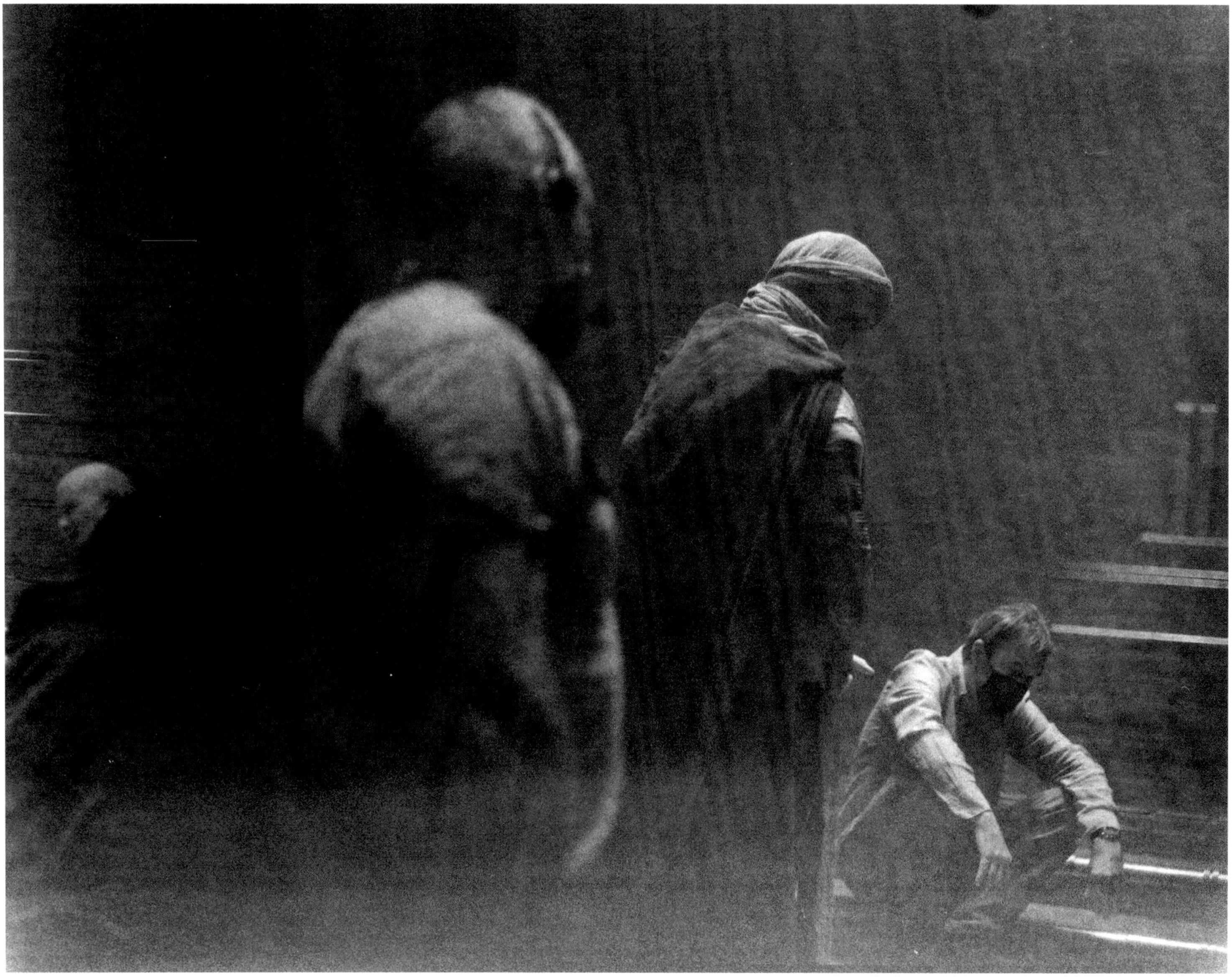

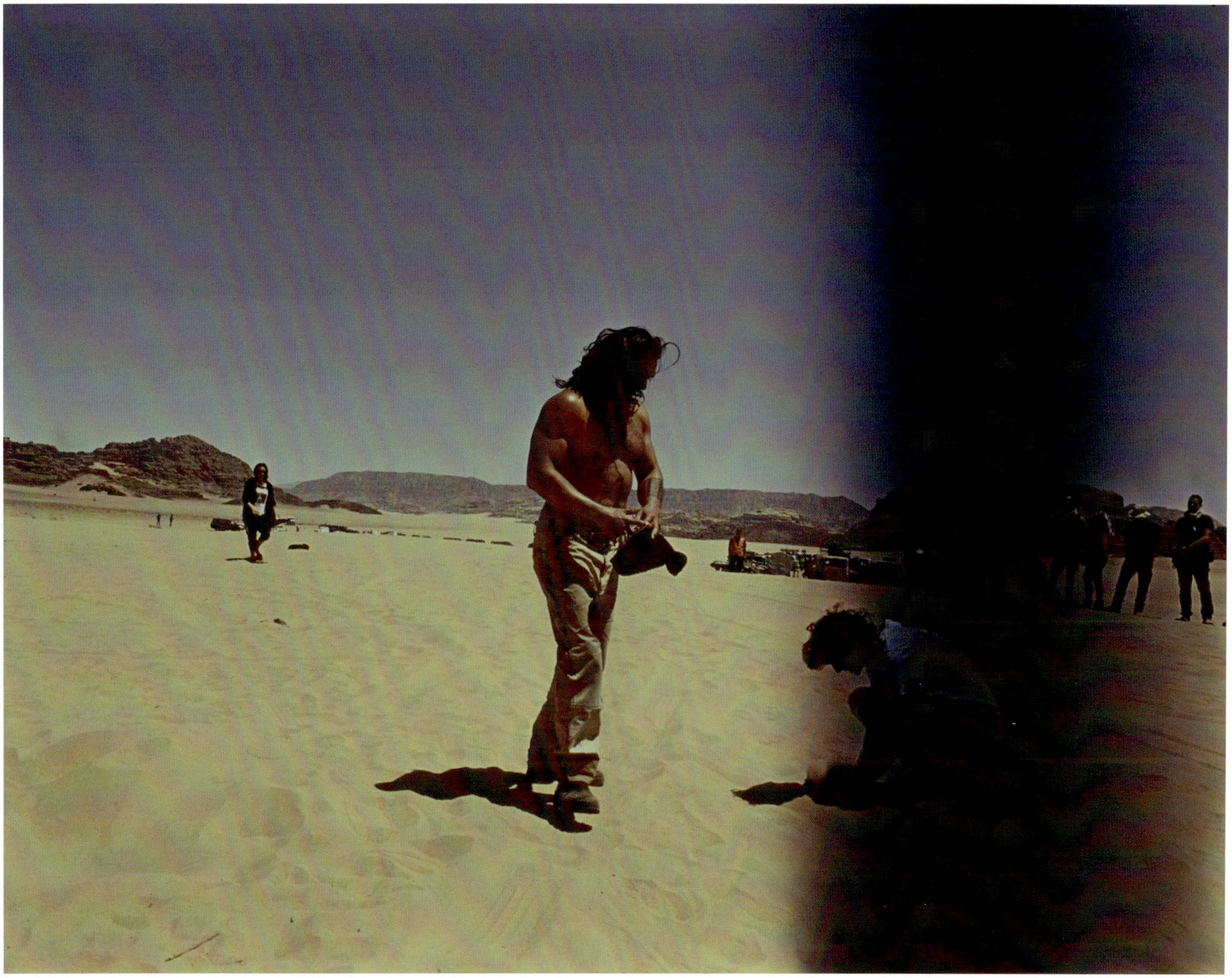

After work in Jordan there was
a hotel we were all staying in.
There was a pool outside and
from my small balcony I could watch
all the goings-on at that pool:
a lanky Timothée running around
with legs like Gumby and a tuft of hair
on his face looking for mischief;
Rebecca with baby, her hair falling
red and against the backdrop of a
Jordanian sunset with her eyes popping
green against the freckled visage of a
pale angel; Denis with jeans rolled up,
feet in water, half smiling,
never looking at a phone; and Javier,
my dear friend, who you would think
owned the hotel the way he
saturated a lounge chair, always
talking, arms passionately flailing.
My dear friend who was the same
Spanish gladiator he was 13 years ago.

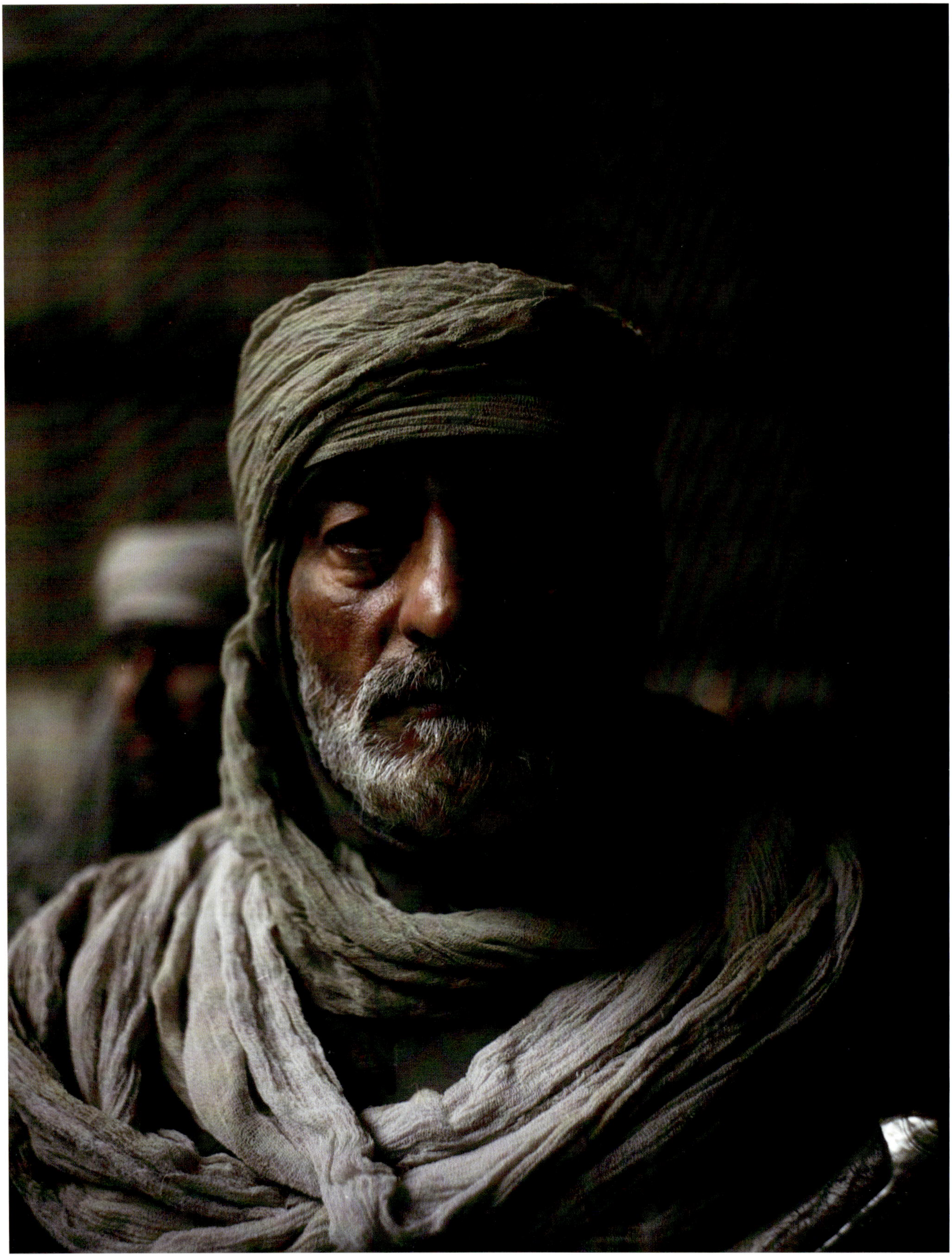

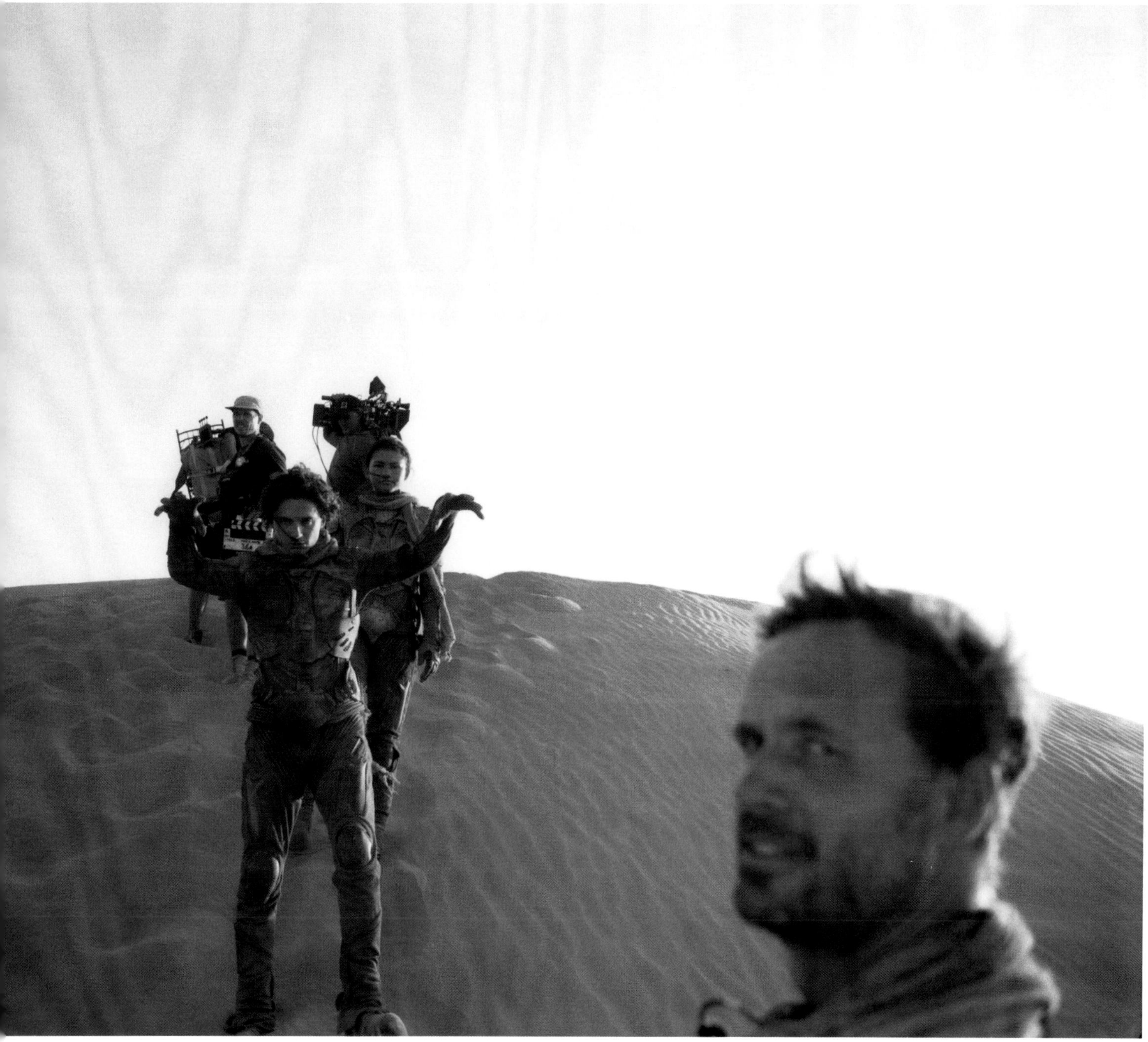

sand, sink, step, slog, burn
onwardly we are pulled toward
the experiment

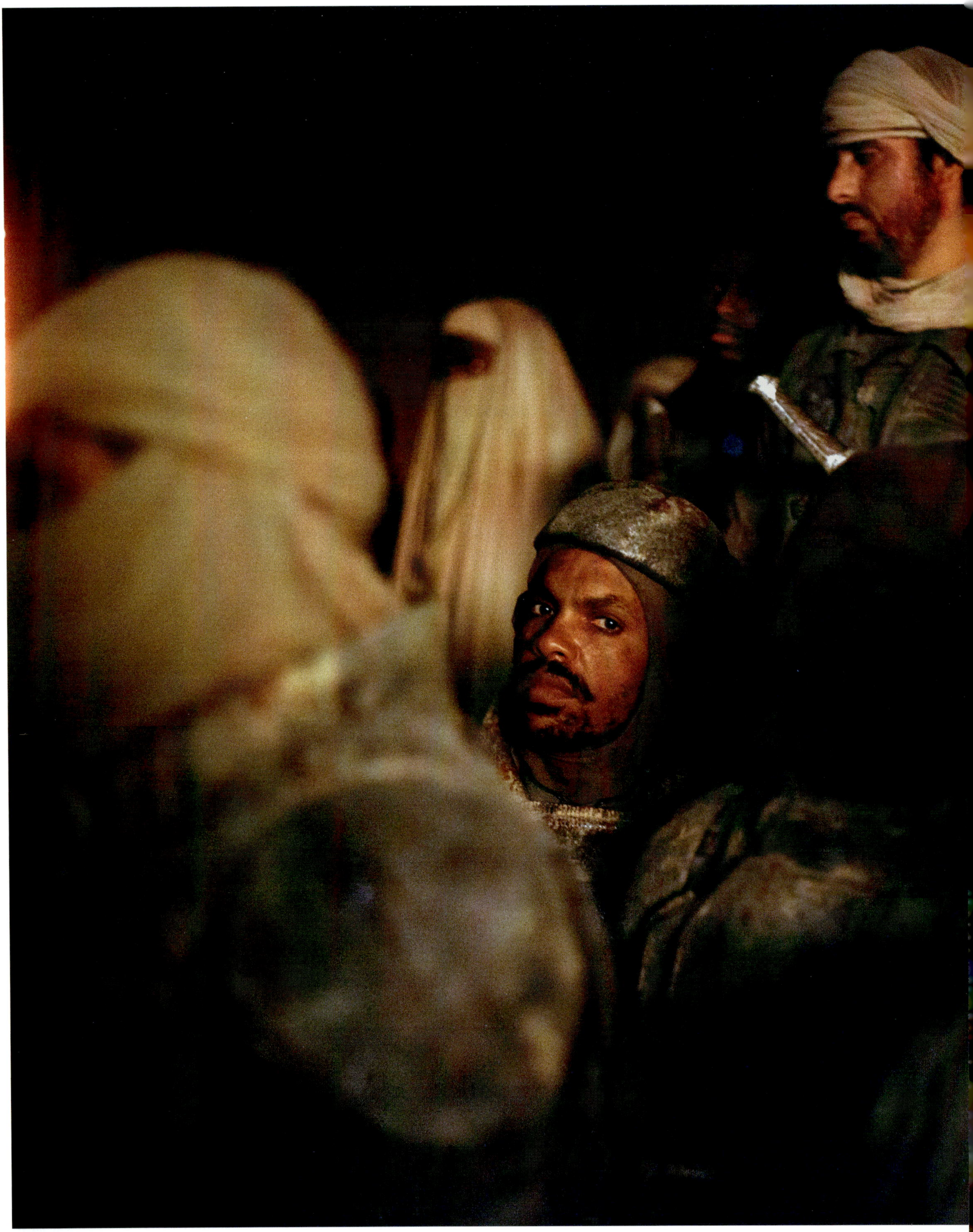

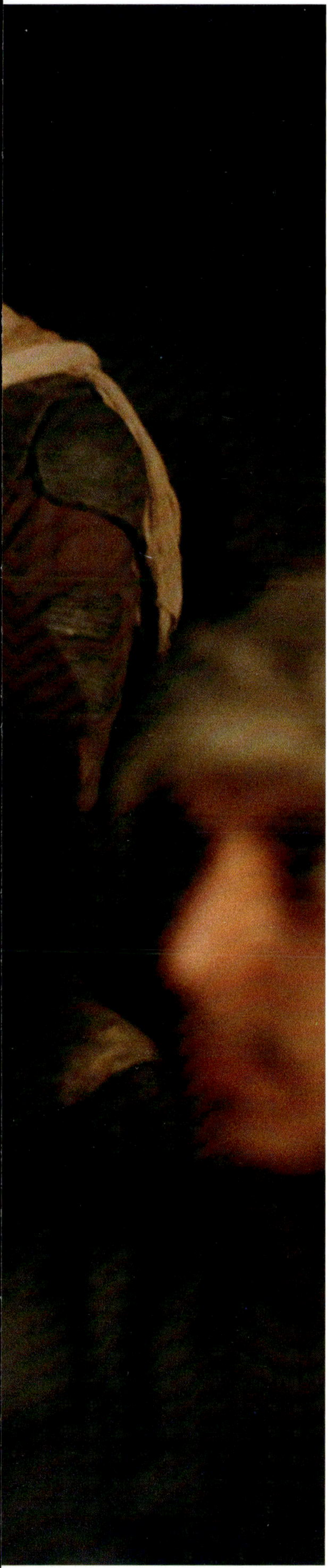

Therein lies a dream
which stretches as far as God;
clenched hands find eyes
closed.

The mornings comes slowly here.
Wrapped in our protective garb,
each step to set sinks in
a quagmire of sand that is
unforgiving. Timothée looks
like an Adonis. Denis, in
his white shirt, is looking
out into the horizon,
a small espresso in his
hand, no expression on
his face but a squinting.
The crew eat power
bars and each has the
last drops of a coffee
in hand.

They talk about last night:
their hotels, the pool, maybe
a gym in town, a stolen kiss
from another crew member.
There's a new reality here
though, every day. The family
that you've inherited, as
if yours had left you on a
dingy corner and as an orphan
you were given away to this
fiction that has instructed
you to act within a circus
for the emotionally chal-
lenged whose imaginations
reign with kaleidoscopic
weather patterns—and
there's always a young
man who struts along with
how I think Giacometti
imagined one of his
sculptures would walk,
with that lithe gait,
who inevitably looks
at you and says:

"I really liked you
in *The Goonies*, man.
That was dope."

And I look out onto
the ornithopter, grab
a crewman's hand, and he
hoists me up. We will
be lifted 40 feet above
the ground with a crane
and I will yell something
to Timothée as we look
down at the thousand-
foot sandworm that's
not there. Tomorrow,
it will be something
else.

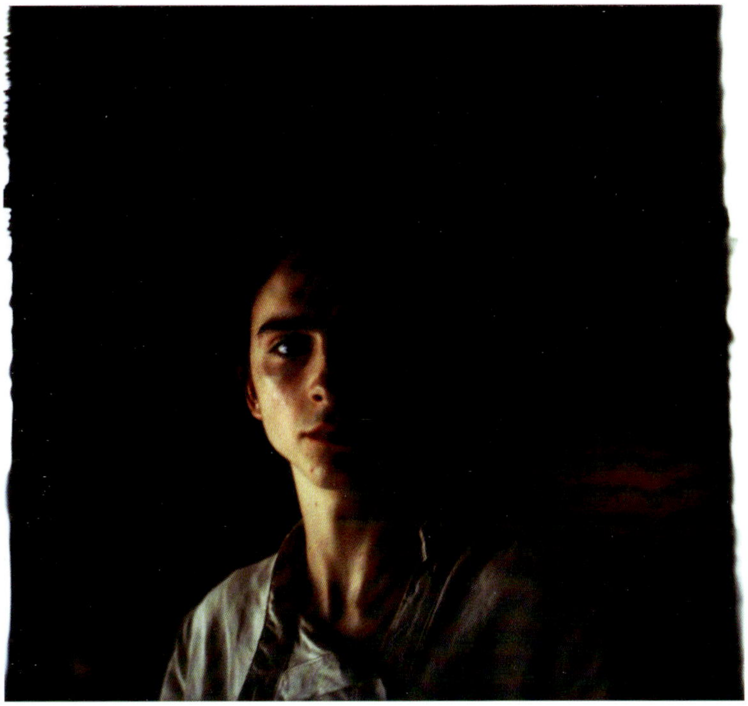

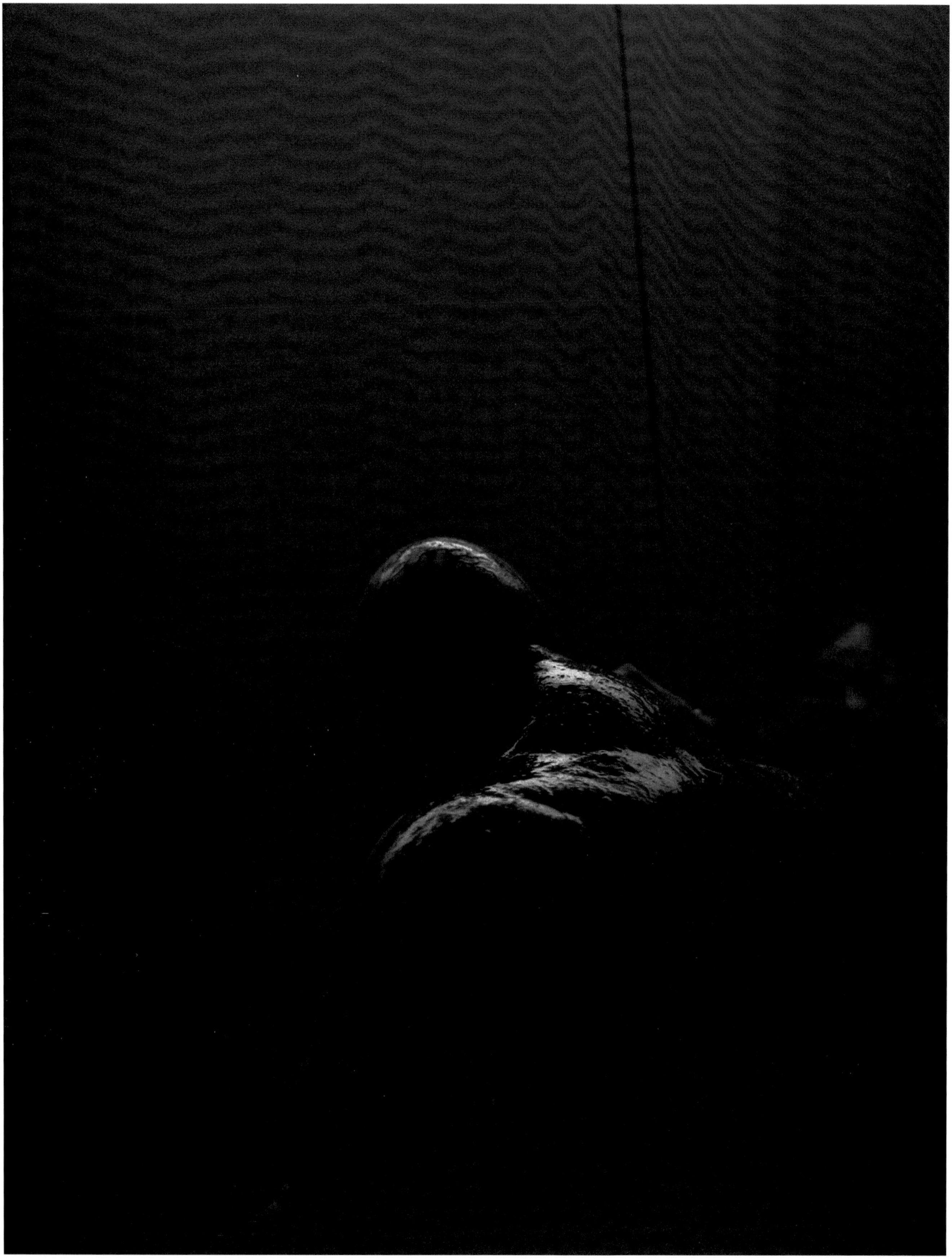

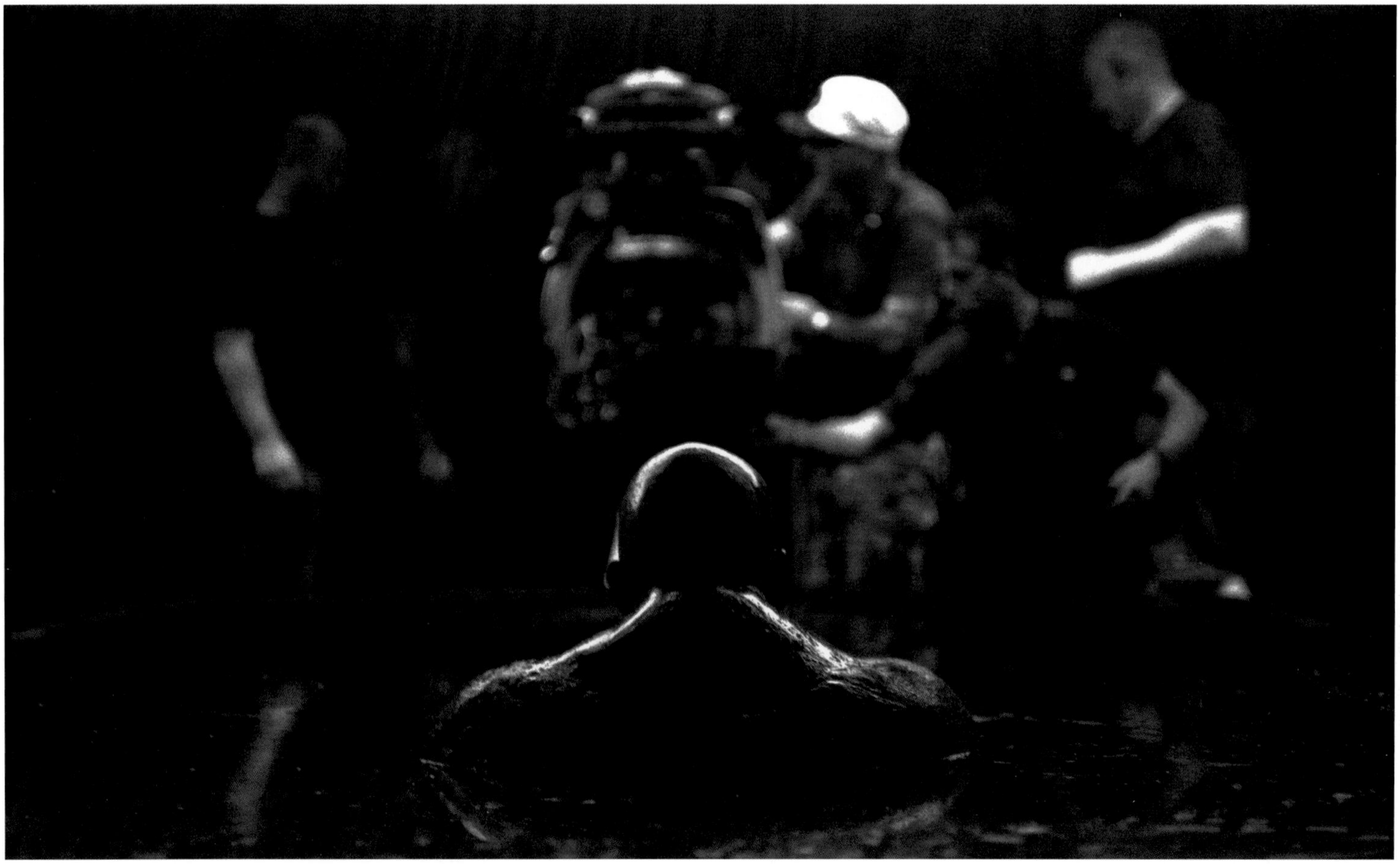

He isn't yelling but has a sternness that she feels in her muscles. She regresses, but the child regressed into knows that she chooses to be here in the name of art. She remembers little performances she used to put on in front of the family when she was just out of diapers: red lipstick, tutus, princess sandals. She tries to wipe the sand on her hands onto her stillsuit. Half of it still clings. She looks up to see if he's looking directly at her, but he is already walking away into another thought. She looks around her, lost, but finds there three other regressed actors that she knows she'll see later when the moment passes and they are back in the hotel lobby volleying celebrity anecdotes that will never cling but, instead, bounce with great glee from plush couch to plush couch.

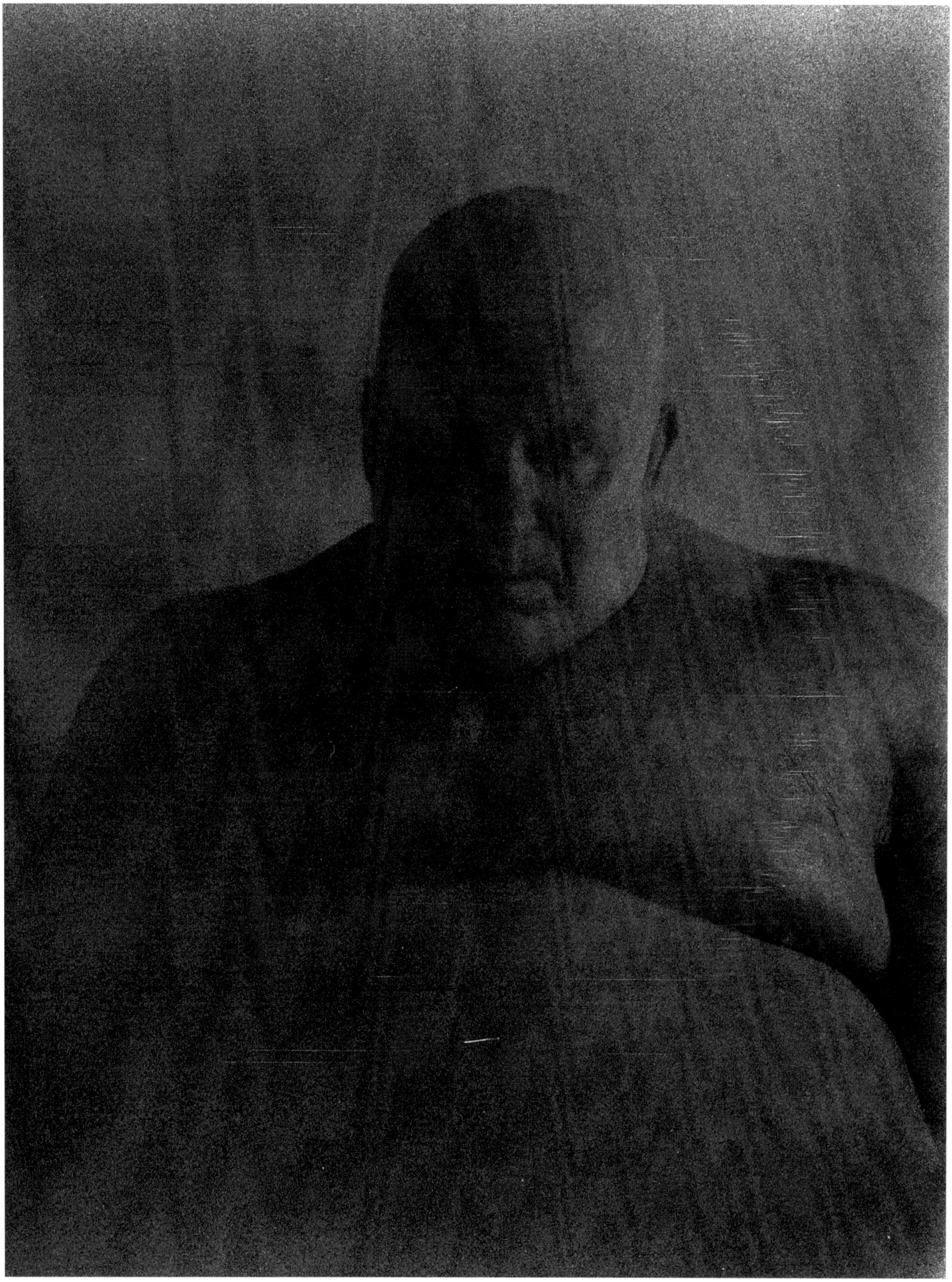

Sleeping held at bay
by our anticipation
of what gem tomorrow holds

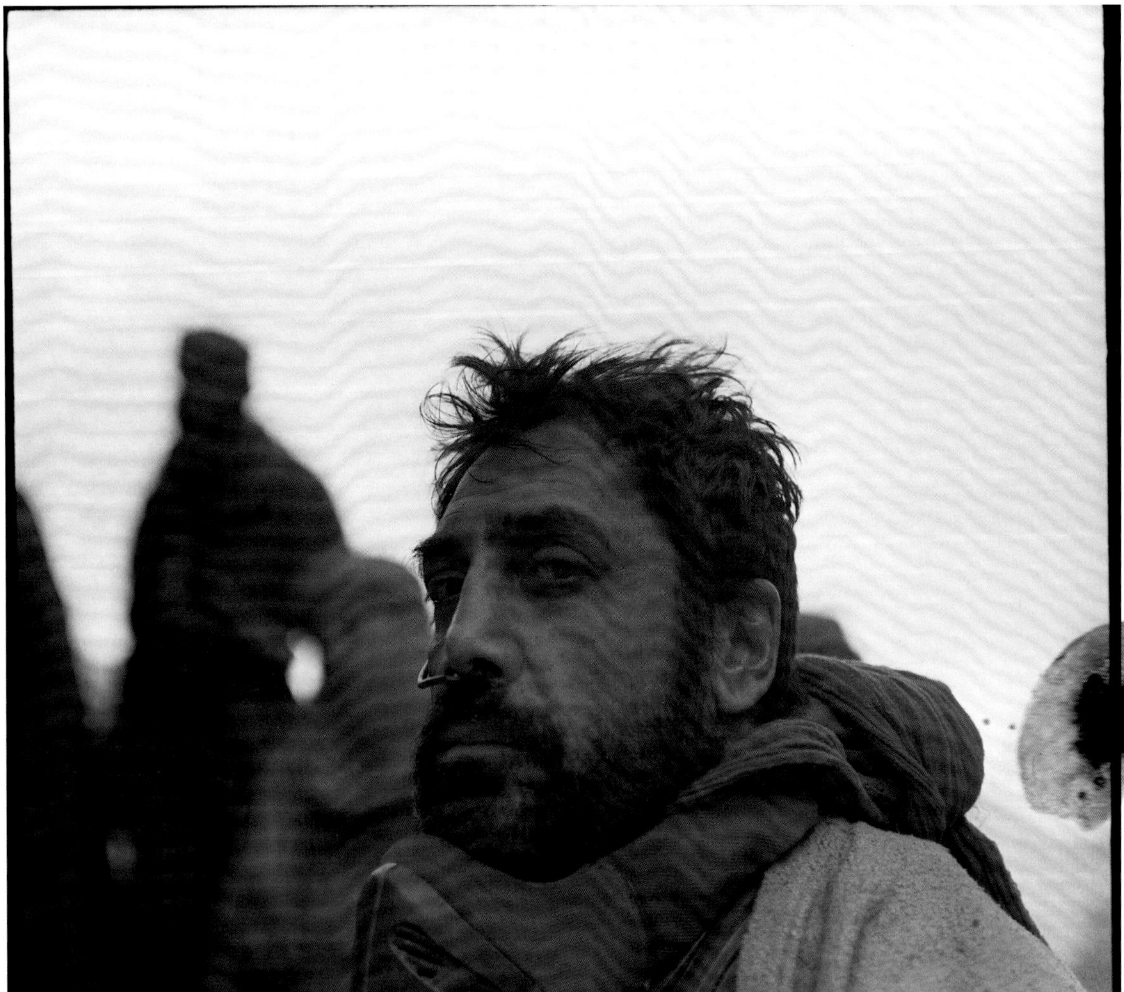

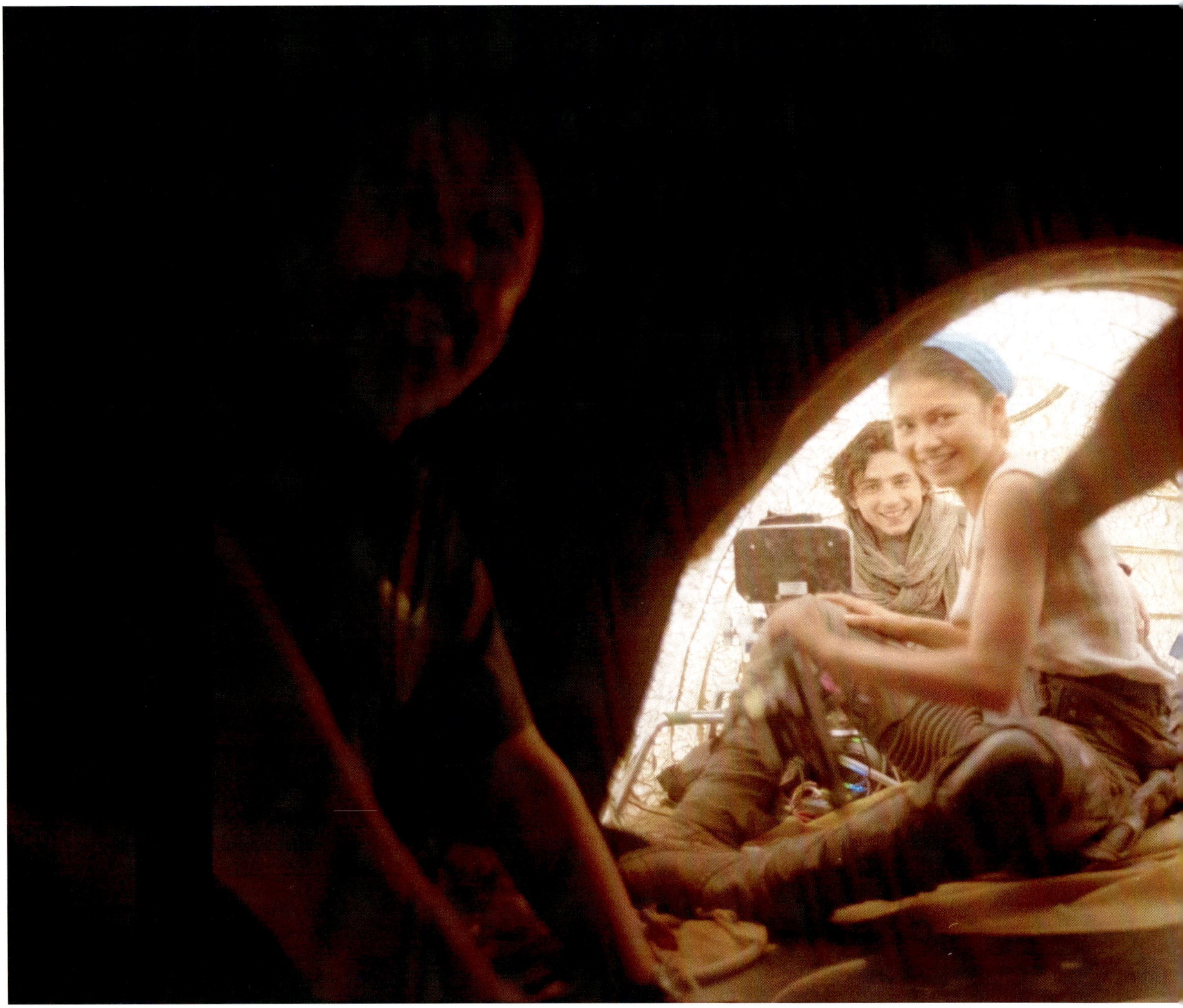

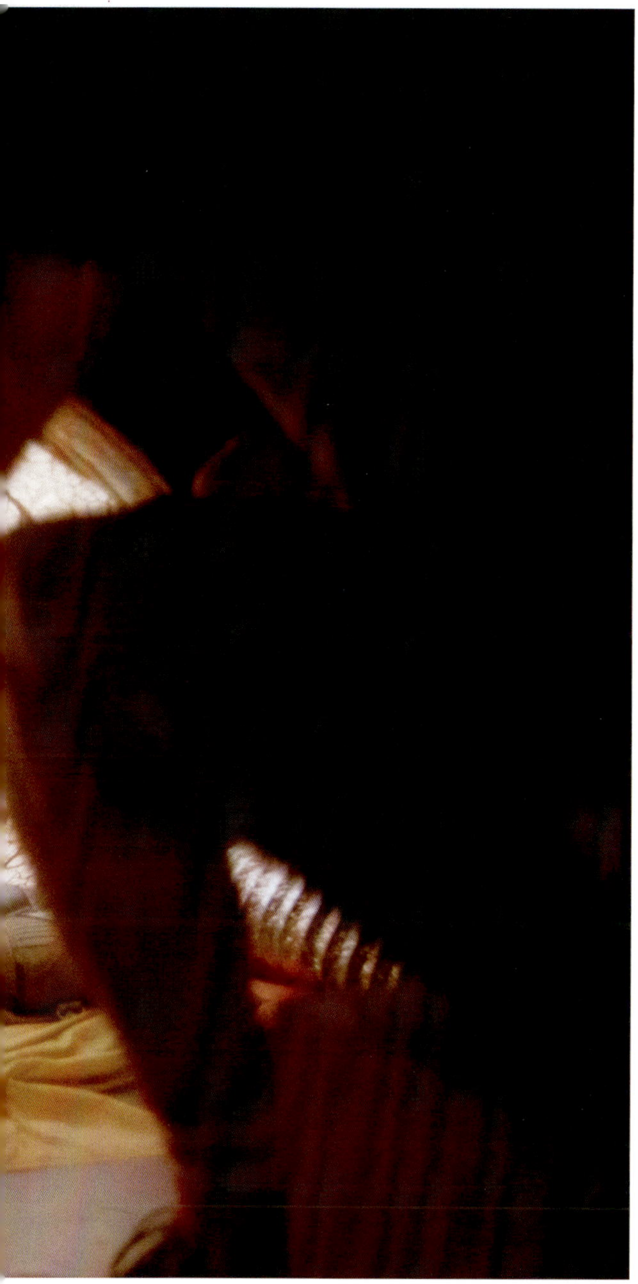

In a hovel naturally dug by years of weather, we squat inside waiting for the dust to settle. The wind has picked up and hot has morphed into a chilly front. The tents off in the distance snap and wave, as we huddle together just as the Bedouins did centuries ago under similar scenarios. The only difference is that we are here under the auspices of objectivity. We play the game of simulating life, hoping as we do that there will be a moment, a hint of a feeling that whatever we are simulating will become us. We will live our own stories somewhere else, at some other time, further away than what even here is.

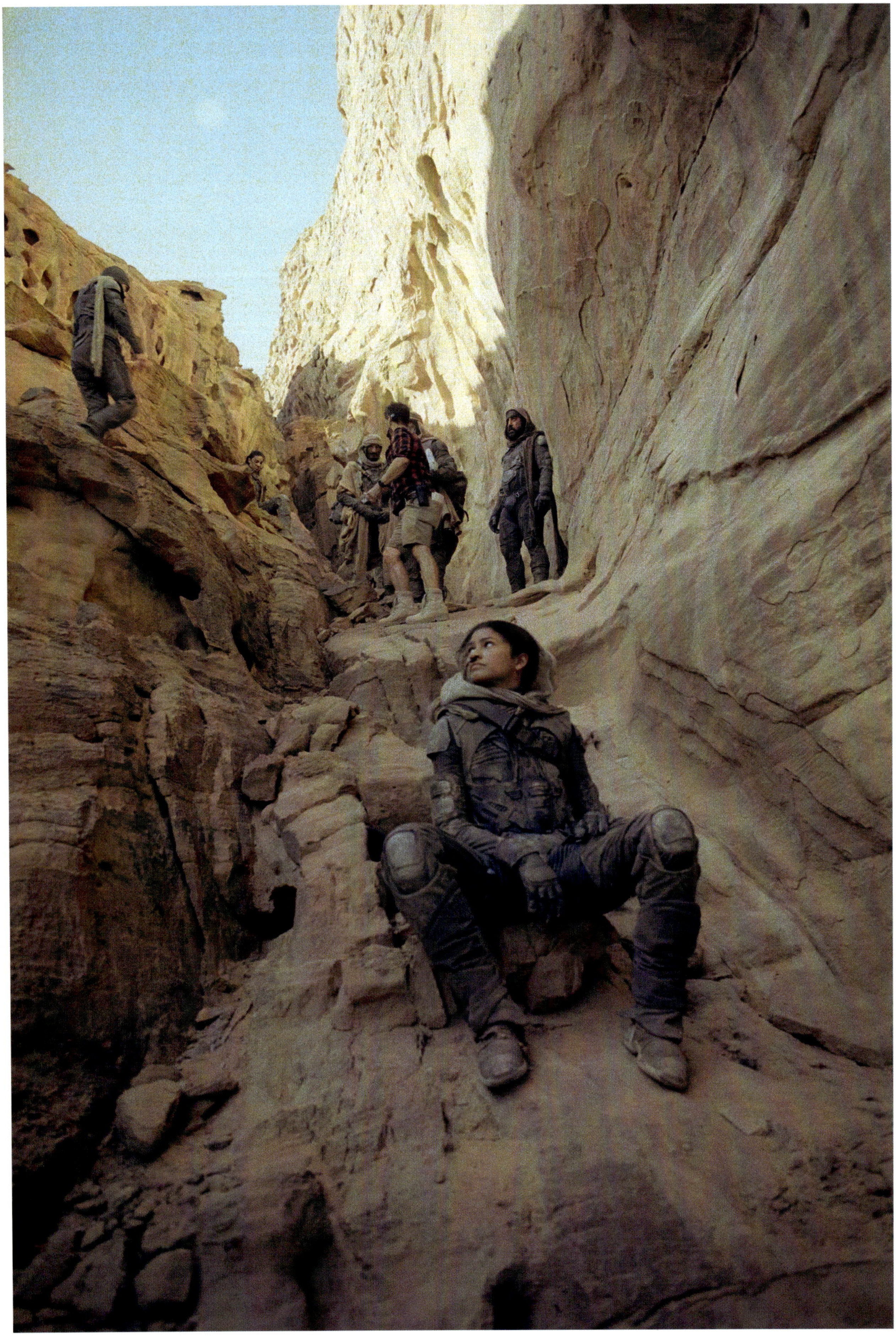

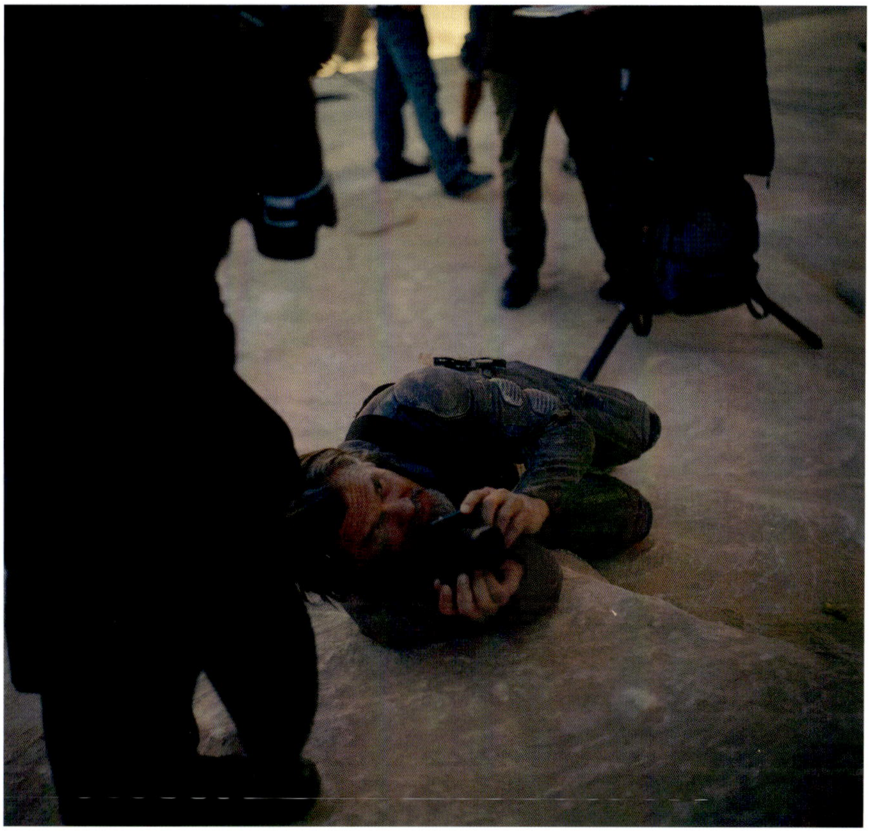

Lie down in the light
As fictional characters
watch you from afar

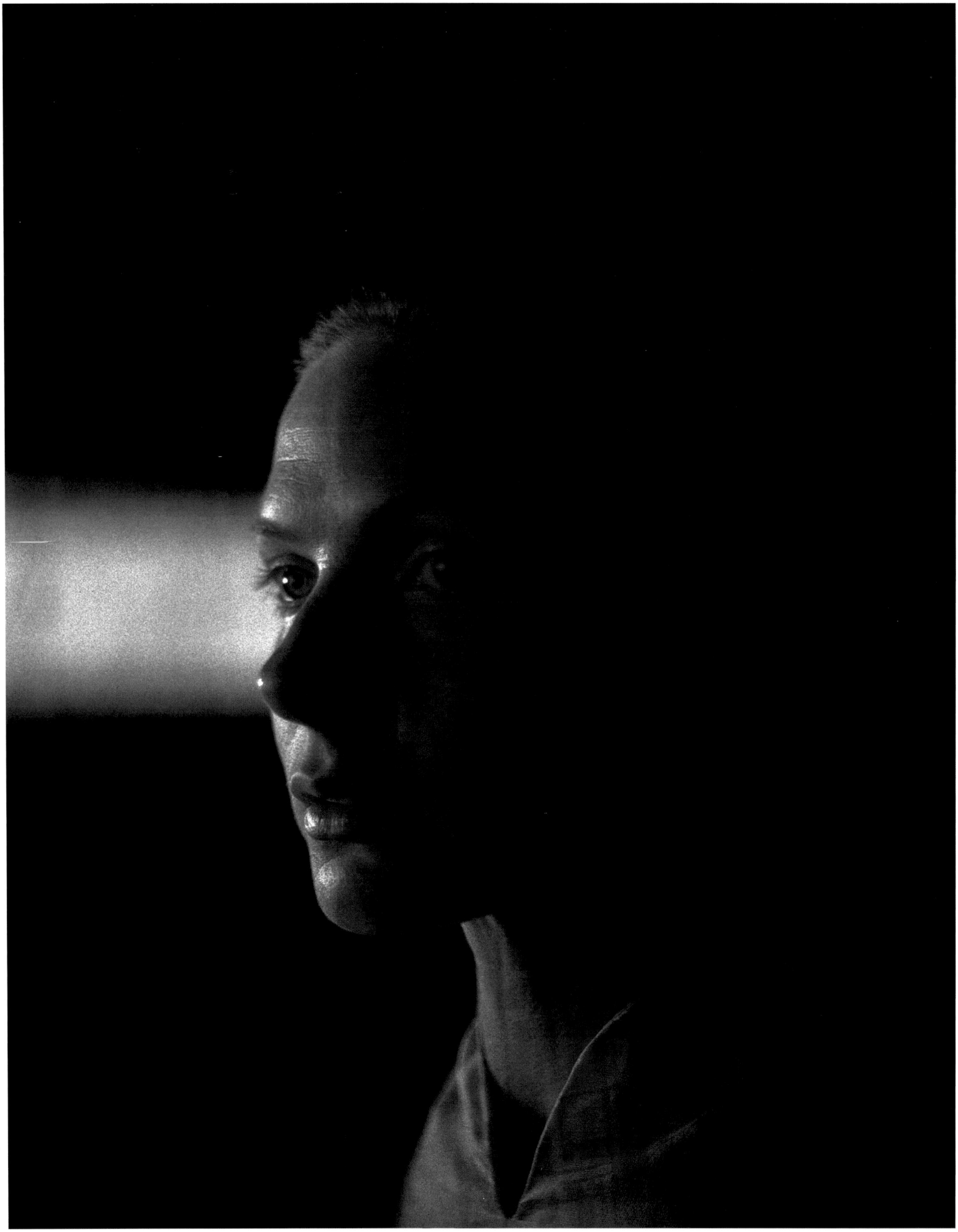

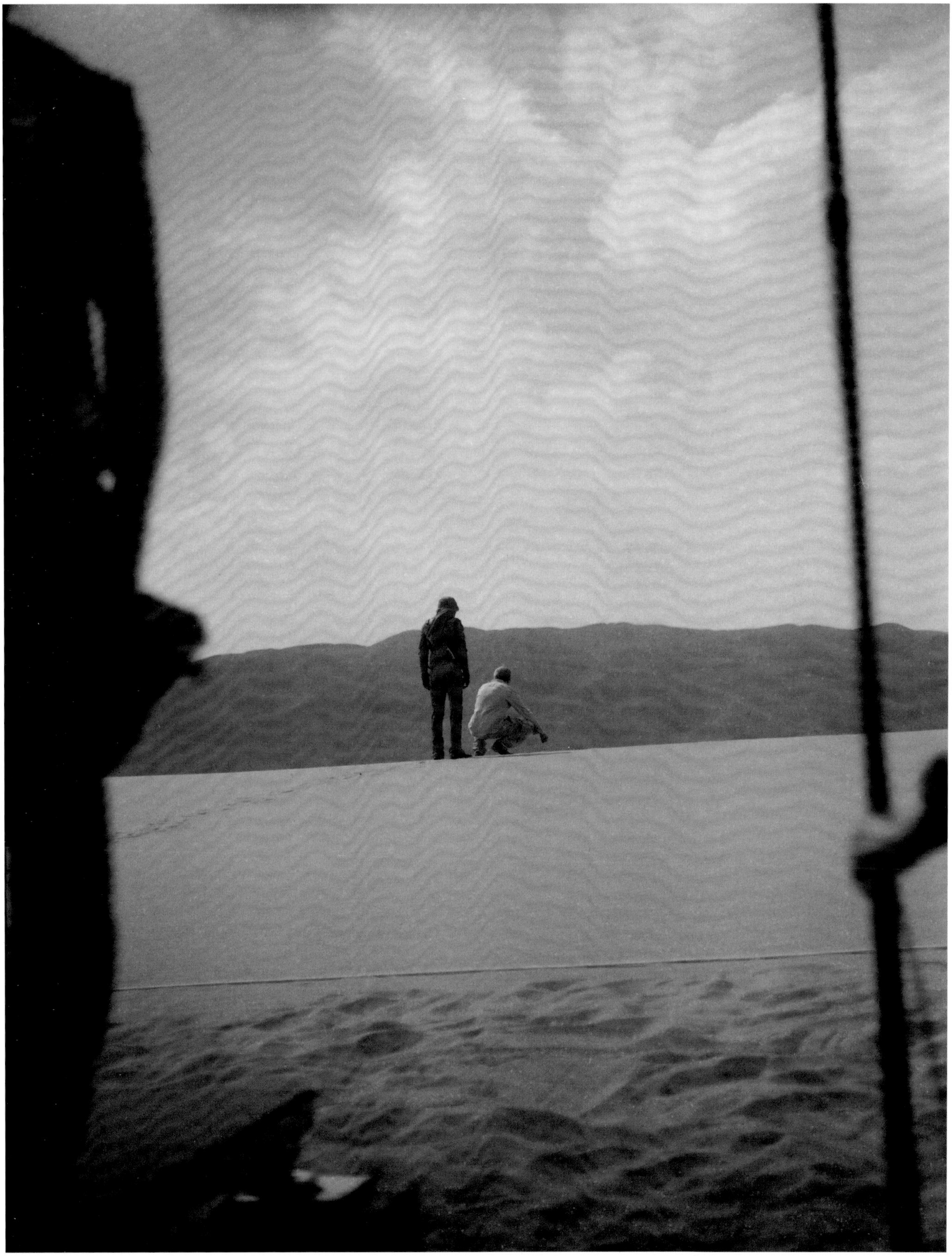

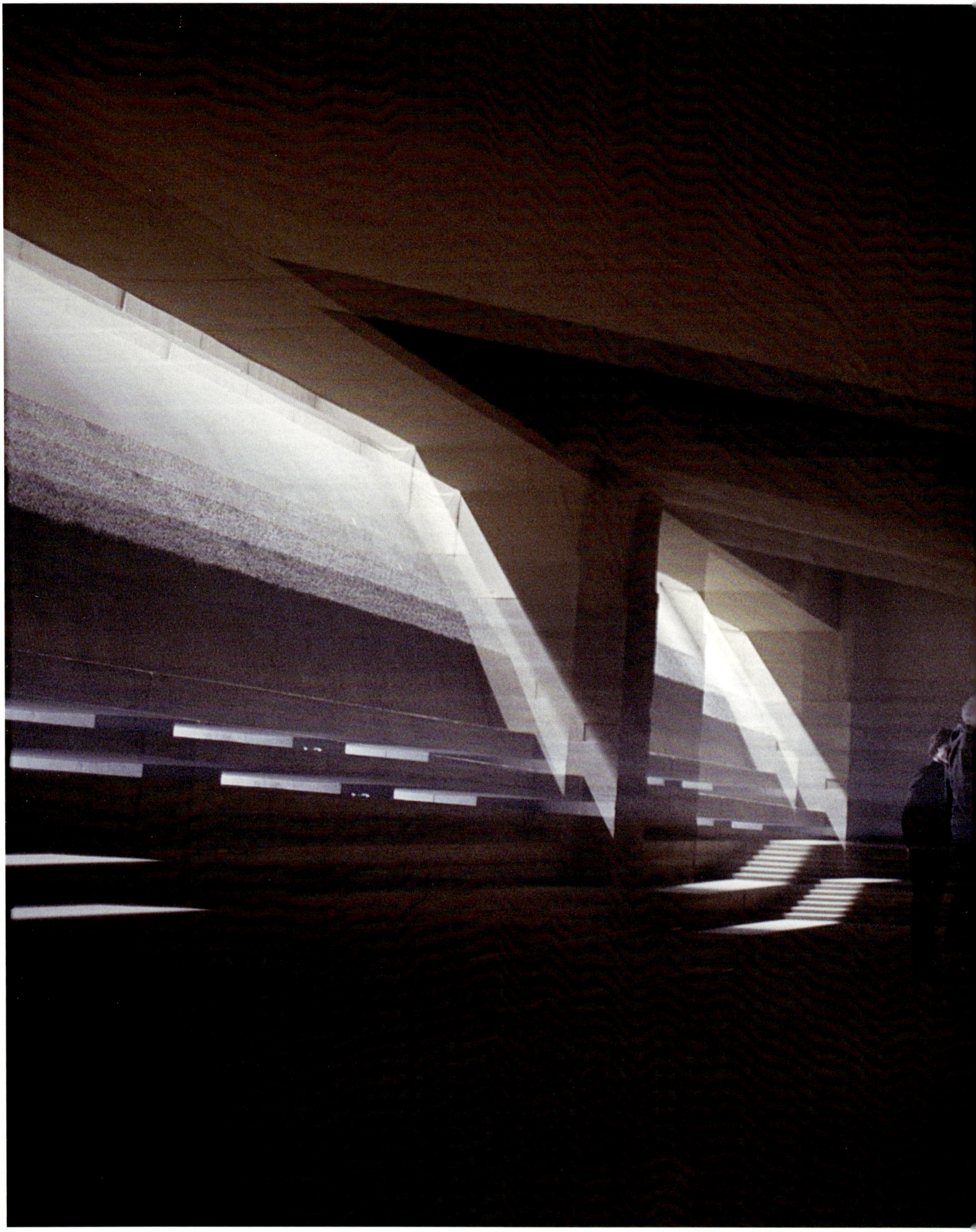

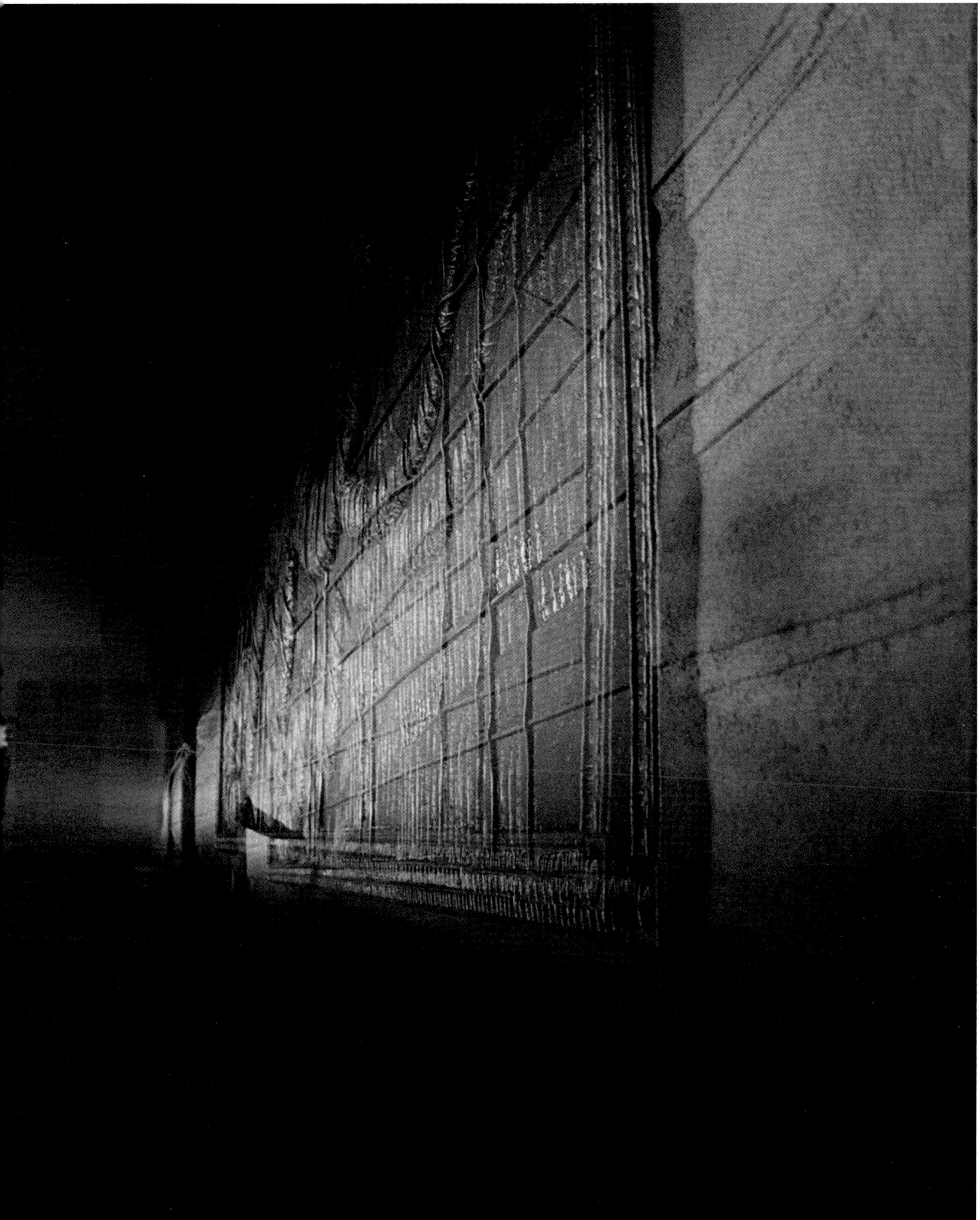

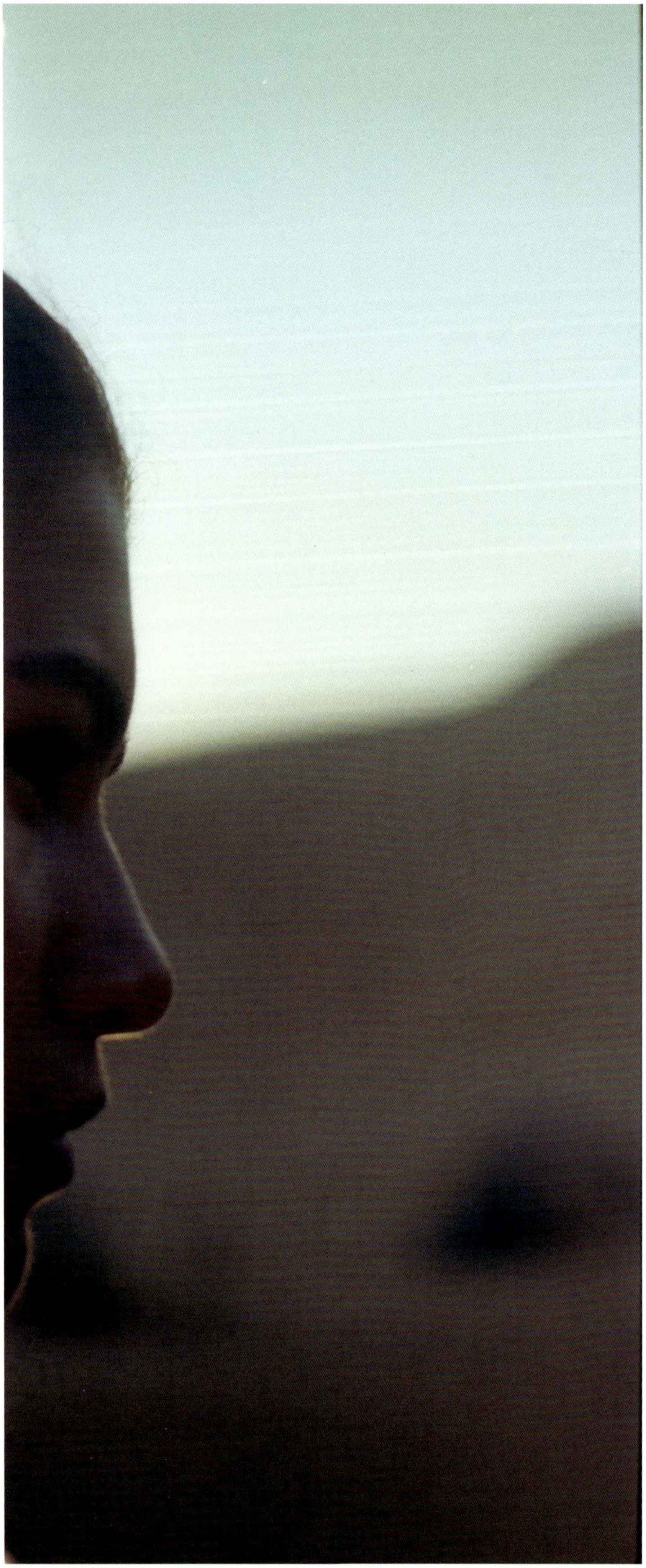

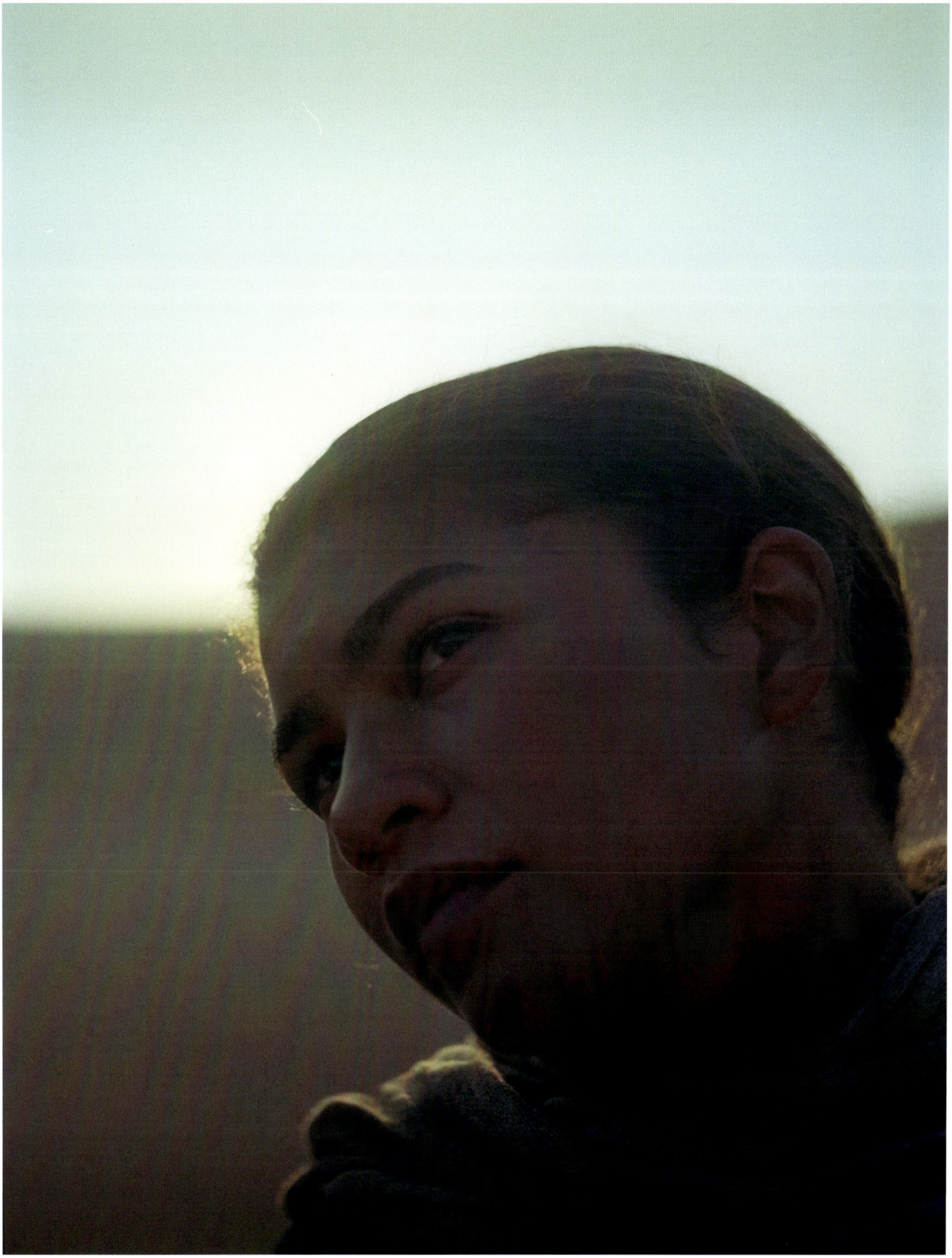

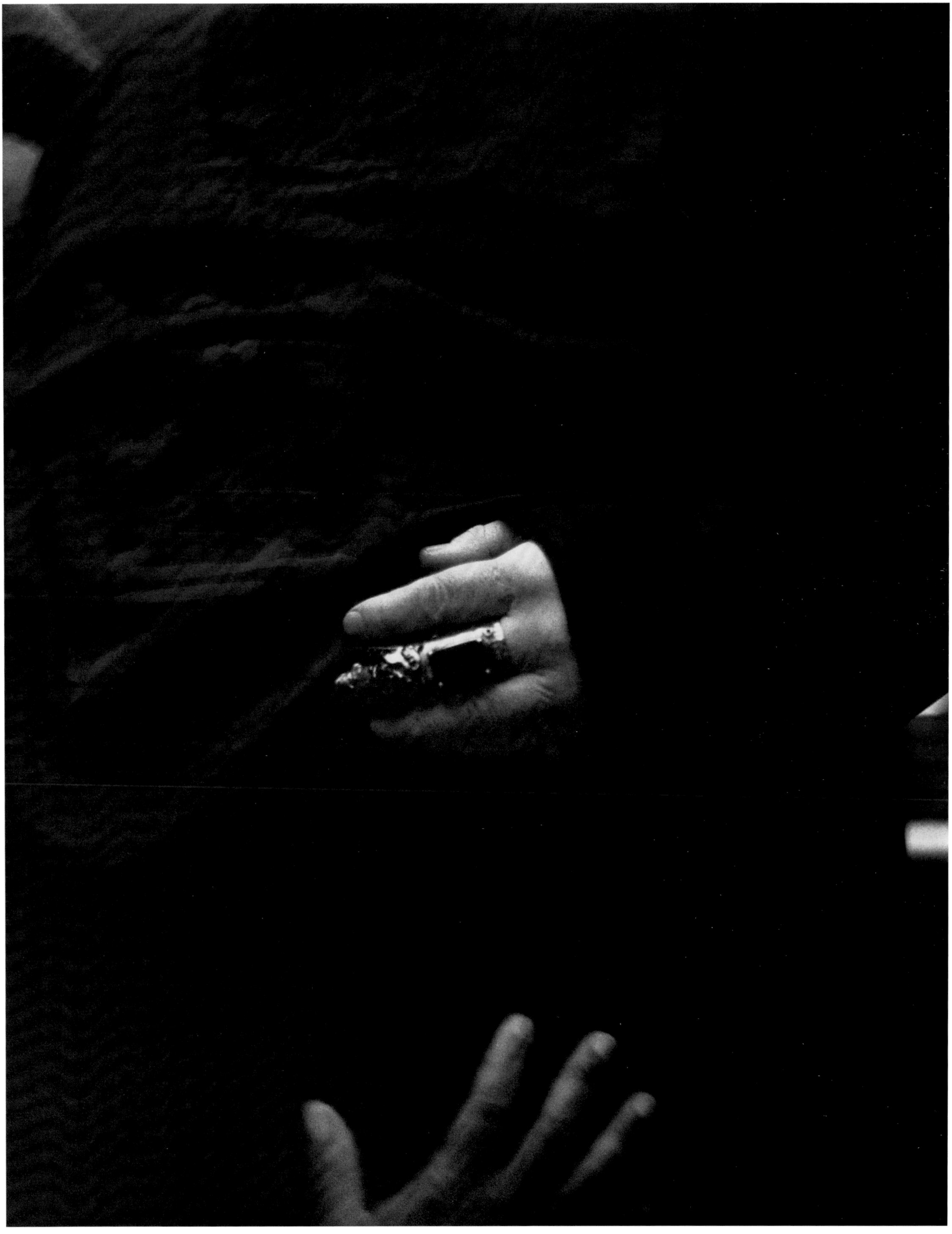

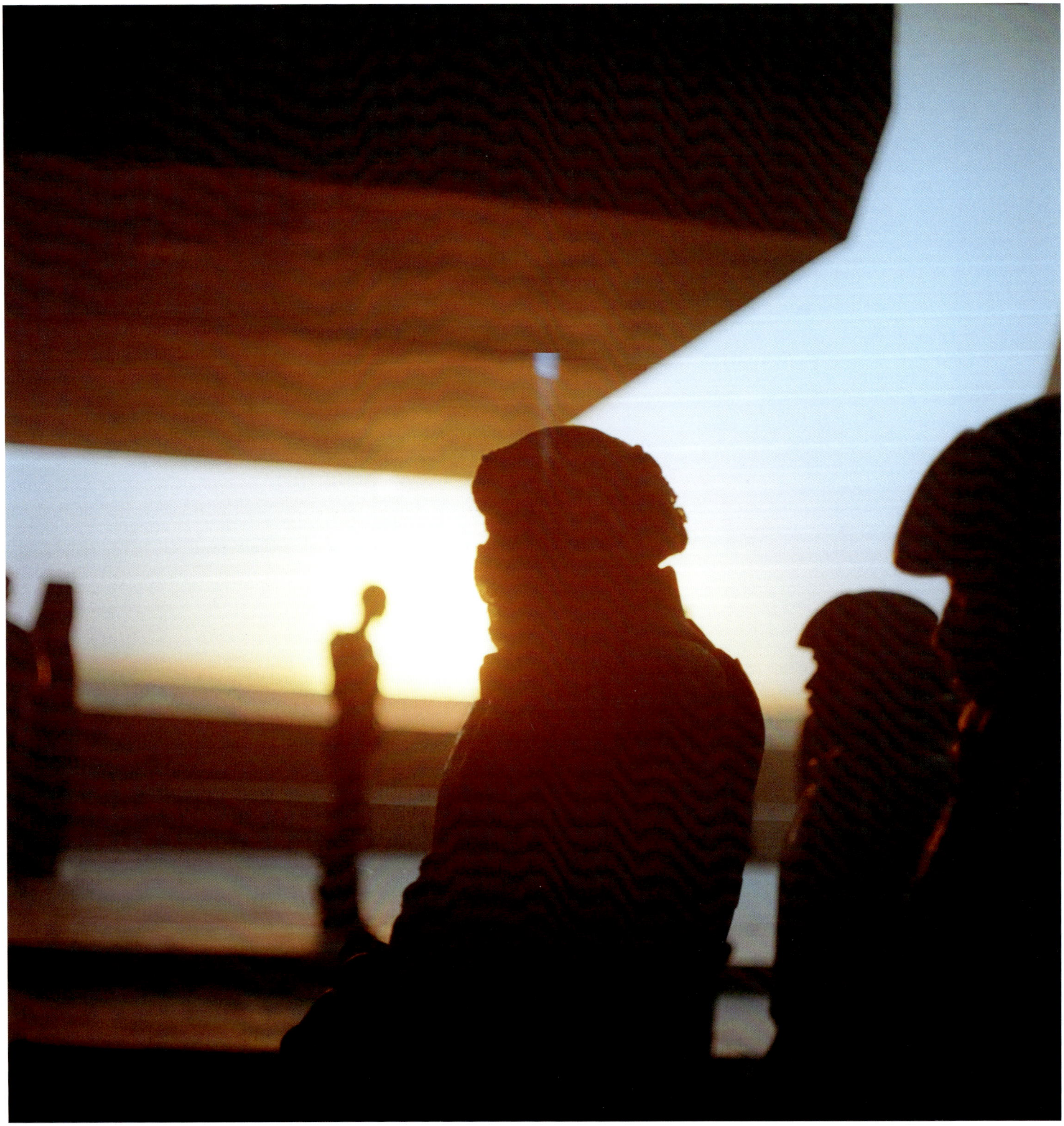

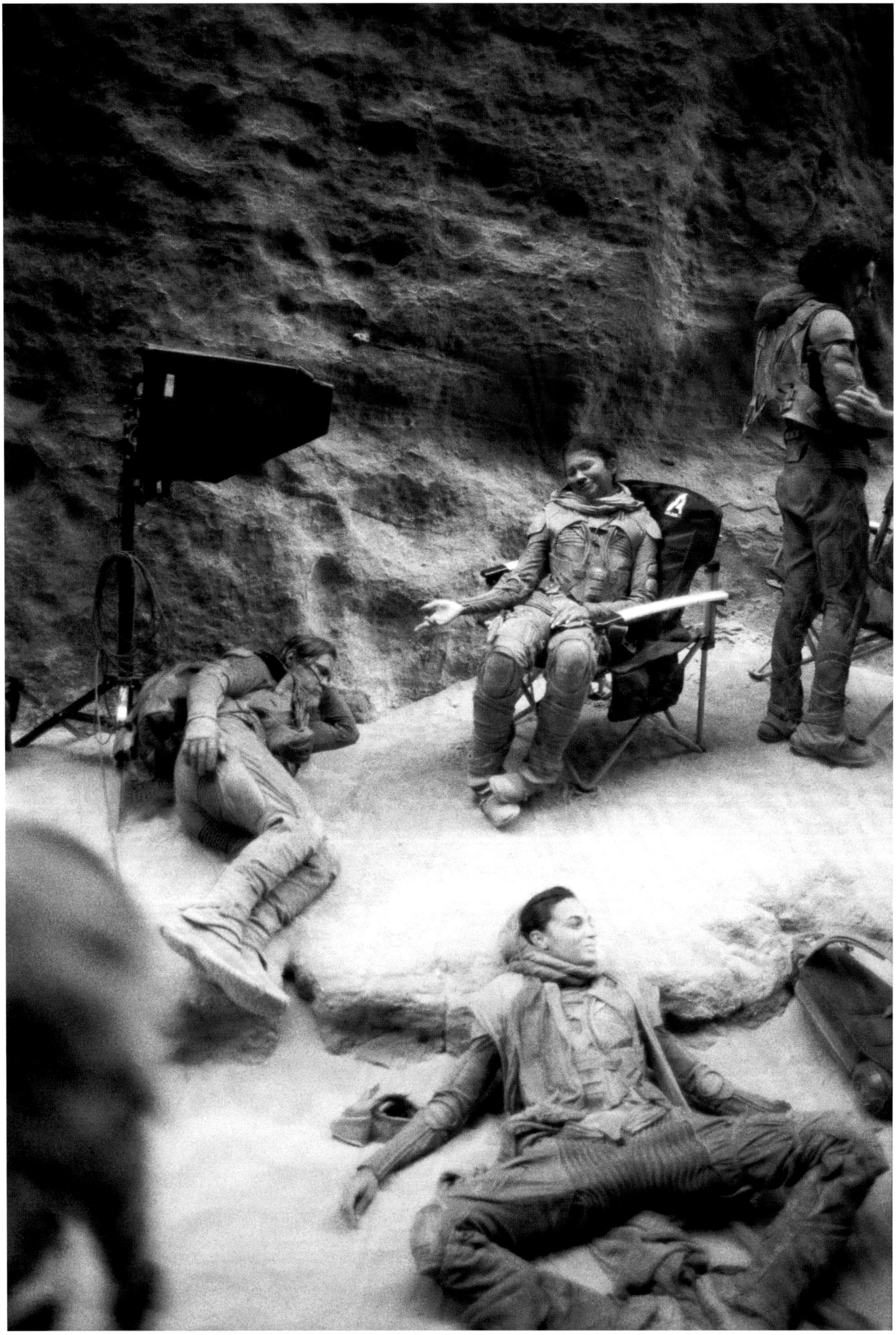

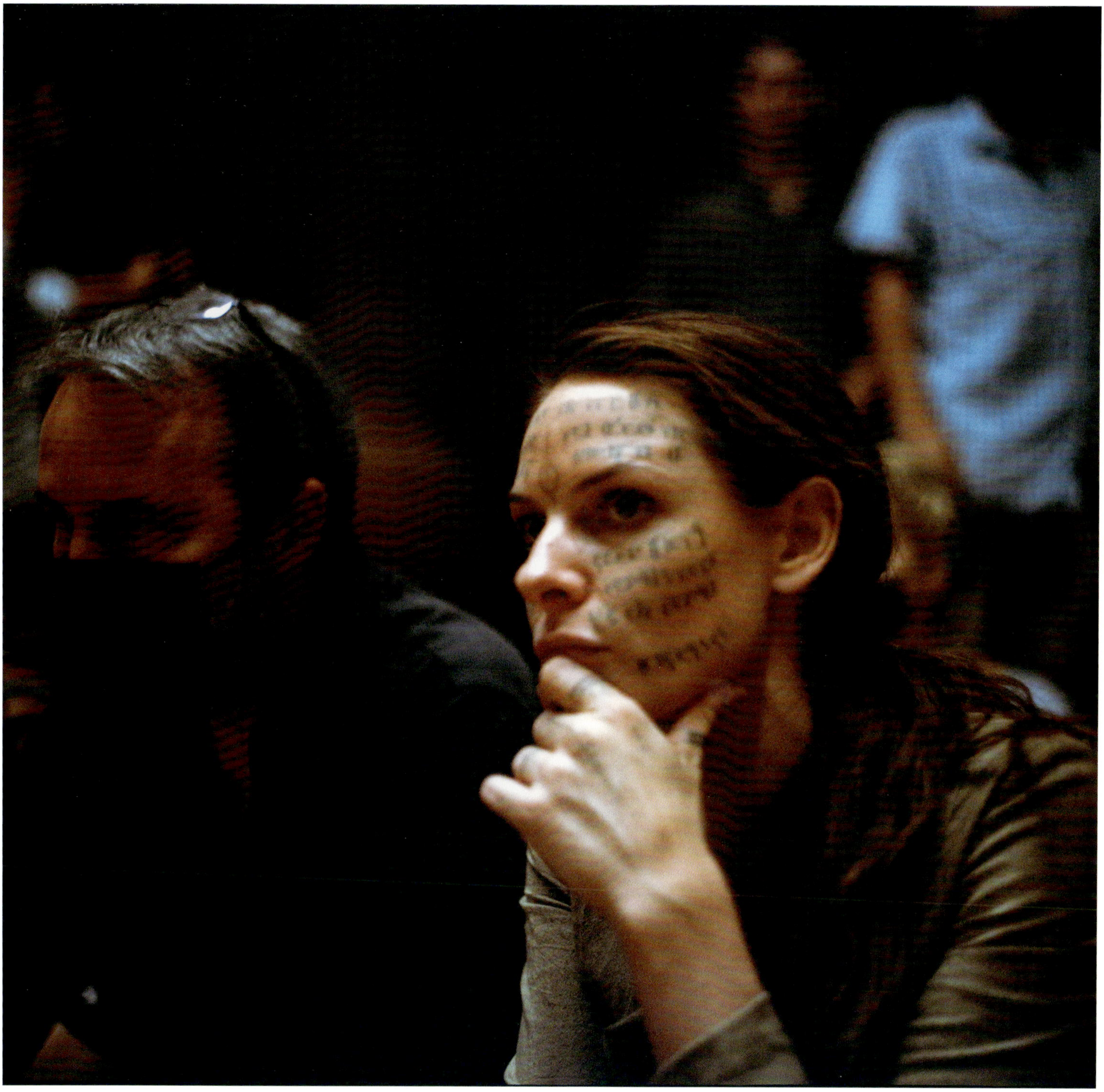

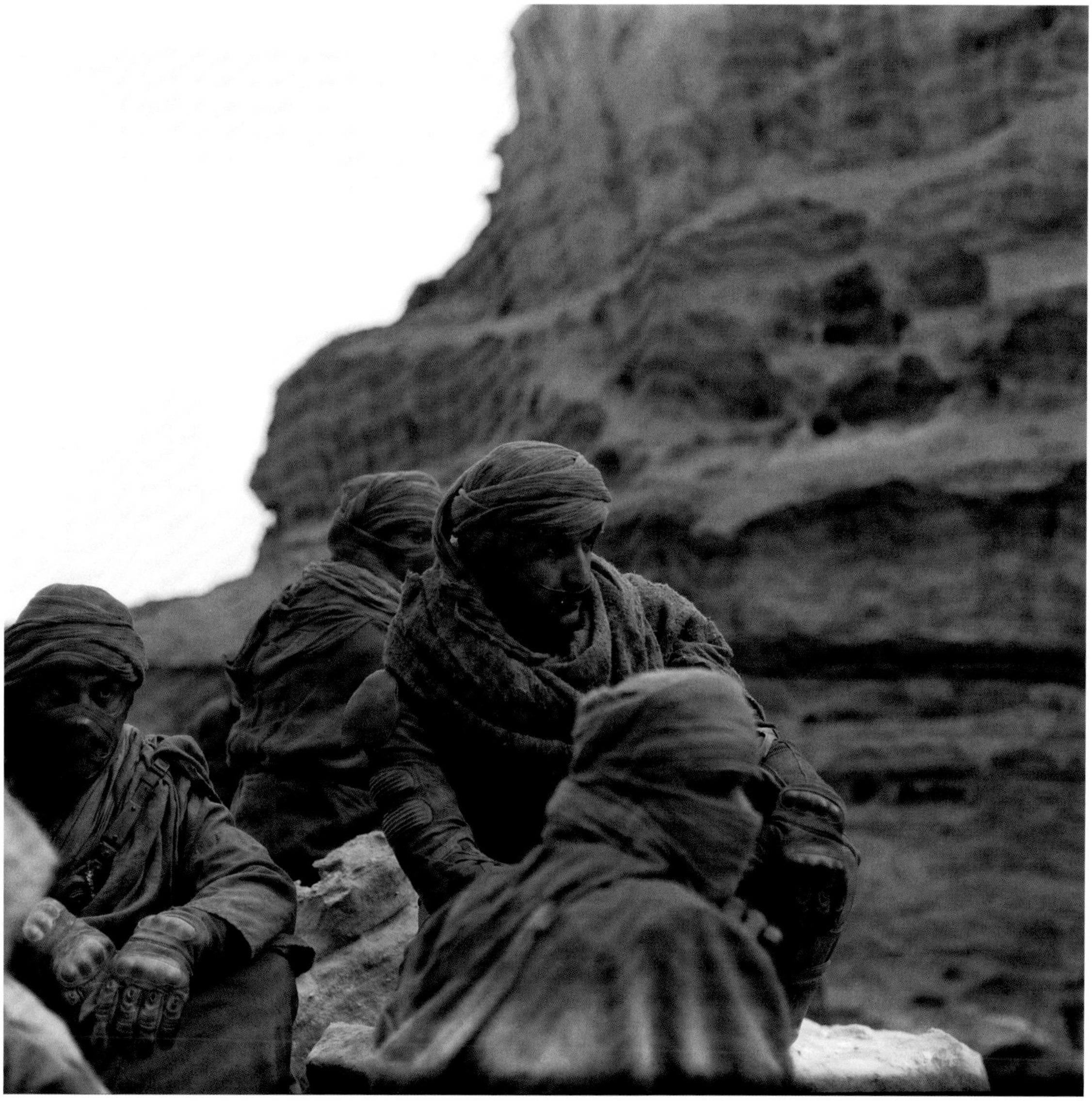

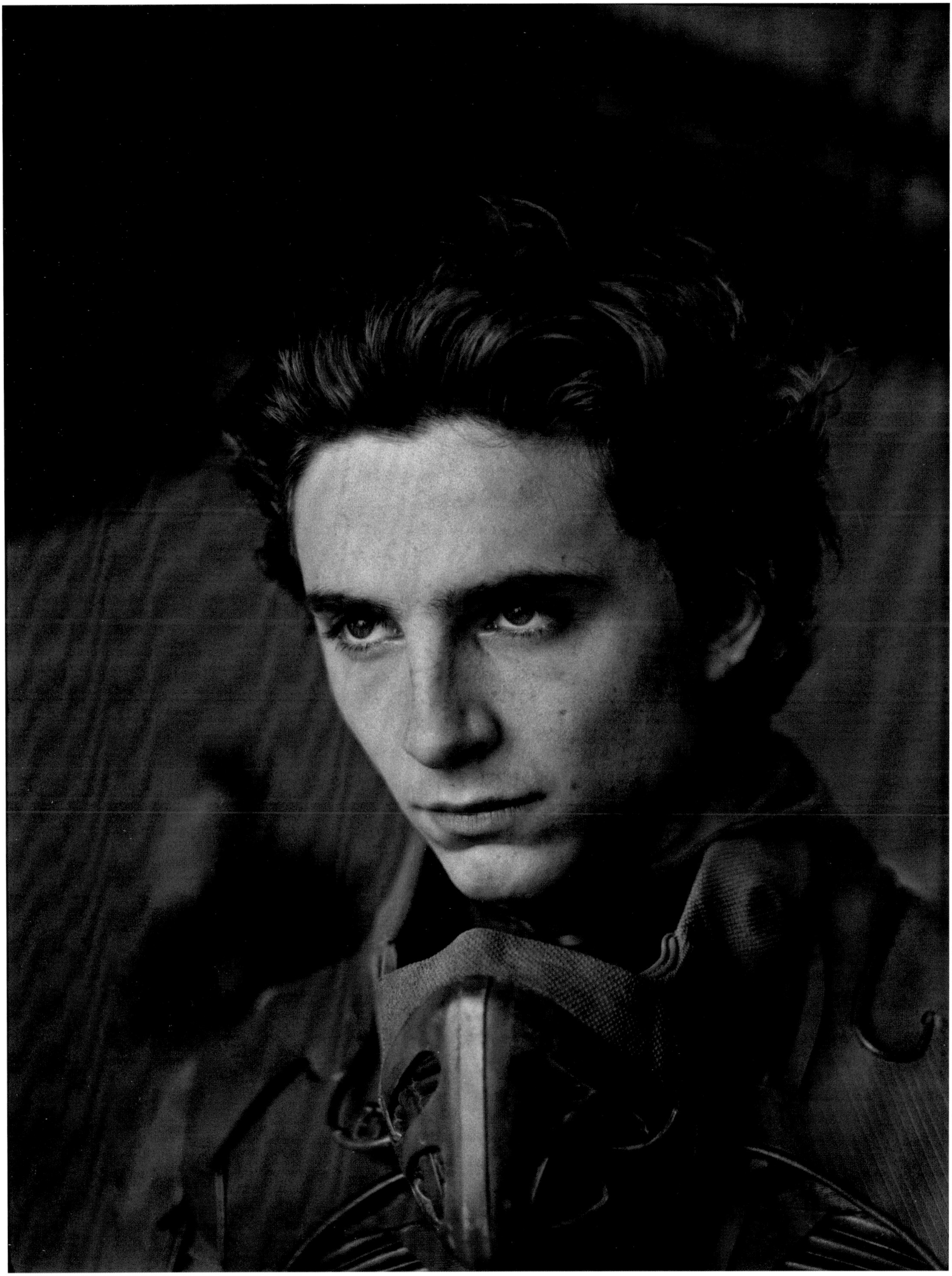

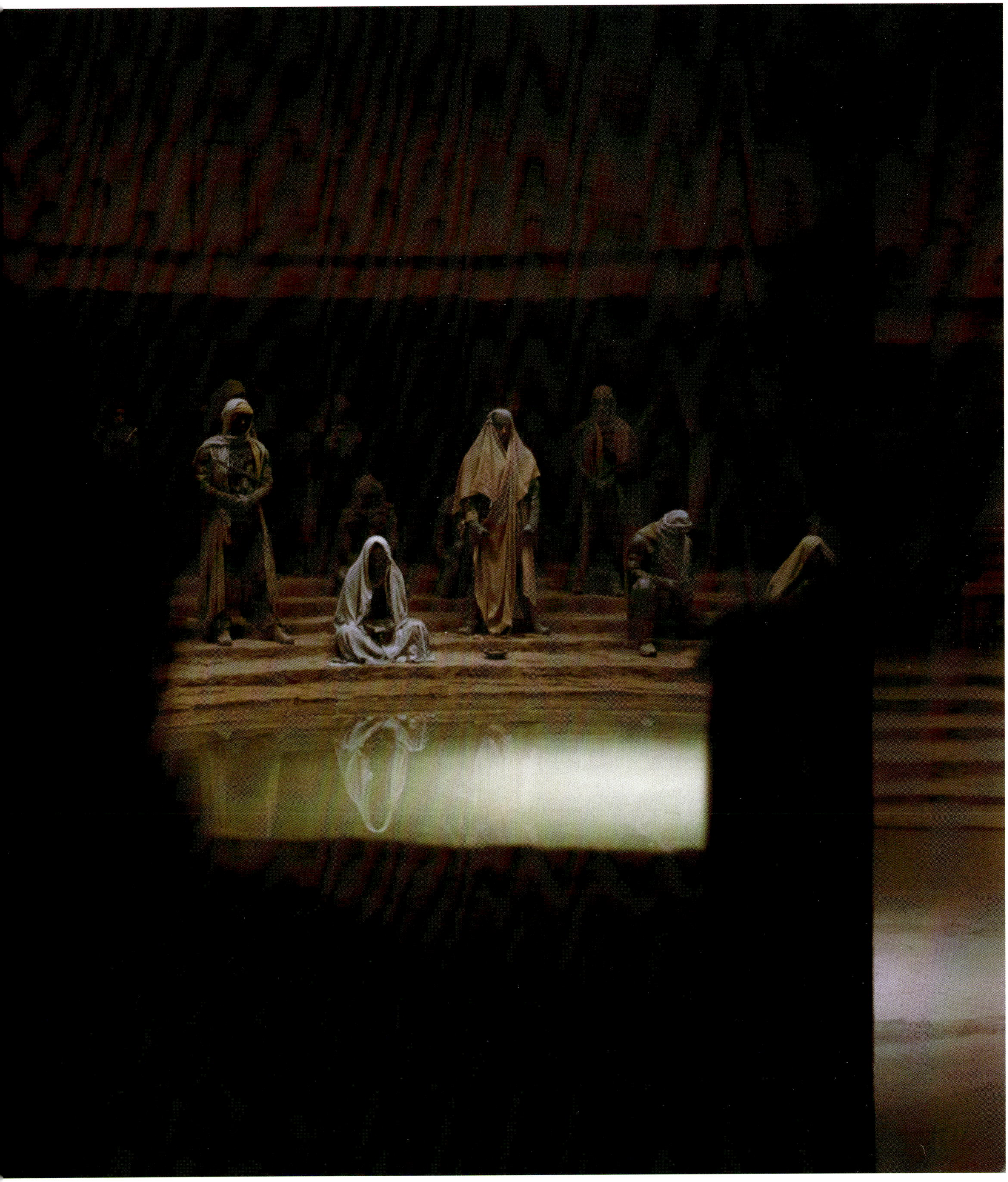

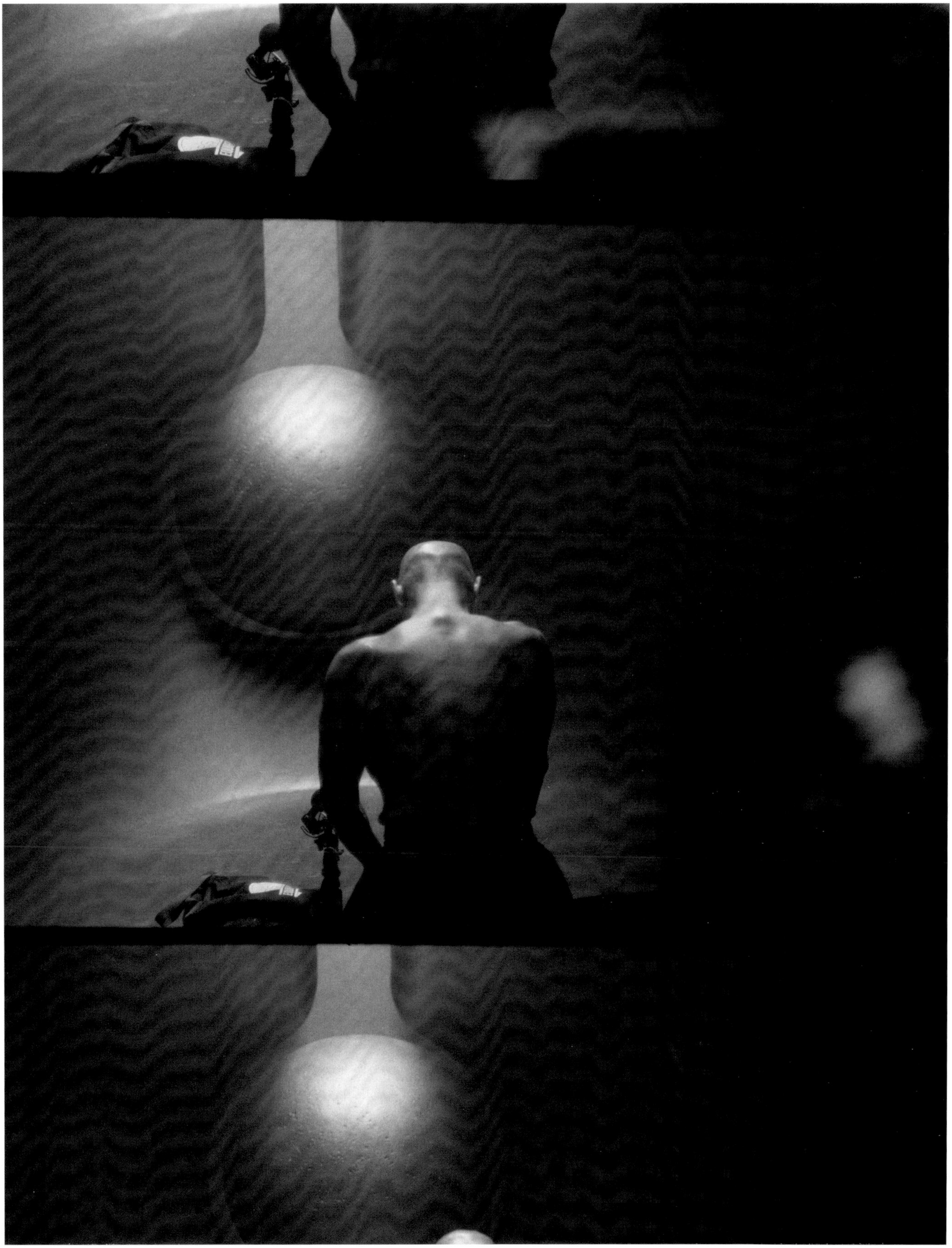

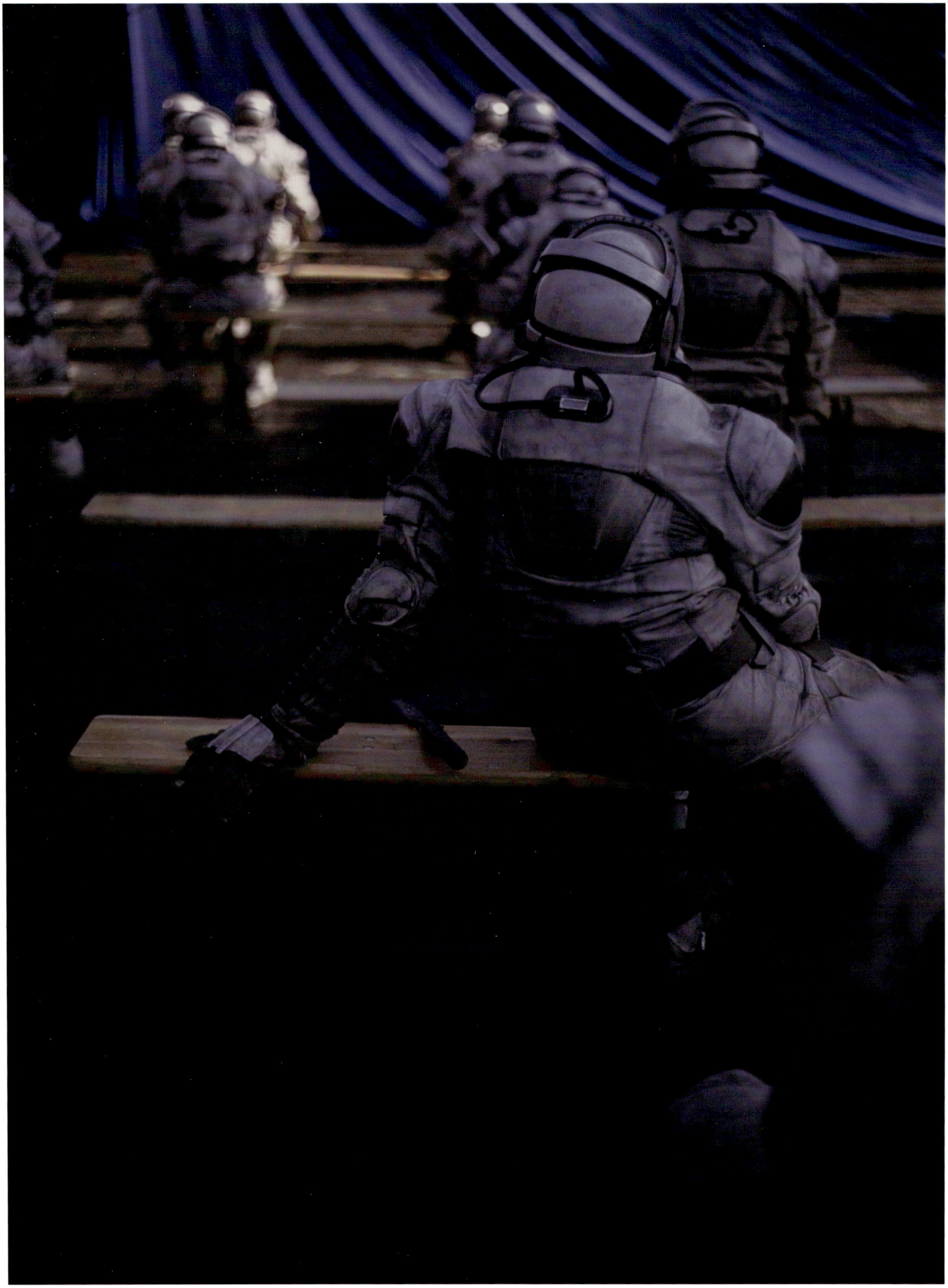

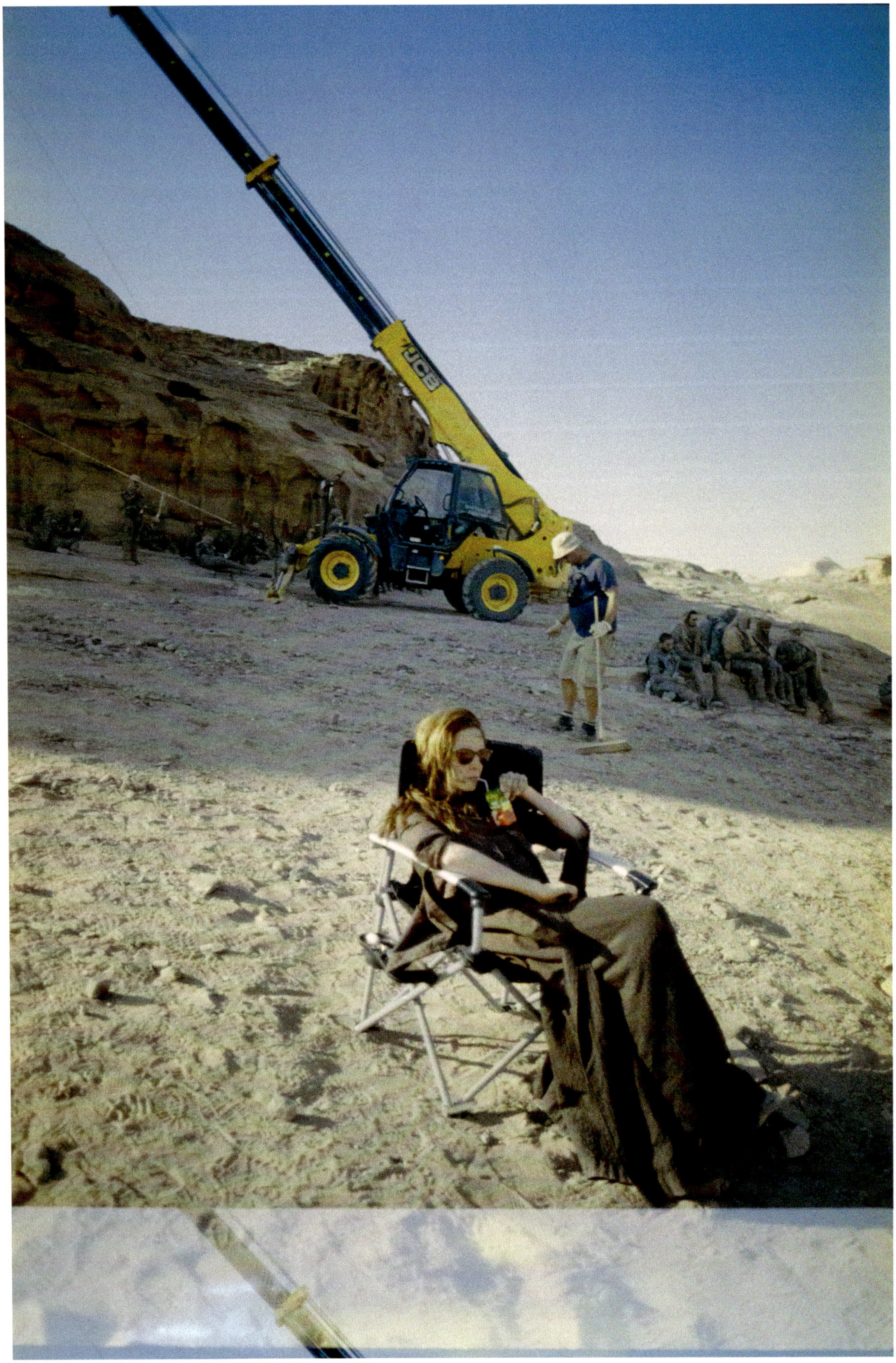
JCB

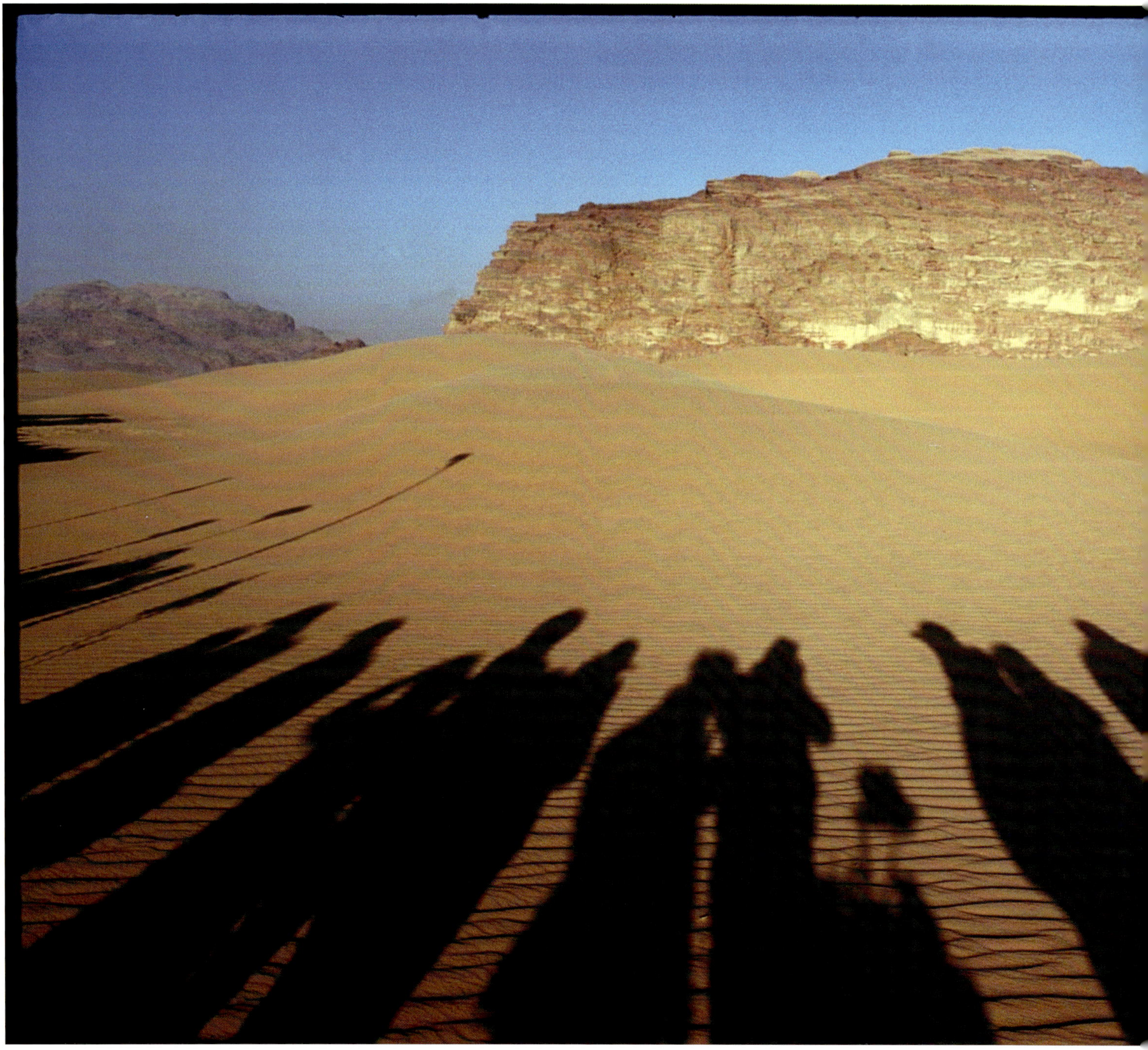

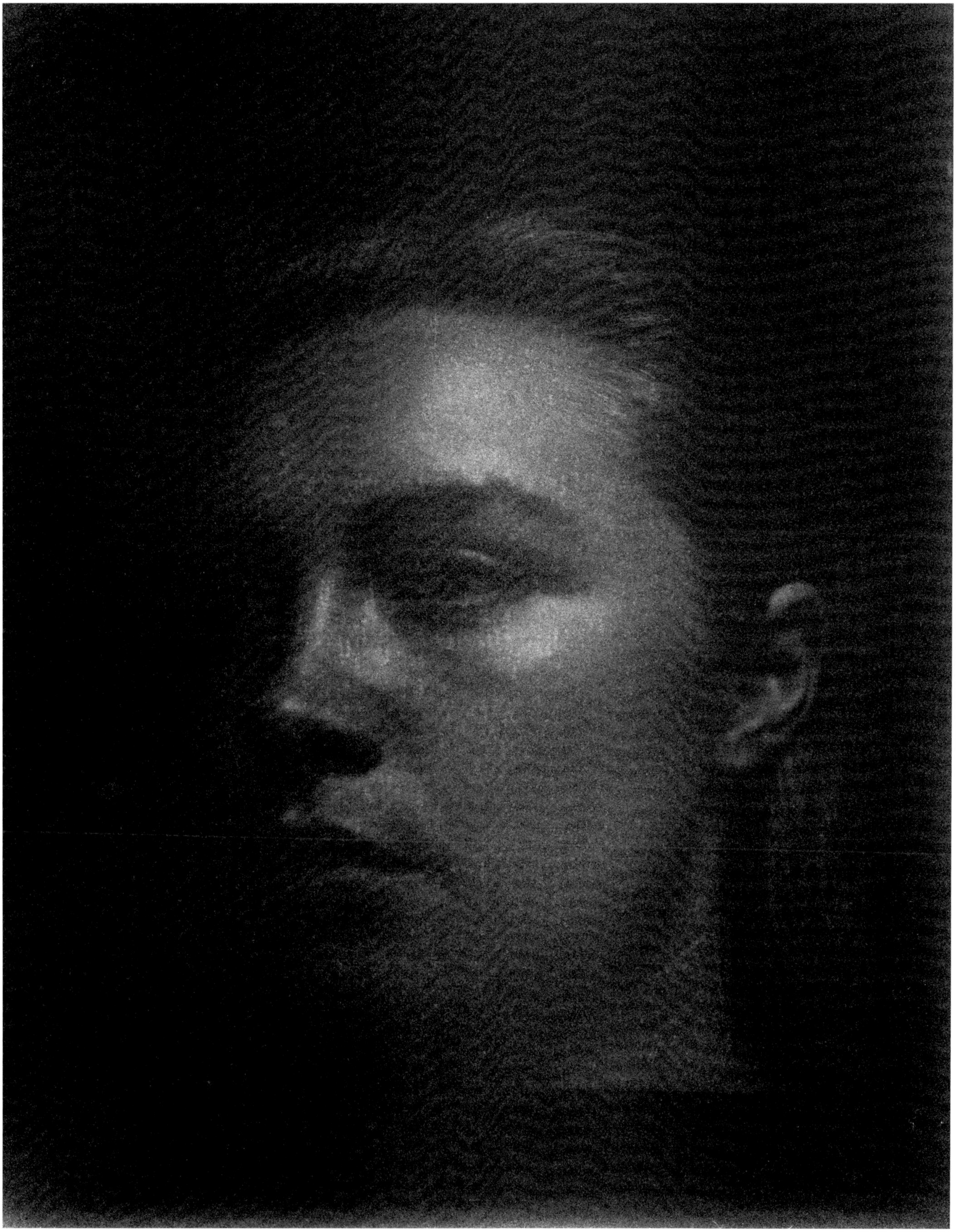

We are in the middle of the desert while my dad is working. I don't really know what he does but sometimes he comes back to the room in a spacesuit while we are eating dinner. My sister hates it. She always backs away. I like knowing that he likes to dress differently than he normally does. It's usually a black shirt, blue jeans, and cowboy boots. This isn't anything like that. He looks more like a dirty astronaut than my dad. There's something scary about him now, and my sister doesn't trust it. Me, though: I like something different. If I'm honest, I like when things don't go my way.

He splays his hand in my periphery as we walk the swishy sand, which I know is a sign to grab his pinky. I do. I'm irritated because I wanted to watch *Bluey* this morning but my Dad likes to start our days roaming through the hotel in search of things that haven't yet been found. He thinks nothing's been found without us finding it. We find everything first. Then, inevitably, we wander outside and keep walking. Another adventure. Another discovery, mostly about our relationship.

We wander outside and start to walk toward the red sand. Every step sinks and every thought burns. We left early but the sun already screams. I feel the heat of the day settling on top of my head as we walk along the edge of a high dune that I know he climbed the face of yesterday. He keeps talking about it. Every step feels like the ground is going to swallow me up. I don't know where we are supposed to be going, but we keep going there.

We are almost at the peak. Dad and I got into an argument because I didn't want to continue walking. He understood what I was saying but he still wouldn't stop. I don't like it when he gets like that. He's like a robot that is broken. He knelt down, patted my head, kissed my cheek with his robot lips, and kept walking. I didn't move for a long time, but then I started to get really hot, so moving was the only way to stay cooler. I didn't tell my dad that, so he thinks it was because whatever he was staying made me walk. It didn't. I made the decision to do it myself.

We're at the top, and I don't care about *Bluey* anymore. I can see everything from up here, and the face of the dune looks straight down. I feel like I could lift my arms and fly all the way back down to the hotel. I know I can't, but I lift my arms anyway. He takes a photo of me. He says he's proud of me. I'm four years old and I know I shouldn't be up here but my dad's a robot and sometimes he's an asshole but I like being the only girl who's at the peak of a dune with my dad before he goes to work. I know I'm the only one. My dad really loves me—I know that—and I love him okay too, like right now. It's hot up here but we sit down for a while and talk about Saturn and Jupiter and all the stars we can't see when the sun is coming up. We imagine a lot of stuff when we're together.

He wants to go down now, but I don't want to. I guess we should, but I tell him five more minutes, and he looks at me for a long time like he's going to say something, but he never does.

I hear footsteps. They are barefooted. The coarse skin slaps the tile, though I know he's trying to be quiet. I want to jump up and scare him, then he will lift me up and nuzzle his face into my neck. We will both laugh. But I don't because my sister and my mom are still asleep. I listen to my breath, how my chest lifts and falls with it. In the bathroom a light comes on behind a closed door. It leaks shards of white geometric figures over the bed. I hear brushing and barely a flow of water. The light turns off but the brushing continues. We ran on the sand yesterday. It was Sunday and my papa never works on Sundays, so he runs with us out in the open where the sun beats down, and the air is thick with a tiring heat. He never wins. It's always me or my sister, but it's mostly me.

A door opens in the dark and I hear footsteps again. The bed sinks at my feet and I hear the shoosh of him putting on his pants. I don't want him to leave. I try to say something, but nothing comes out. His socks. His shoes. A spoon hitting a bowl. The small refrigerator in the kitchen opens, but I don't hear it shut. Muted crunching. Silence. Suddenly, lips on my forehead come out from the dark. I reach my head up to touch his hair, which is long for his work. He puts his hand on my heart and puts a little more weight on it than is just the weight of his hand, then it's gone. Silence.

When the sun comes up and Mama and my sister awaken, I'll still have my hands where my papa's were, on my chest. I'll ask my mom if we can watch cartoons because there's sand all around us, as far as the eye can see. I'll look out there today and see if I can see my papa way off in the distance somewhere dressed in his dirty astronaut suit. I know he's crying somewhere because he likes playing with us more than he likes doing anything else. When I sing, he cries. When I look at him in the eyes, he cries too.

He'll come home after we've gotten into bed and Mama has read four or five books to us. He'll come home and he'll place his lips on my forehead, and his hand on my chest and put more weight on it than just the weight of his hand, and I'll go to sleep before he ever takes it off, if he ever takes it off.

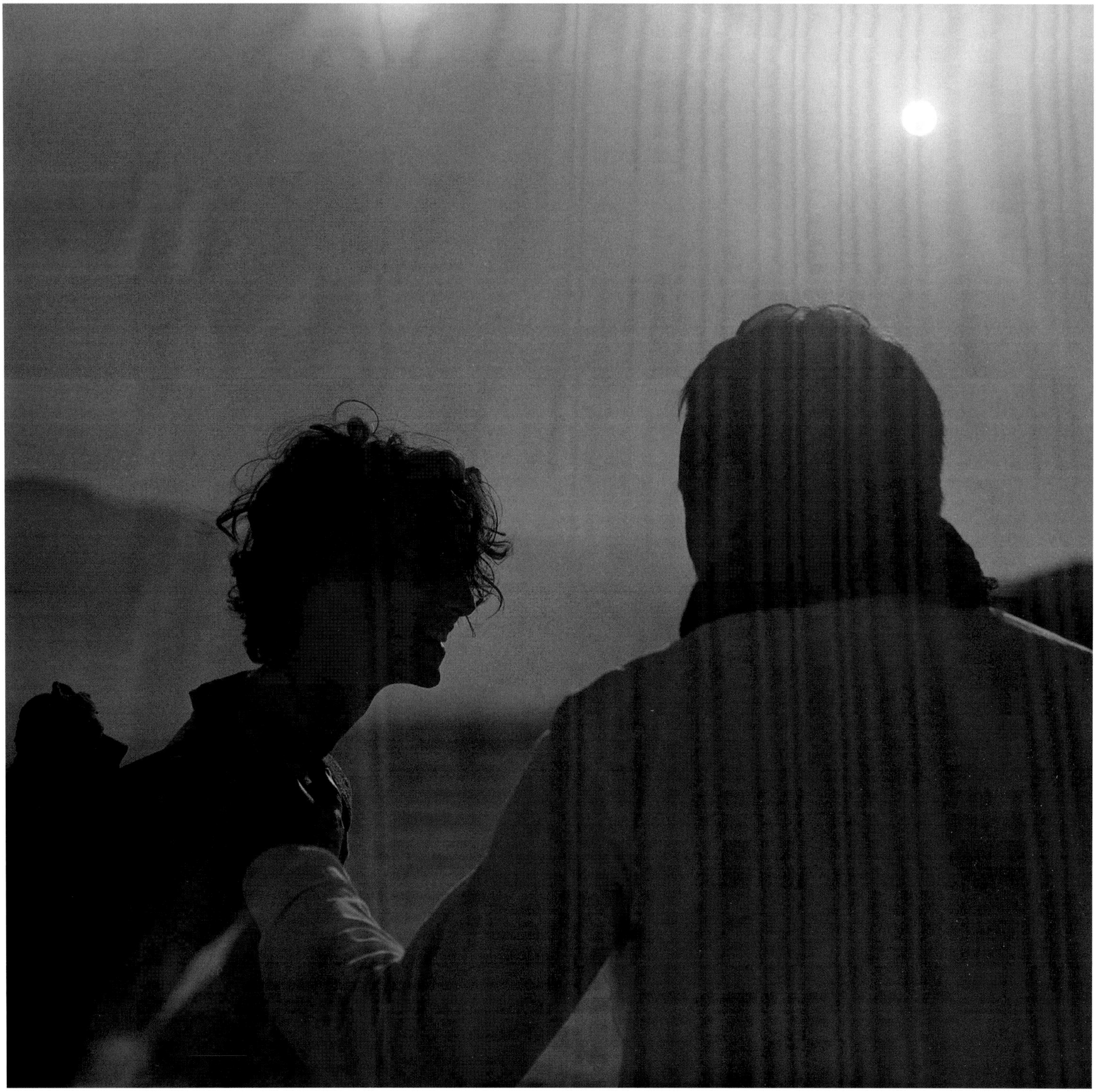

The production takes hold of the shadow's whim and lies exhausted onto the dune's now blackish pitch. Black painted figures slide down the topography, morphed into what might have been a Francis Bacon swath of colors: wild with turbulence, insaned with myopia. We have been sucked right into the phantasmagoria that Frank Herbert created and we are melting with the heat in a spastic laughter; with brother and sisterhood, we hold hands, our equipment, tilt our heads to the sun, Hollywood no longer having a hold on us, and abandon ourselves to the spice of the sand: caliche ahead, limestone, sand and new home/here, inhaling/exhaling the black release of our personalities growing by the minute at our feet as the sun also rises. There will be no going home, nor any need to.

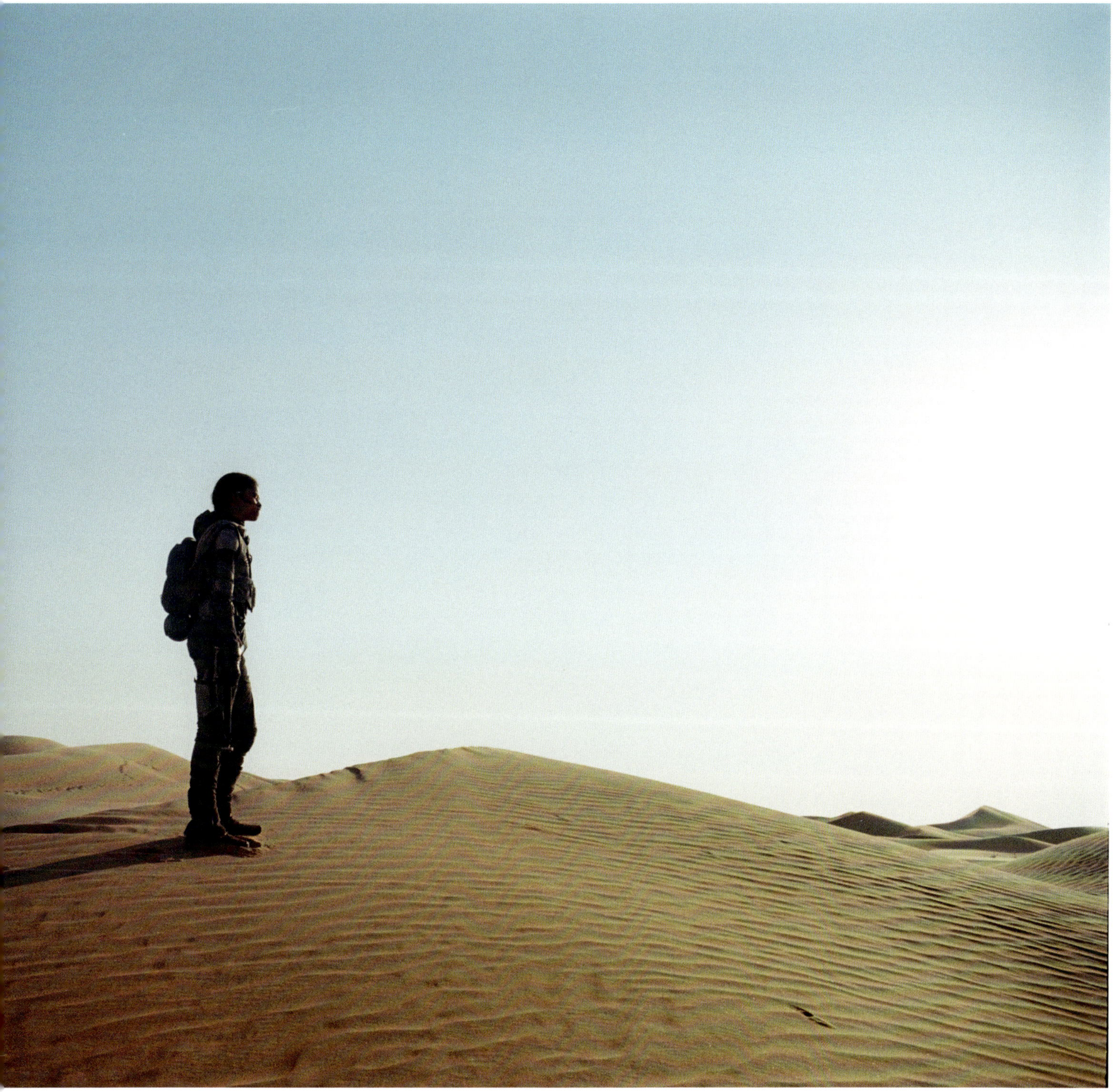

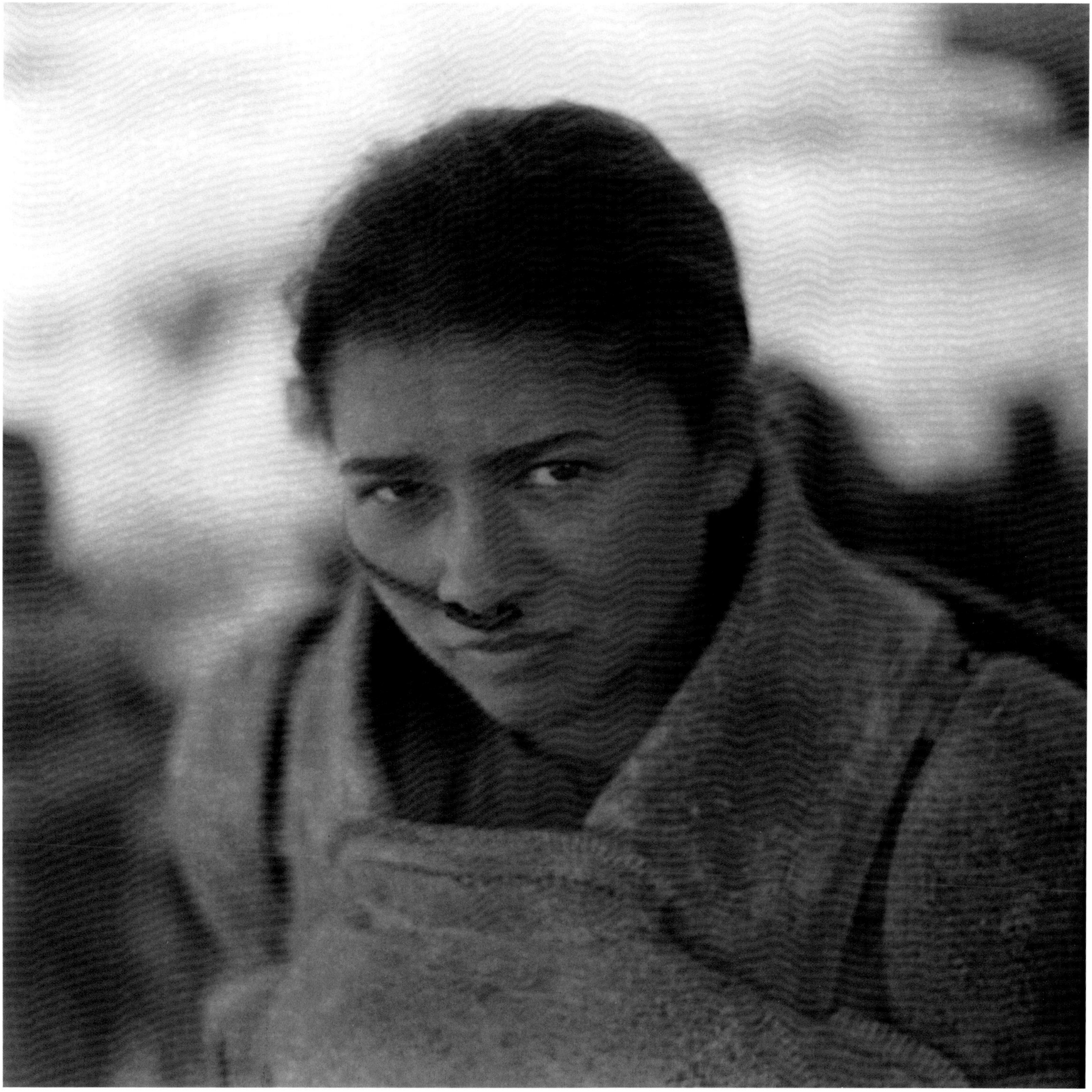

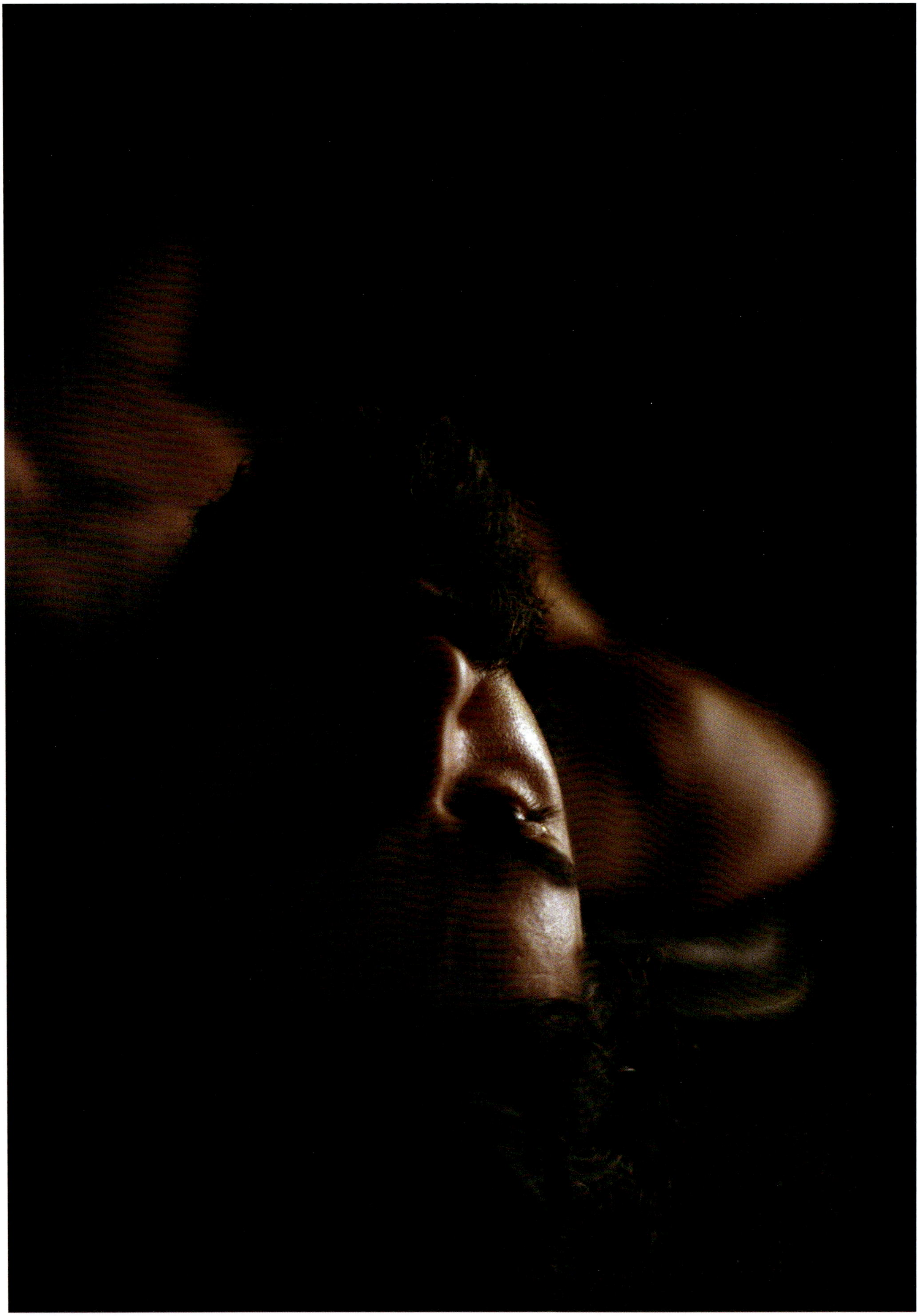

Oscar is doing squats outside
in the cold in Hungary.

His buddy has brought something
that is a pad, bands, and a bar to
simulate squats.

I watch them
do it out
the window
of my trailer.
I hope they
don't knock
on my door.

He does.
Damn it.

I'm outside now performing
the squats. "Wow, you're in good shape!"
16, 17, 18 … I finish. Gerry comes out.
He's worked with Johnny Depp and other
great actors.

He's paid to remind
actors why they should always
balance on the verge of businessmen
and inmates. He's paid.
The guy doing the squats now is paid.
Oscar and I are paid. We're all paid
for doing something.

For now, squatting.

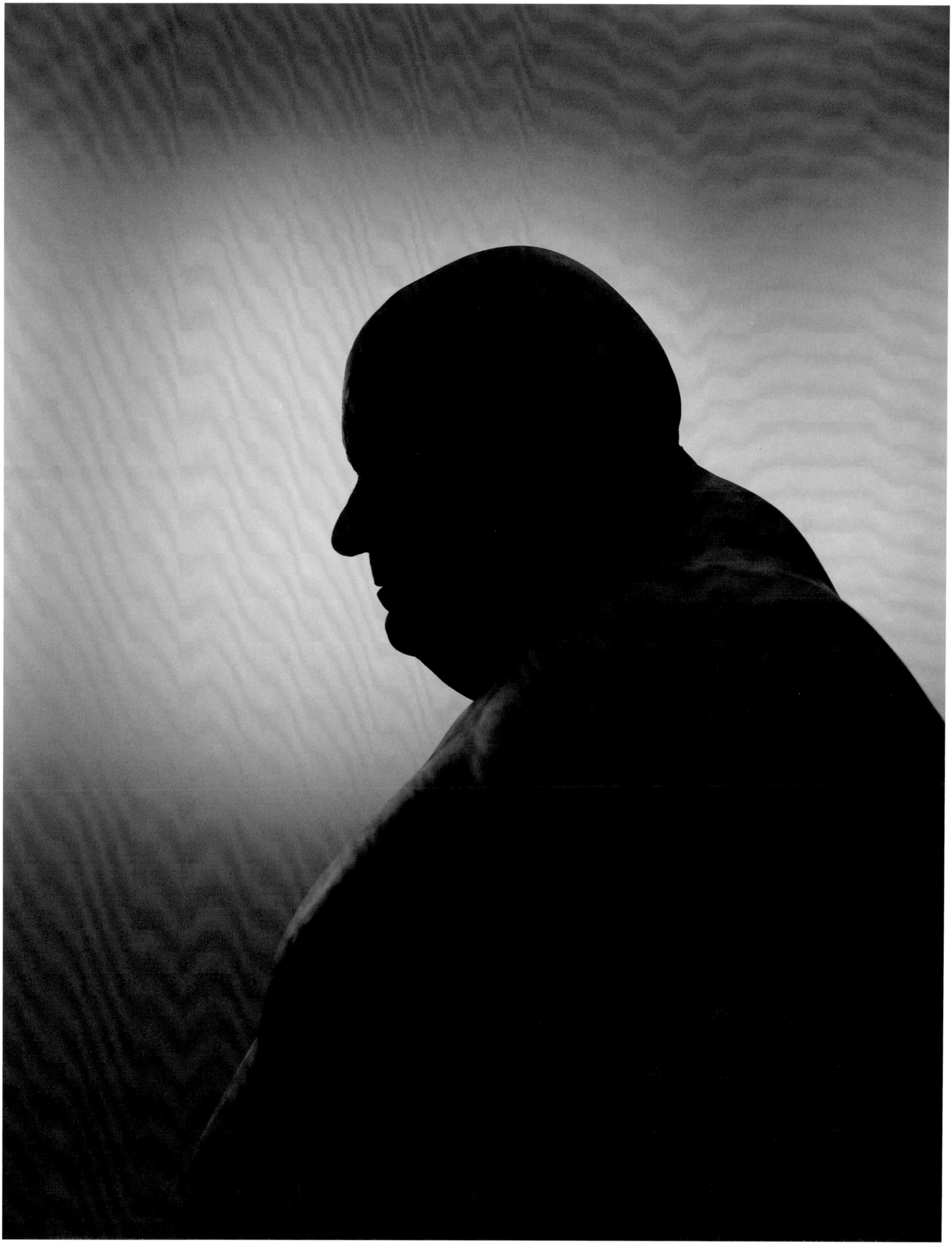

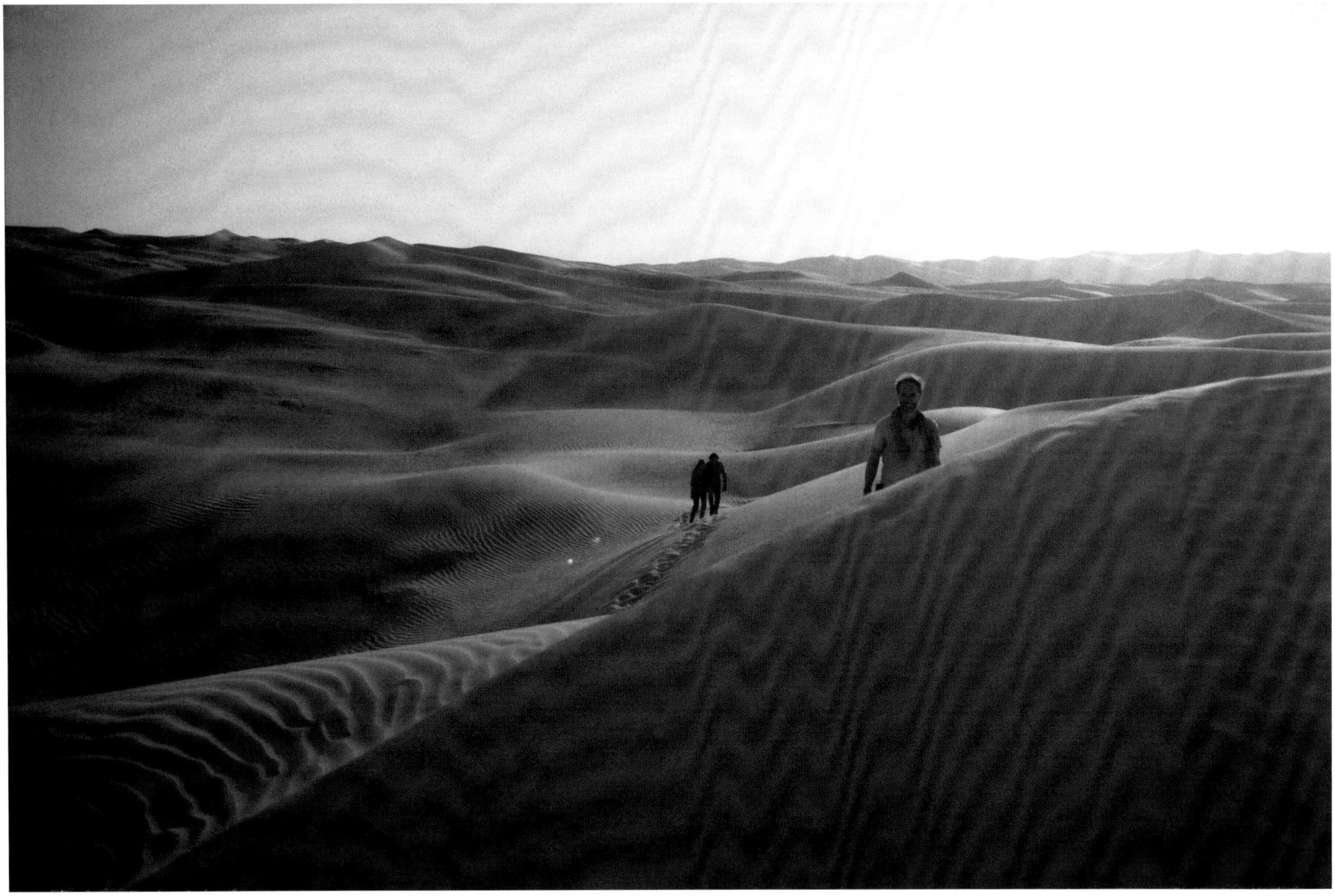

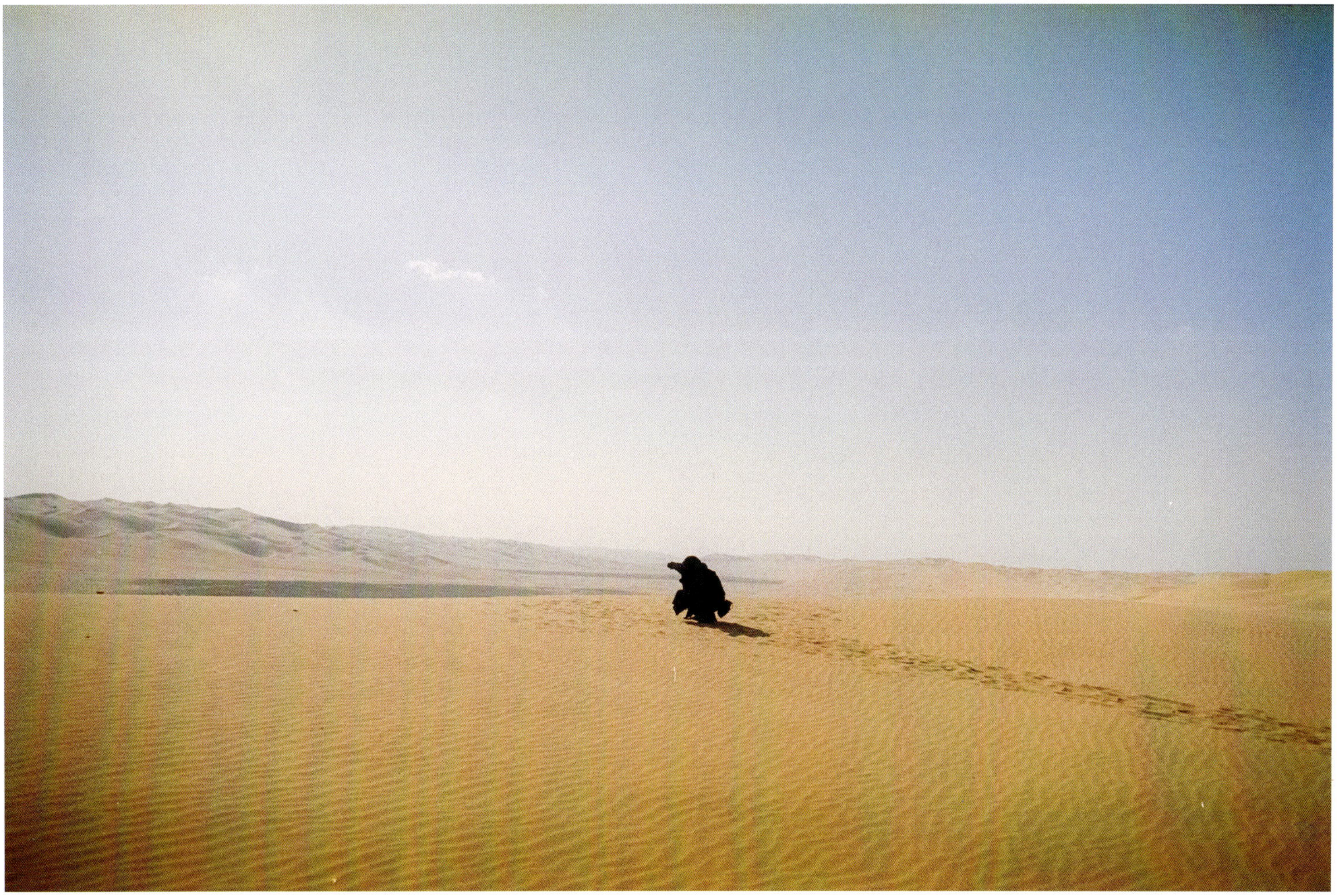

Long paths of footprints echo into the distance. There are sandbags nobody uses to travel down the face of a dune because we are all adept at the sink-footed steps needed to float with the least amount of energy to conserve for the upward bottomless battle to the peak at the other side. We are all better athletes now, but we are nothing compared to those who live here. They are the same people we see on the sides of the roads we drive along to work, tending to sheep, or walking alongside their camel. They have nothing of the luxuries even our poorest don out there in the States. Electricity doesn't run through some of these villages. What do they do when the sun goes down? They sleep. They sleep and they dream. Or maybe under candlelight they write in a similar journal to mine about the goings-on of their day: a 15-mile walk in 105-degree heat; another infant born without a hospital nearby; or the weekly gathering of neighbors for a dessert prepared by the children made of oatmeal and colorful spices grown in a closet.

We heave upwardly carrying what we can. We grab at the sand as if the sand might not move just once. But the reality is it is setting the mind up for the shaming of its life: the realization that we are not set up at all for this. The desert here demands a certain disposition. You can visit with your stargazing blindness, or you can walk among the galaxies that have peppered centuries of these people with an interior perseverance that nobody, not even hardest of perpetrations, will be able to break the spirit of a little hardship.

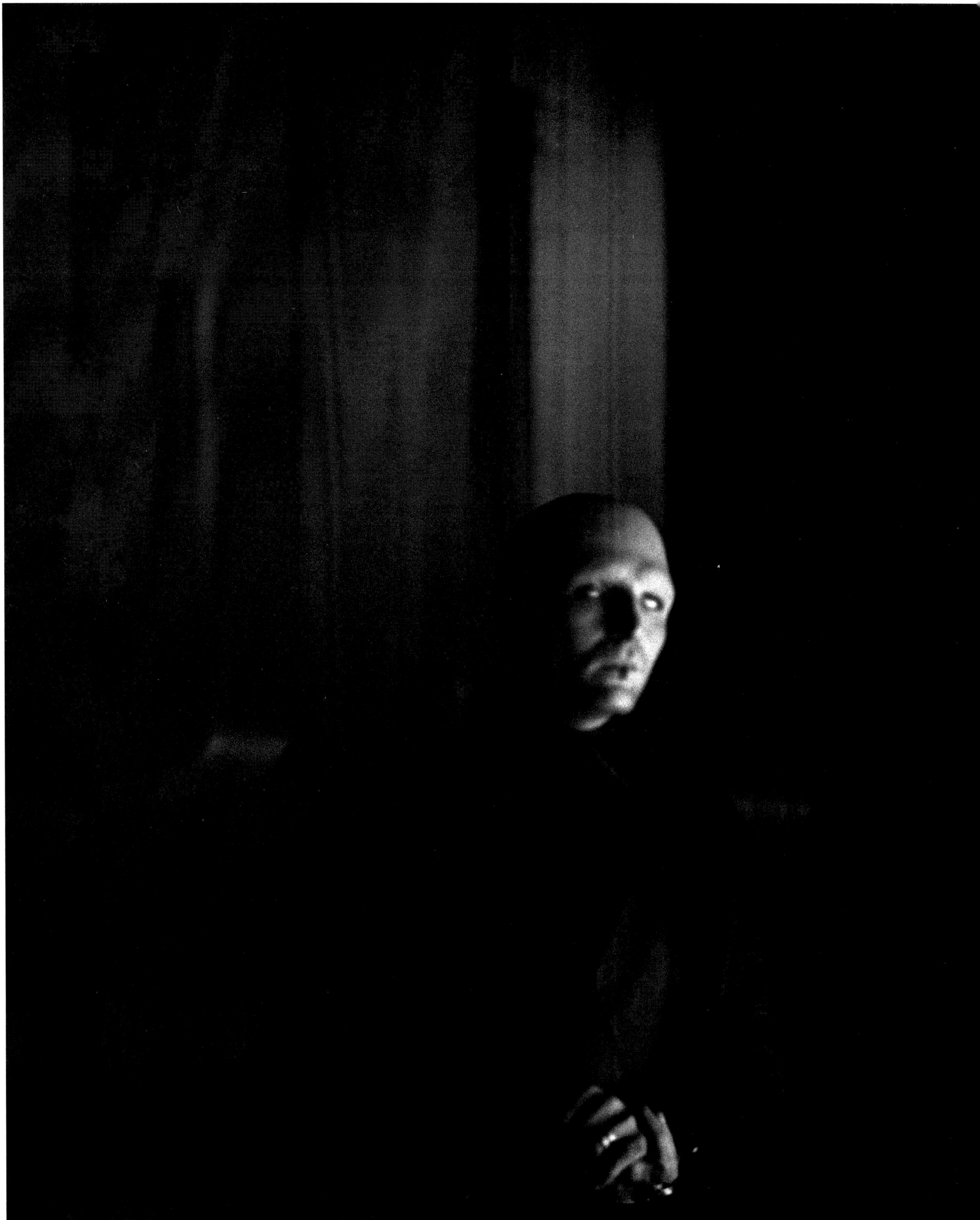

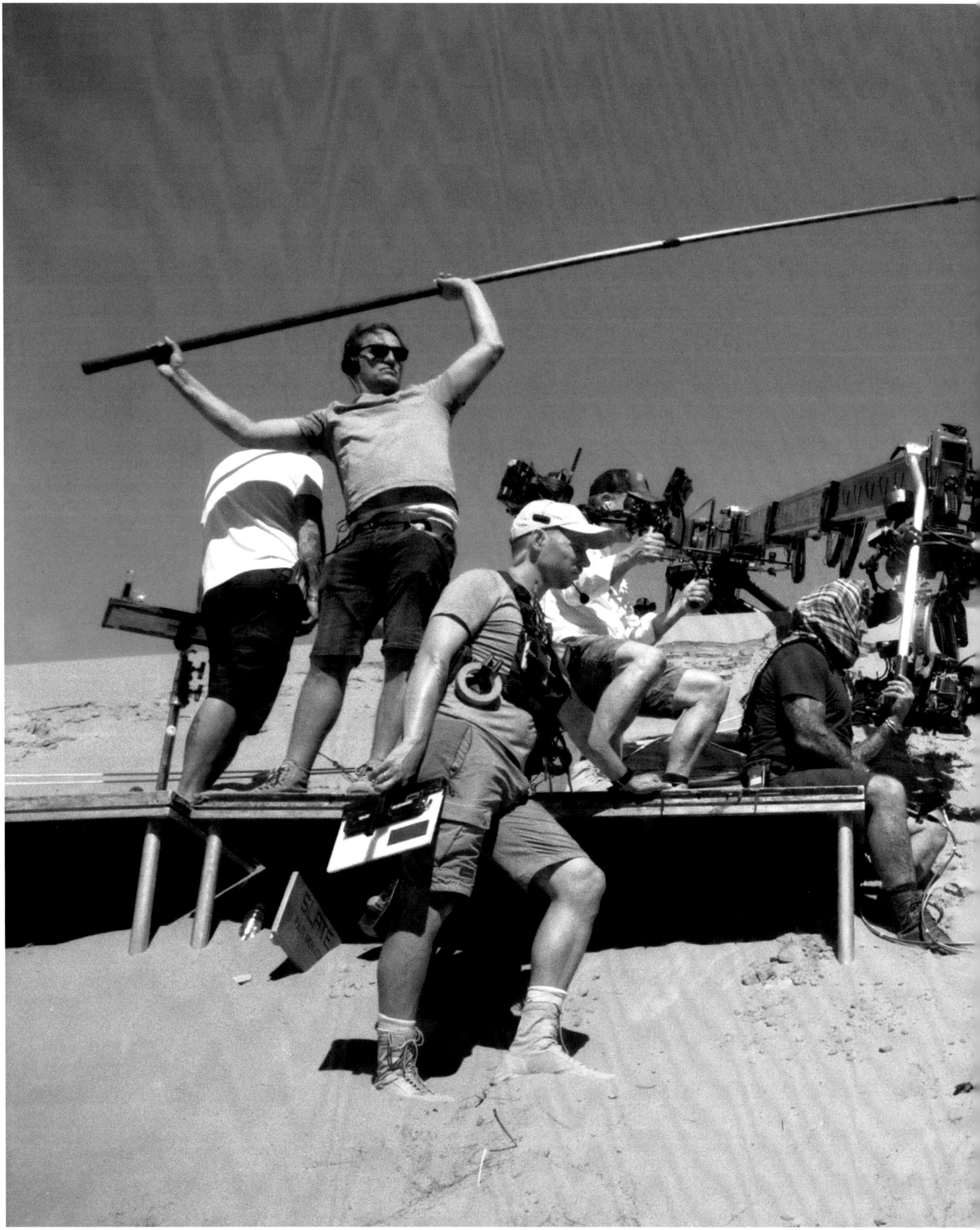

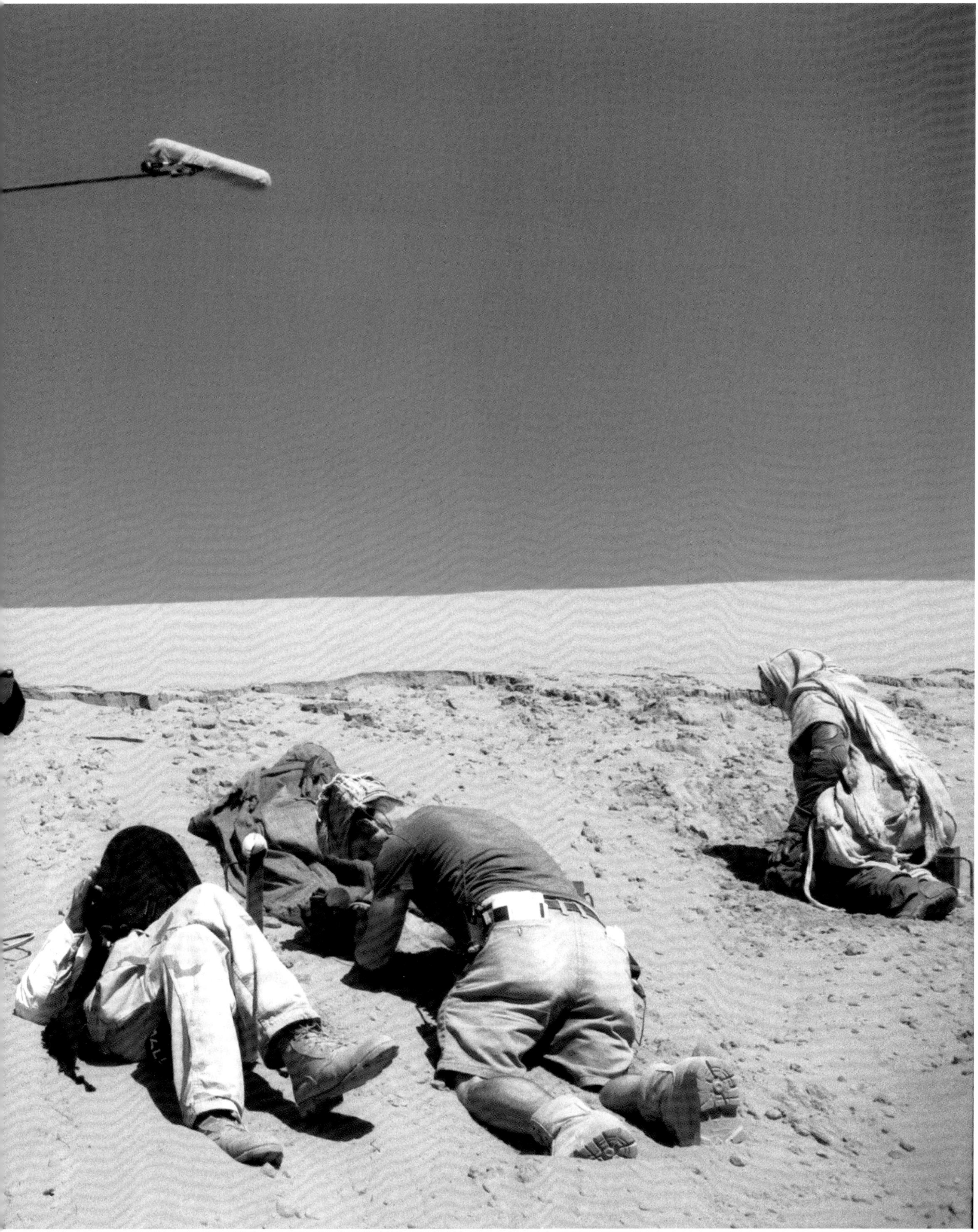

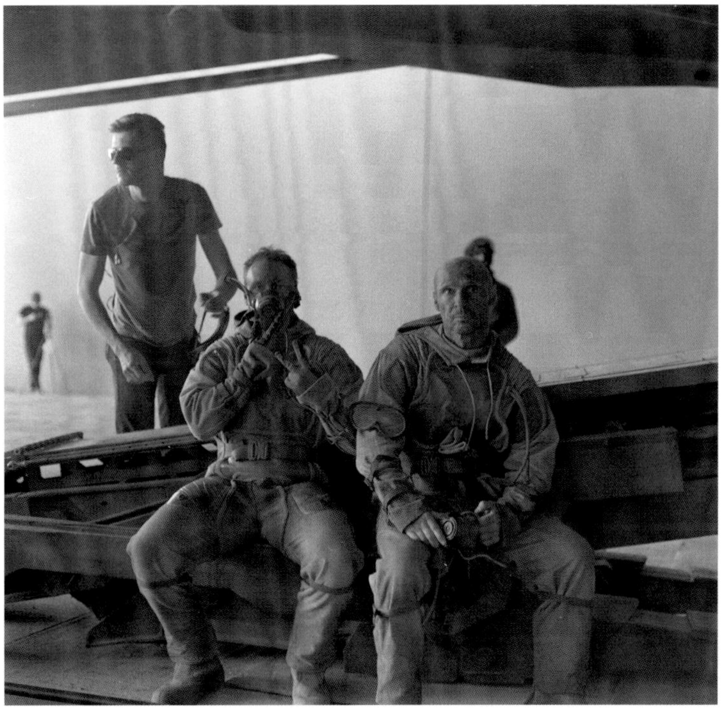

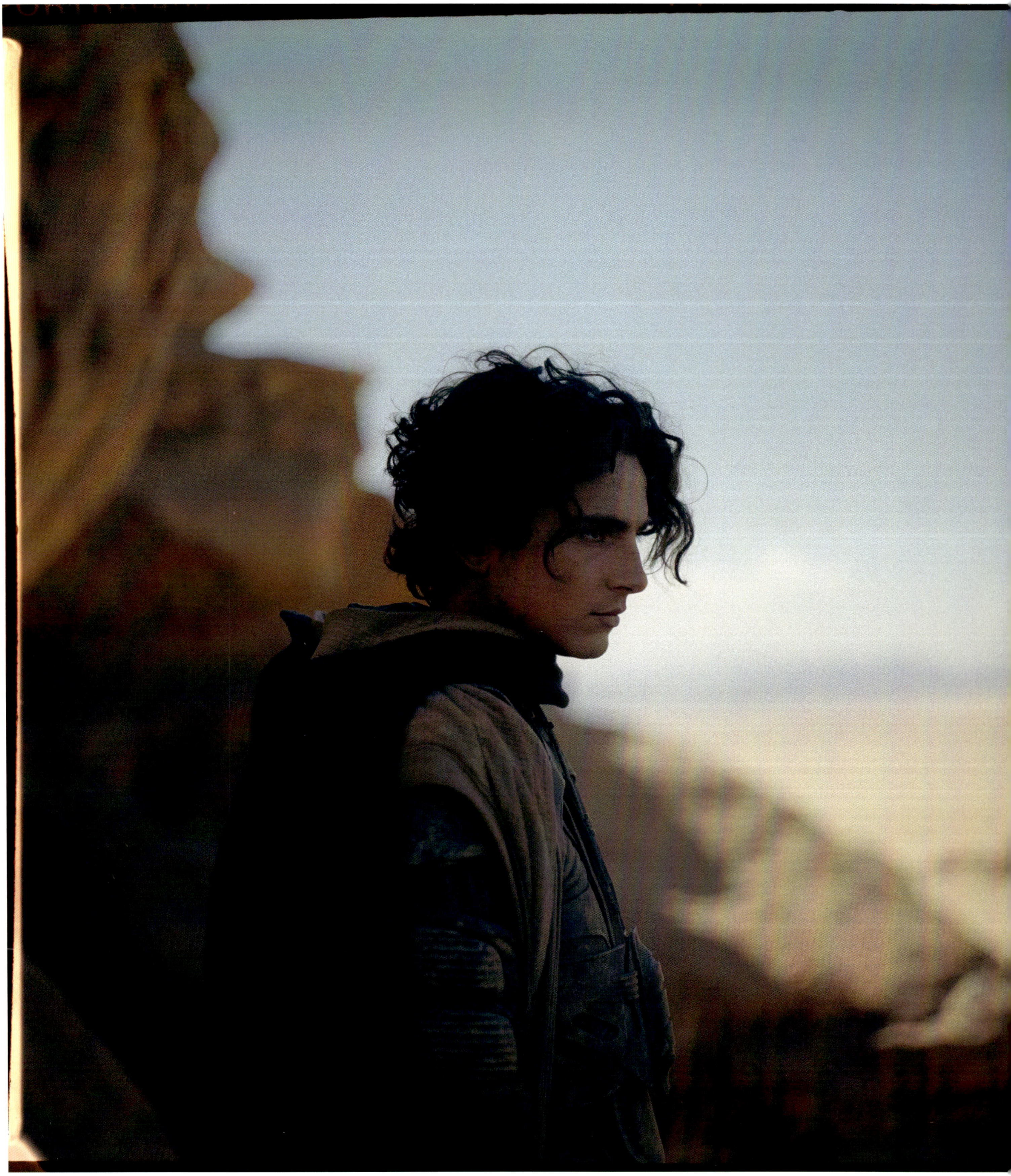

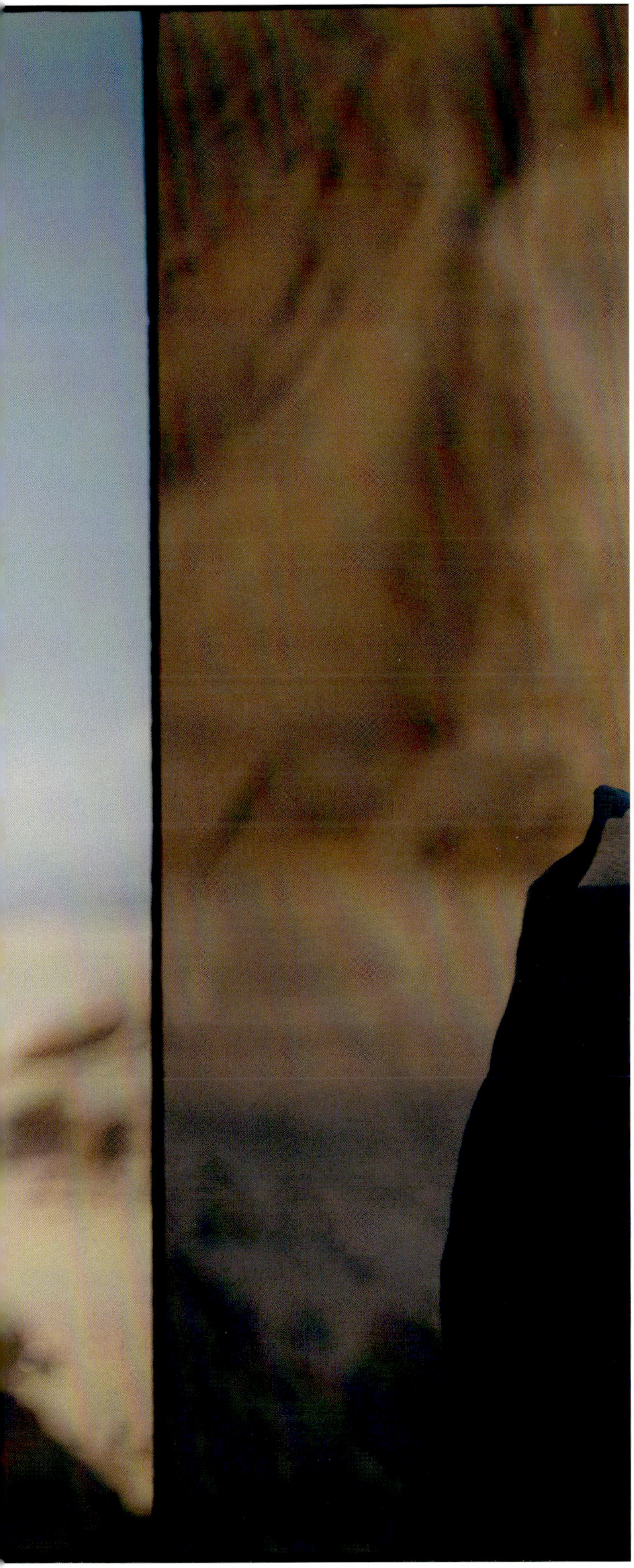

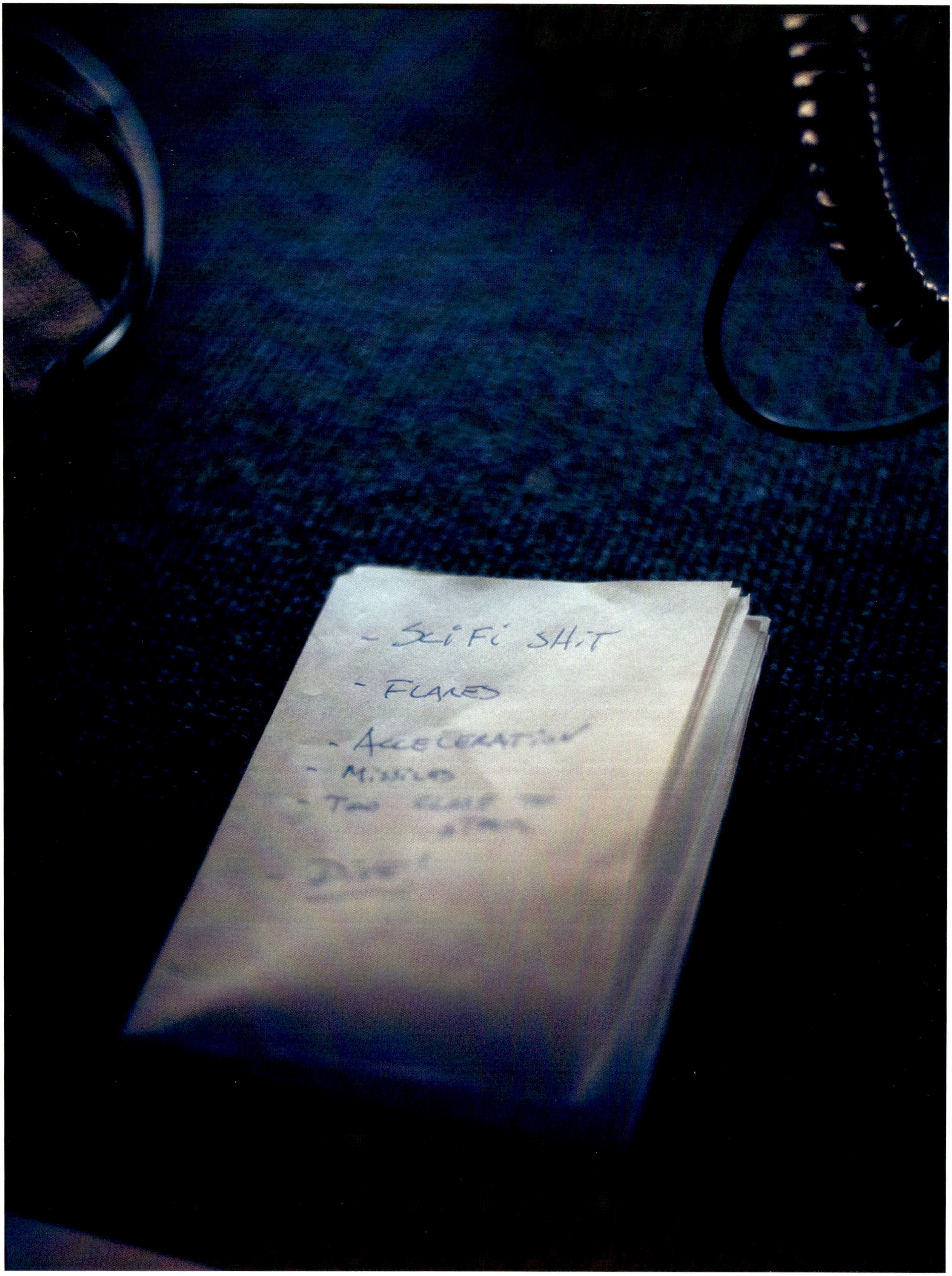
- SCIFI SHIT
- FLARES
- ACCELERATION
- MISSILES

one day it will dawn:
birds chirp but swallow a new
worm come home for more

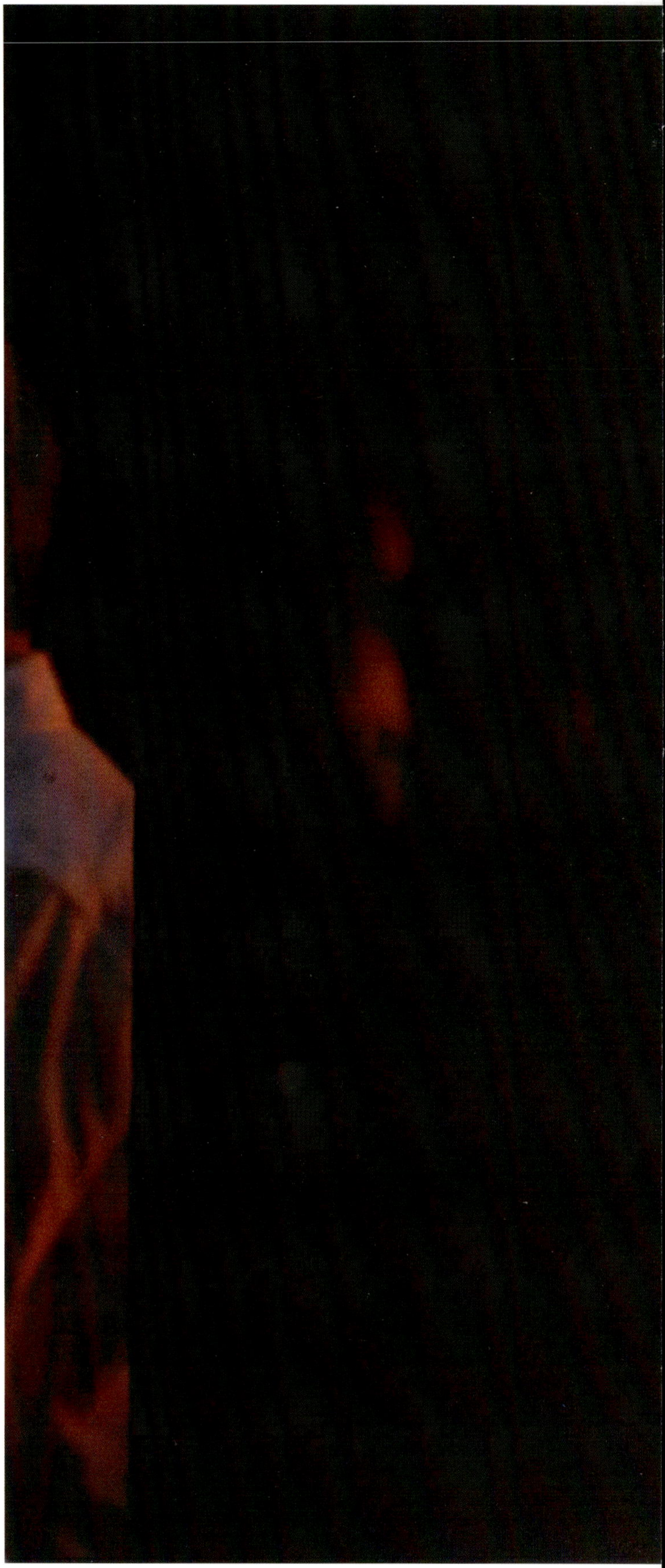

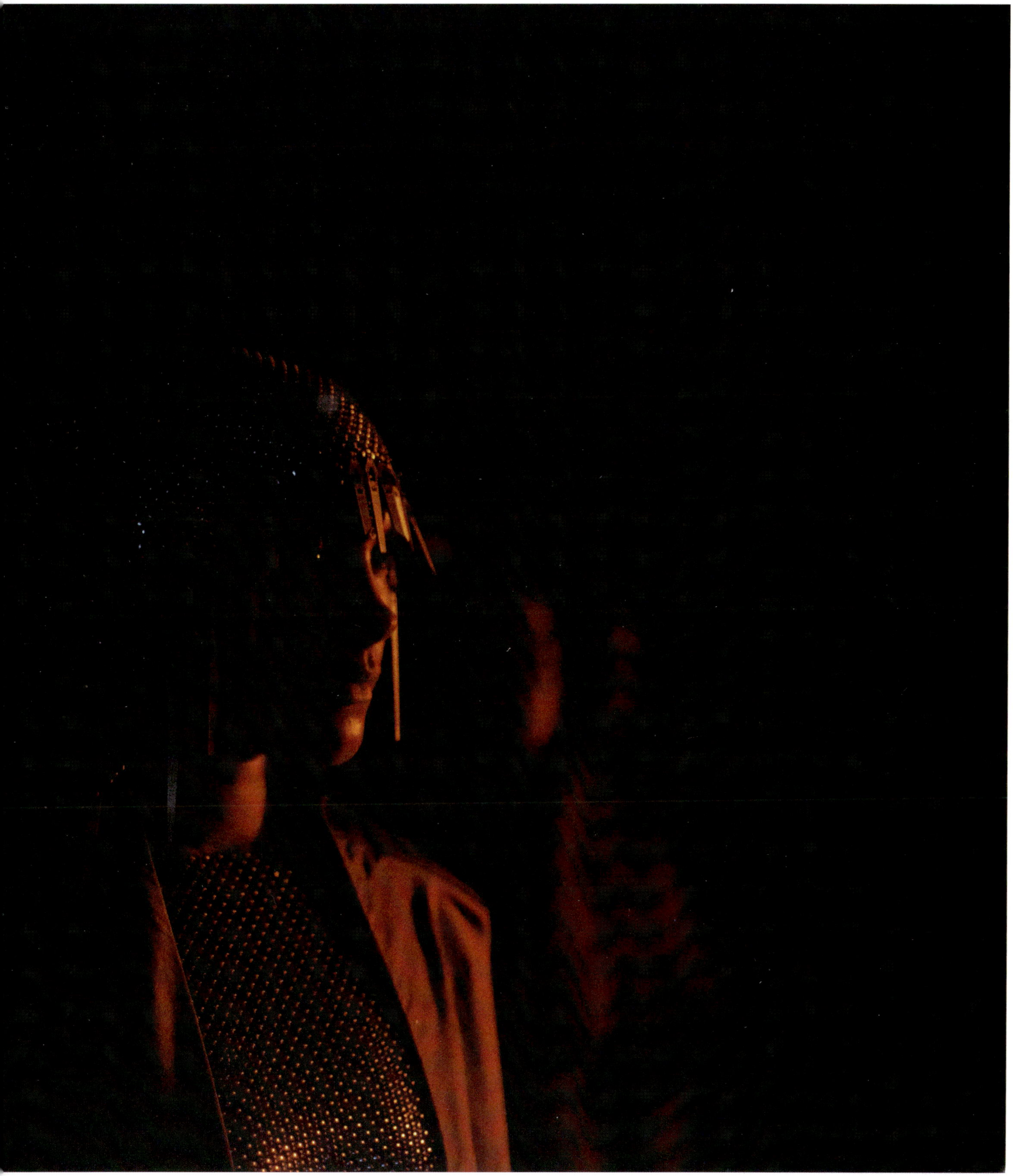

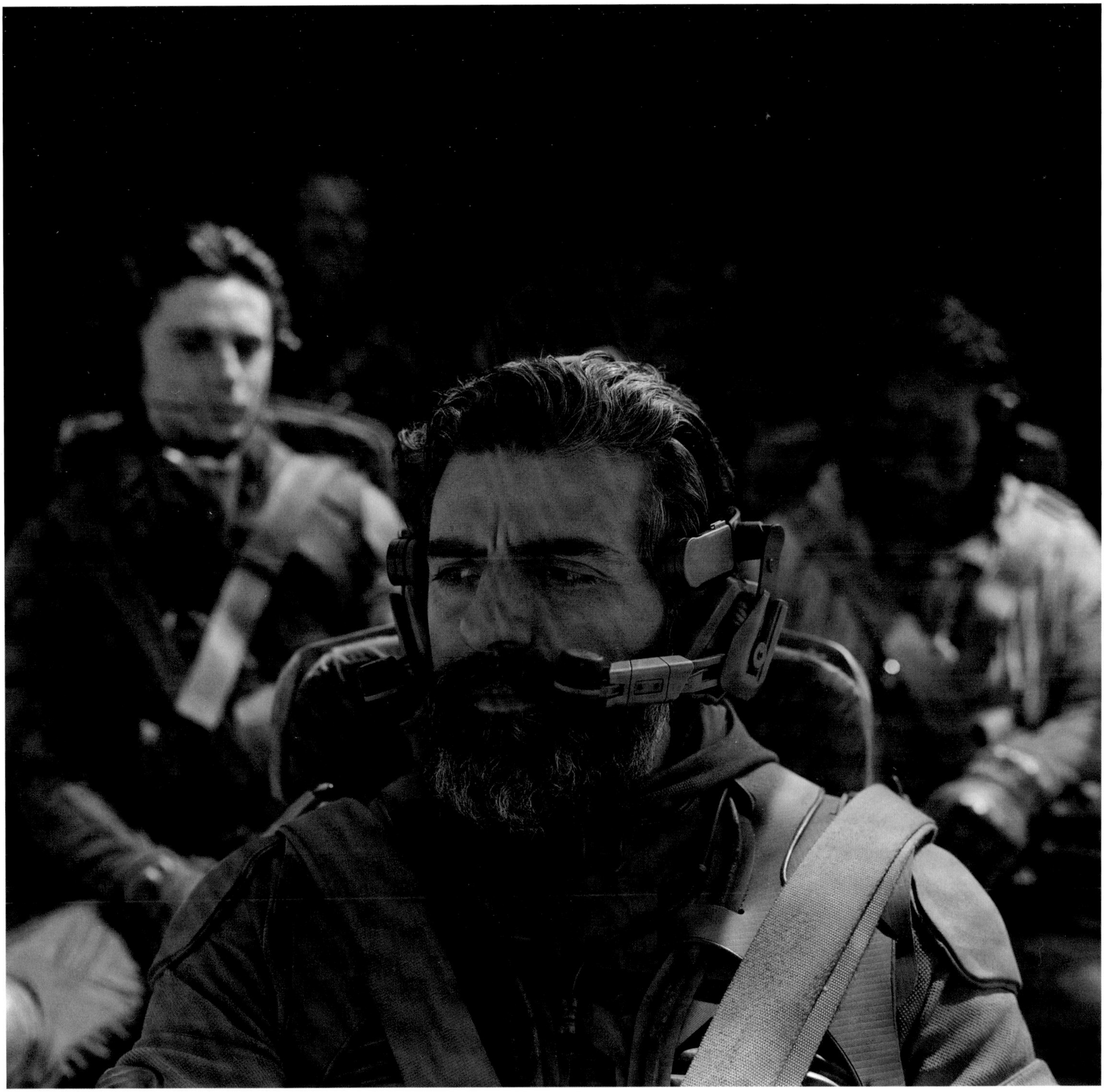

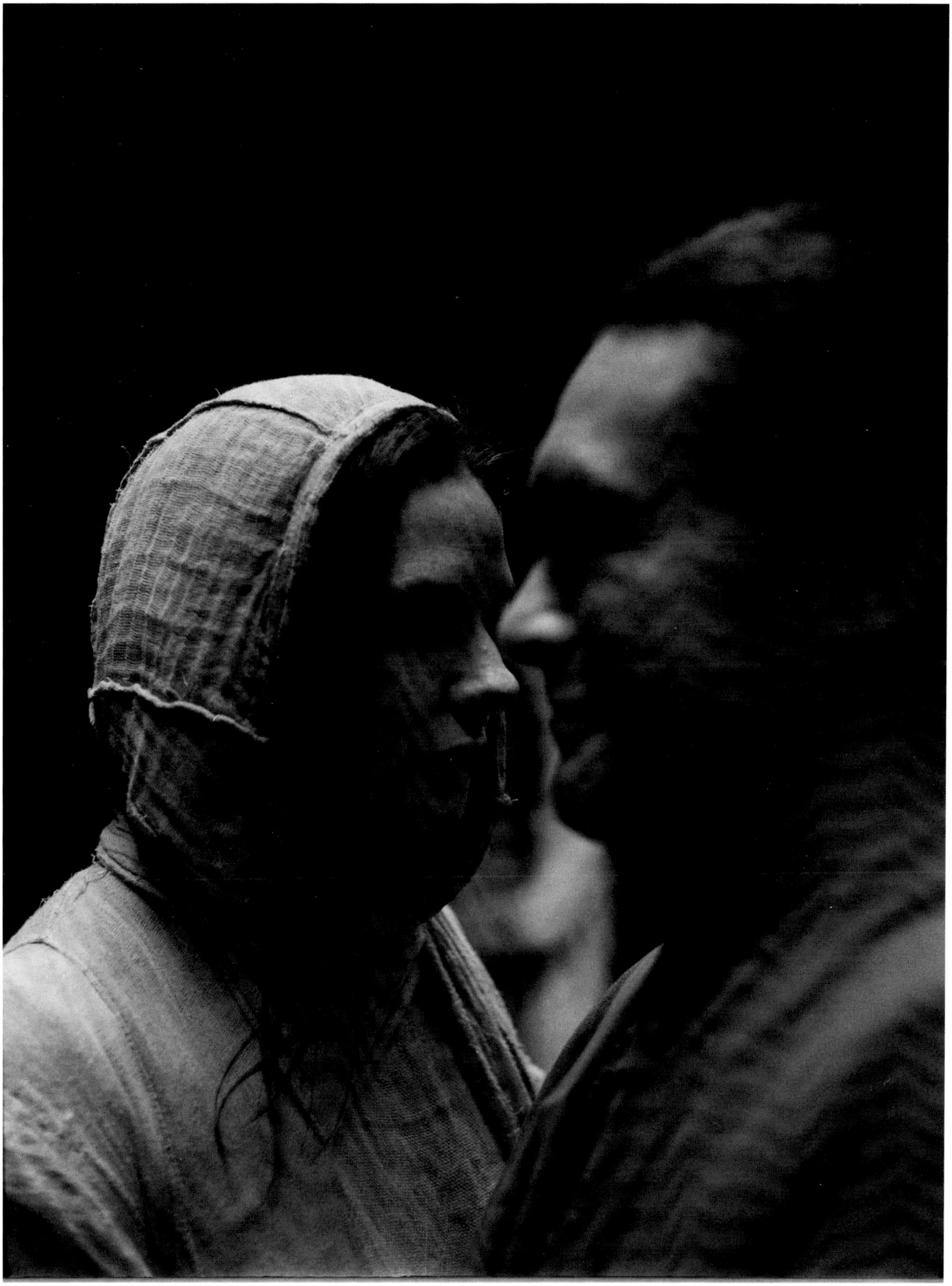

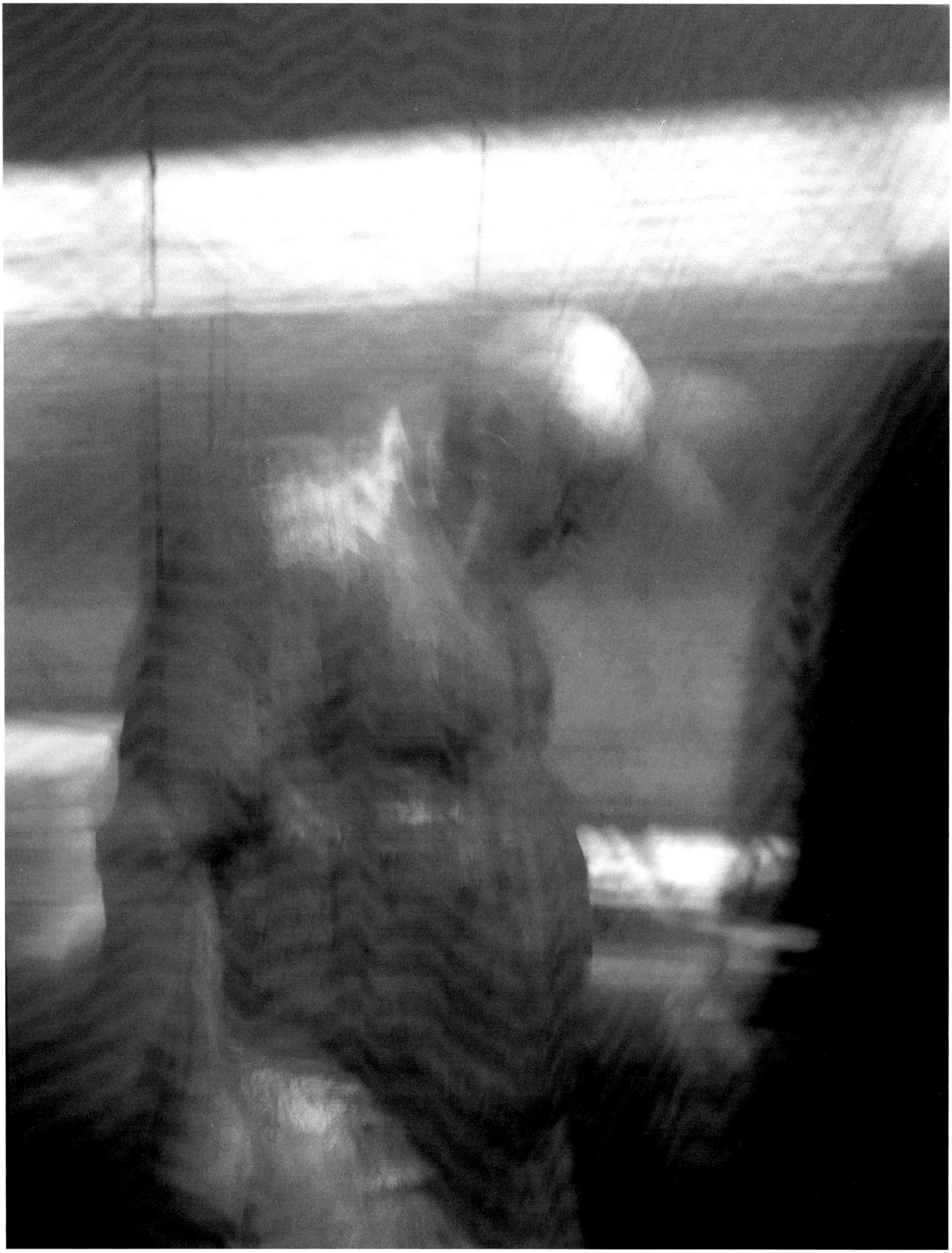

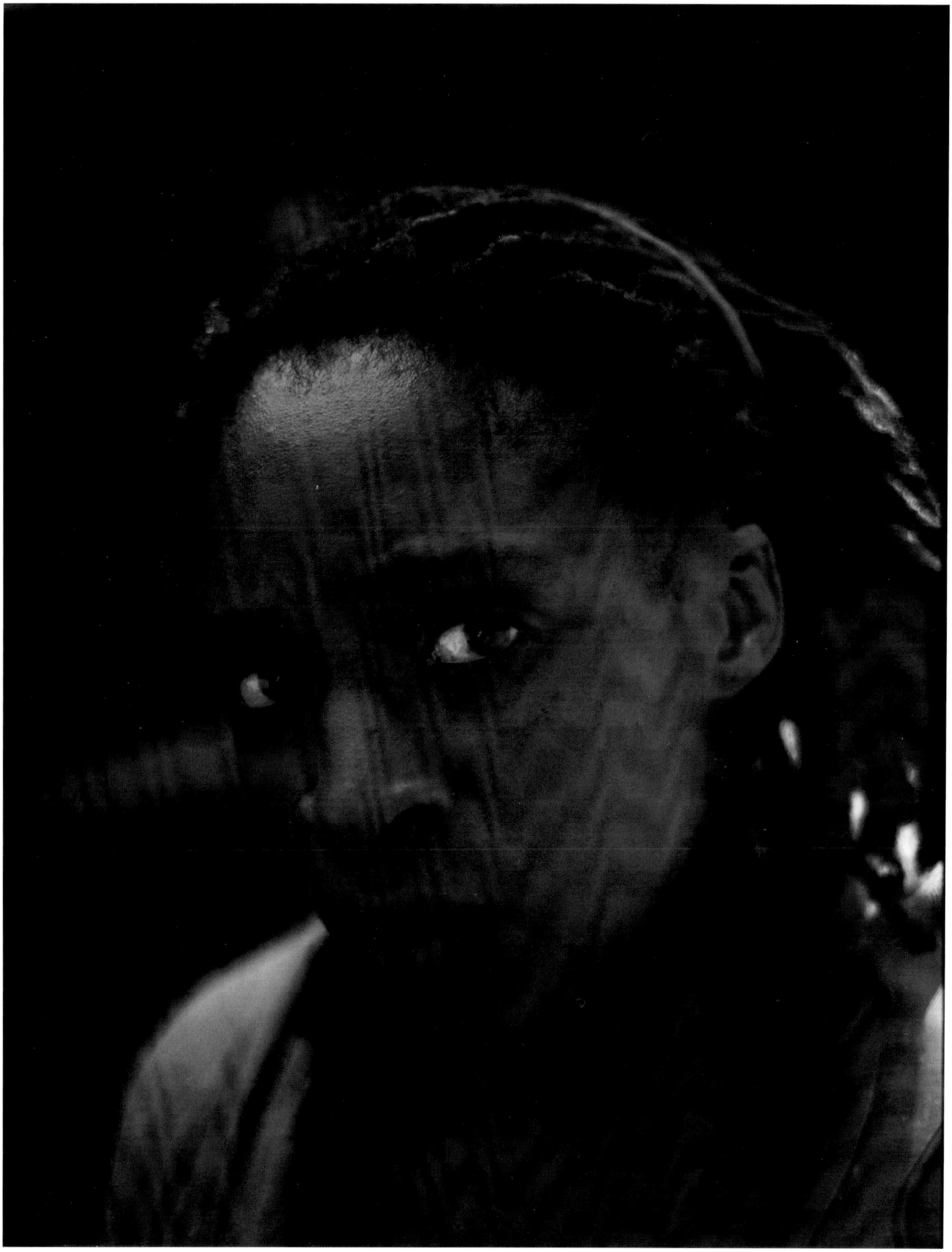

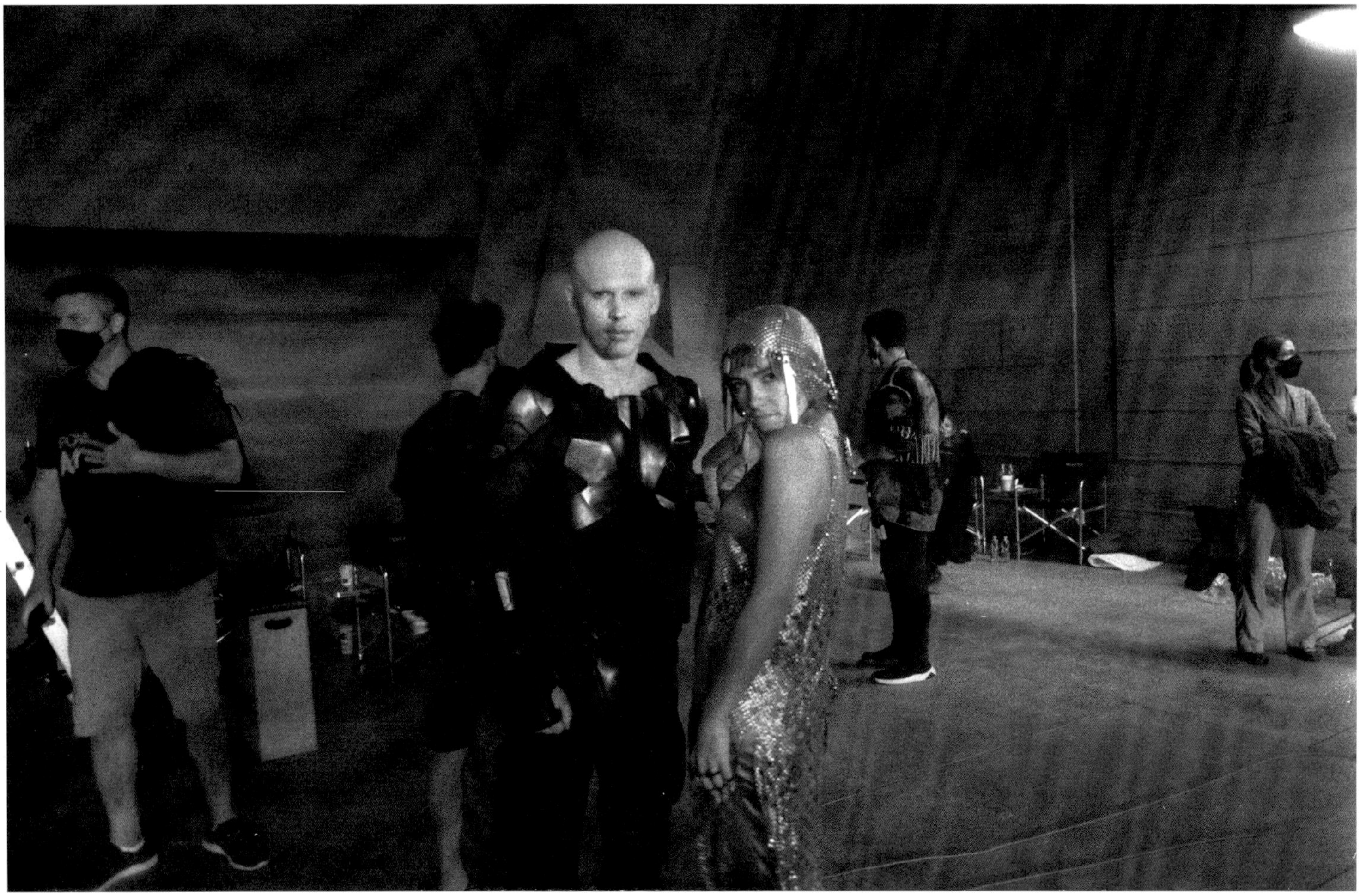

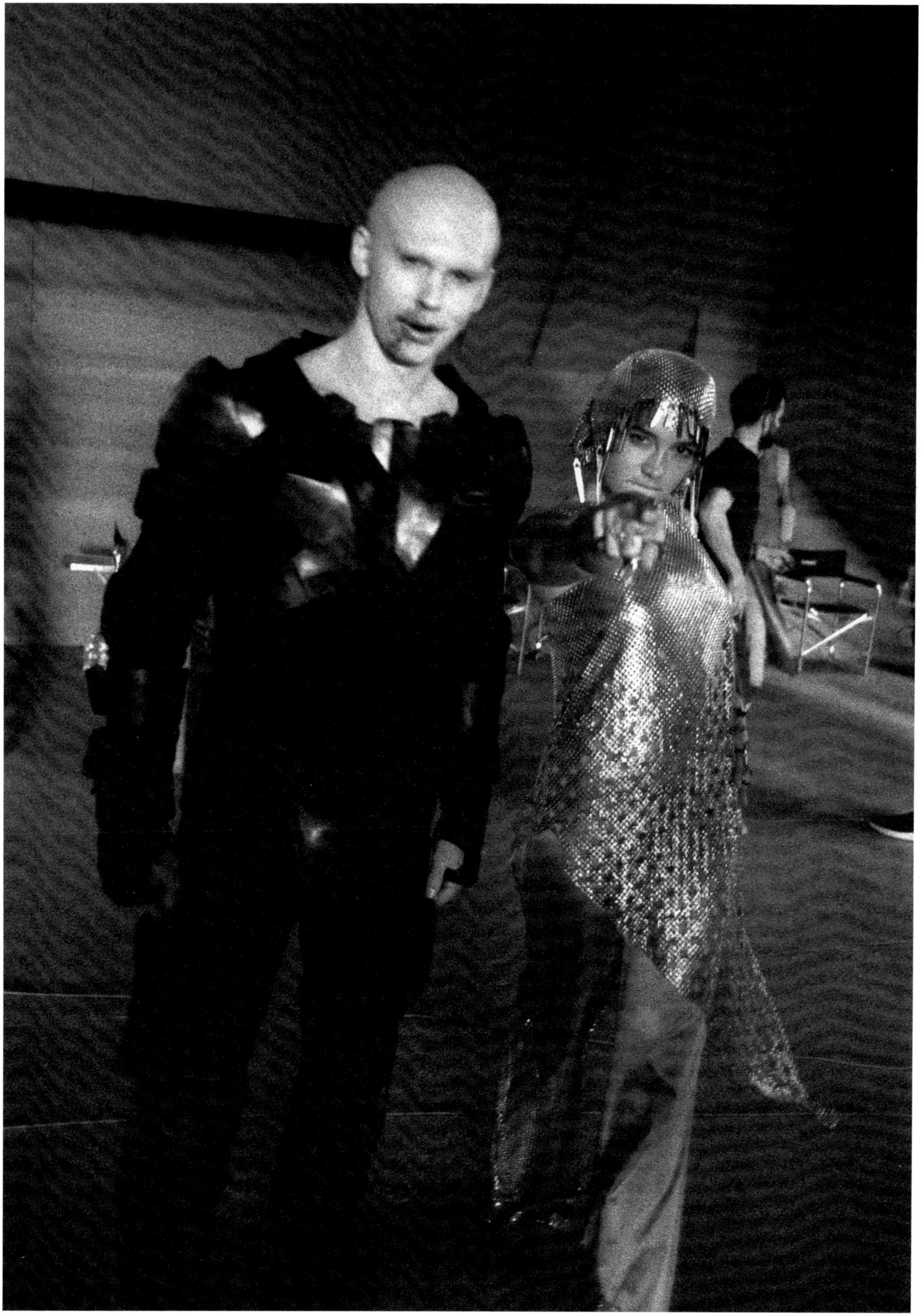

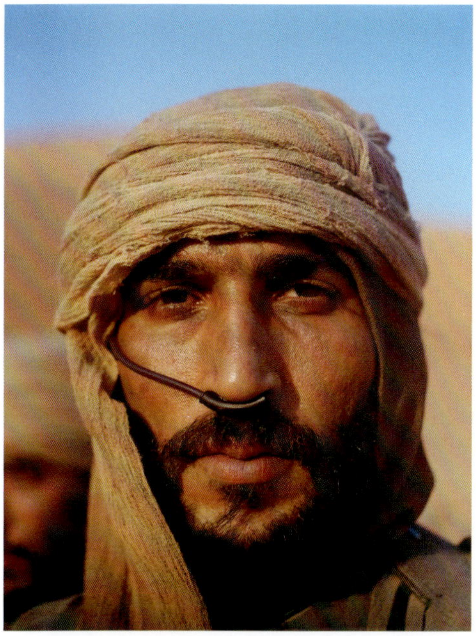
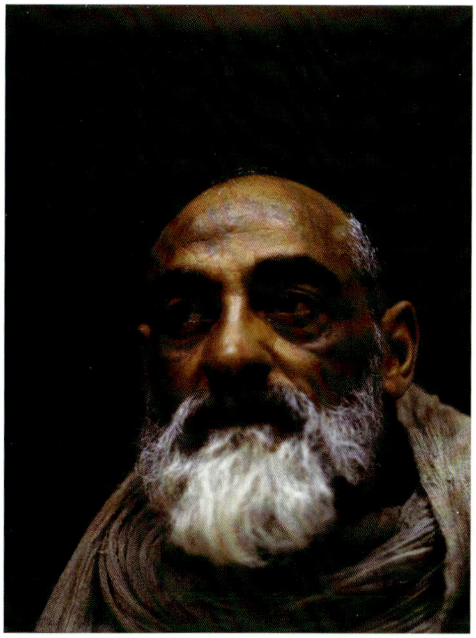
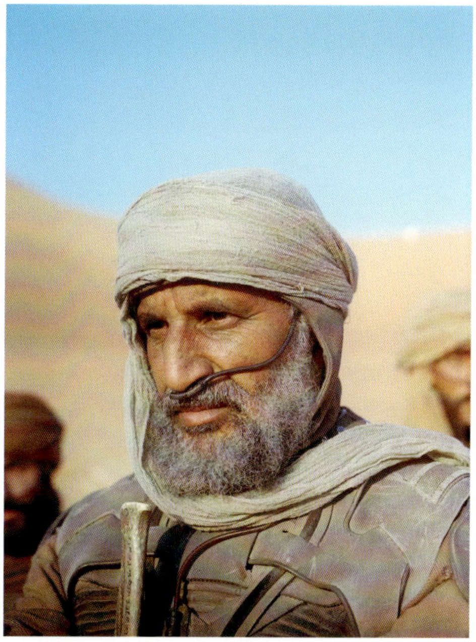
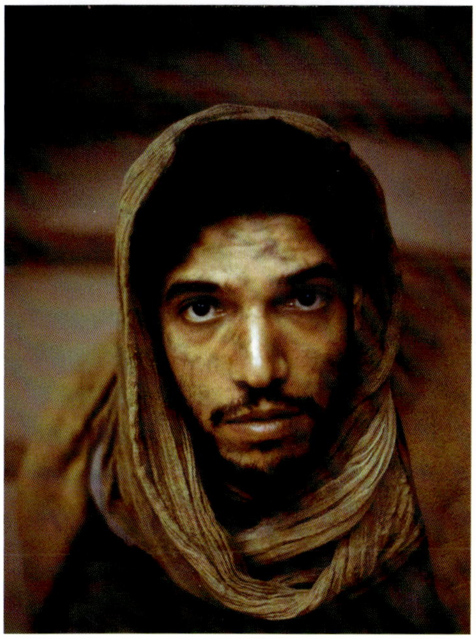
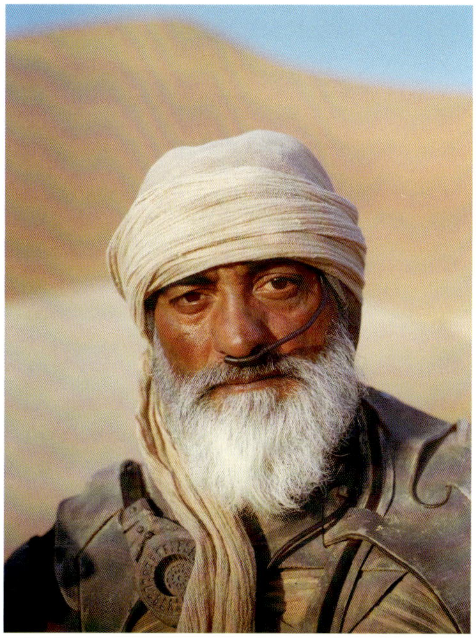
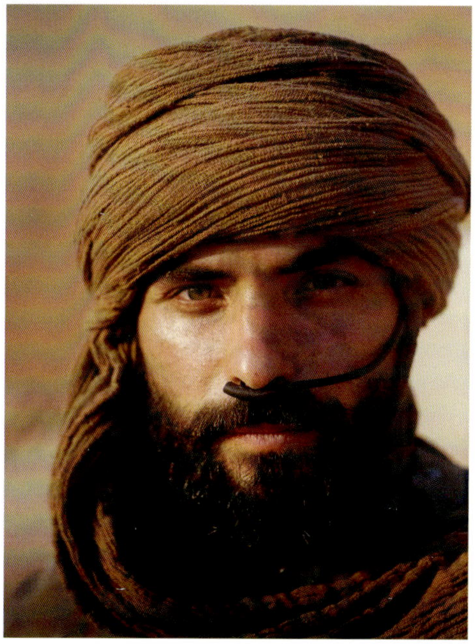

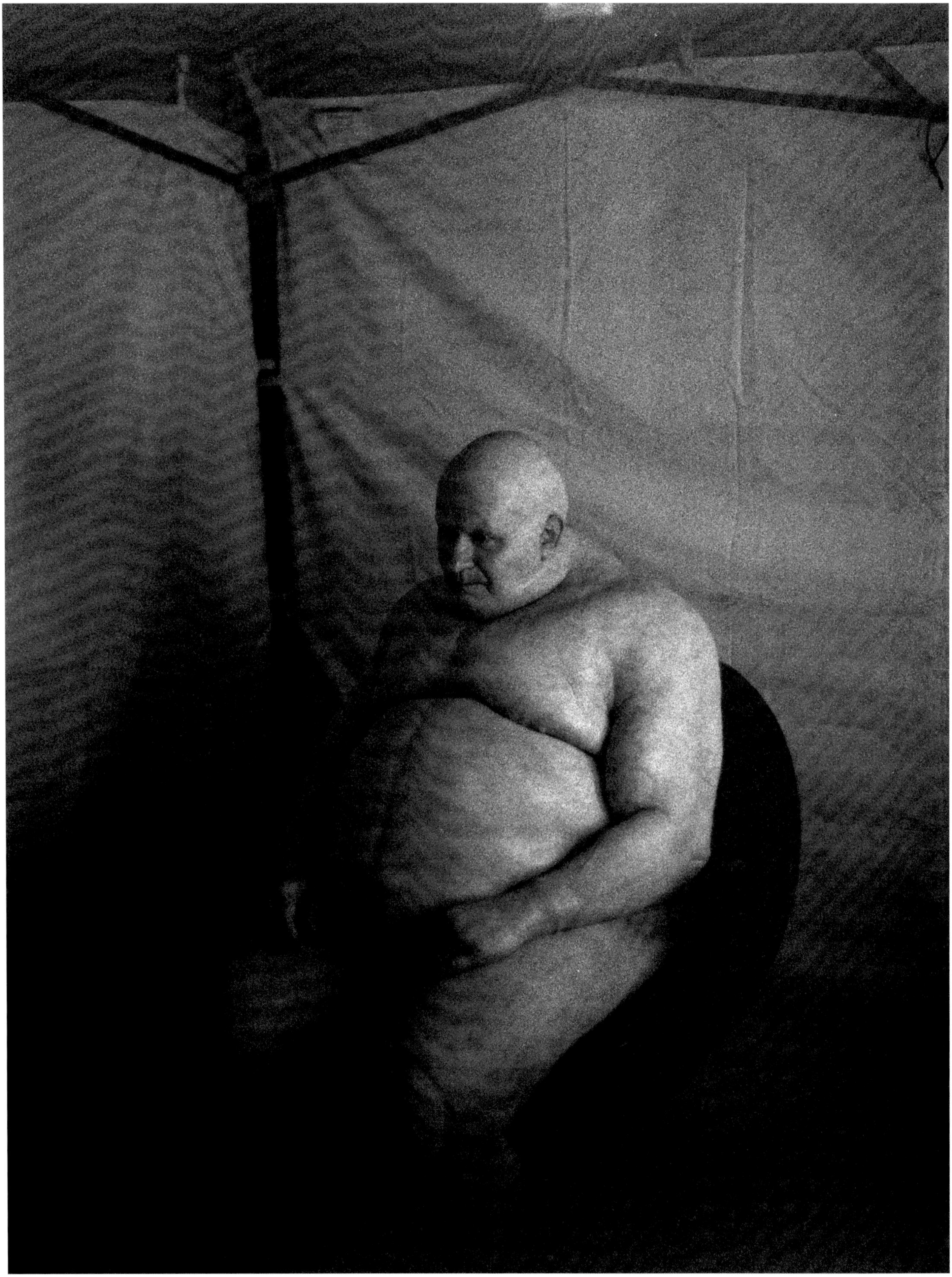

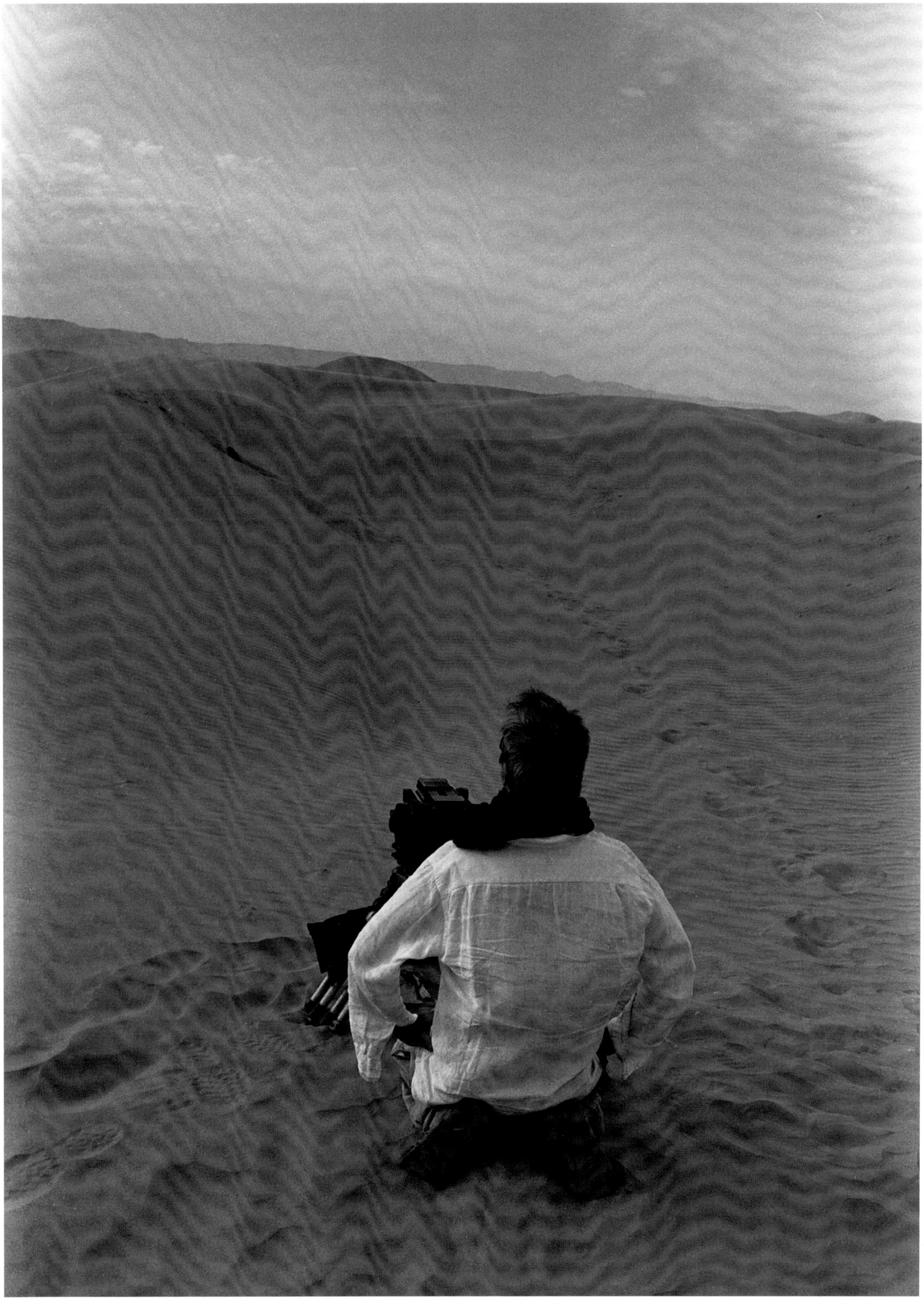

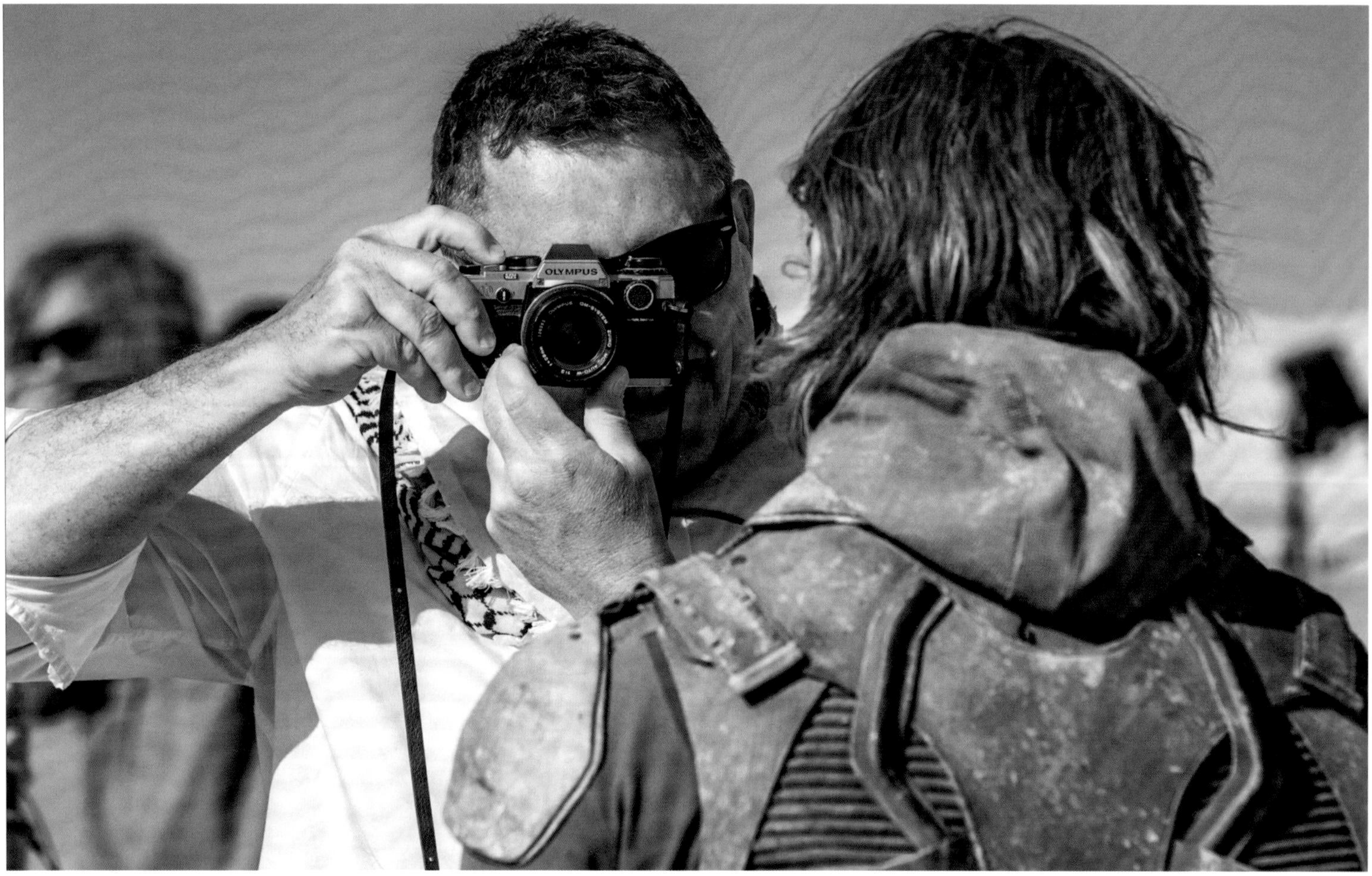

Photo by Niko Tavernise

Greig Fraser

The great photographer Robert Capa said: "If your pictures aren't good enough, you aren't close enough." And such is the mentality of Greig Fraser, our DP. There was an added benefit of being the director of photography, which enabled him to already be close: asking us how our night or day was, and if we knew of any restaurants in the area that were good to visit because his family just got into town. It wasn't a manipulation, but he was gaining your trust: "Ah, wait, just stand there for a second!" and he'd get his shot. You never even really batted an eye at it. It felt like it was part of his job, like holding a light meter to your face —click— eight inches away, and there'd he'd go again. One day it was with a camera he'd bought at a flea market somewhere in Budapest, and on another day it'd be another camera he'd found on the boardwalk along Venice Beach before he left. Always film. There's something about perpetually staying on top of understanding how light behaves with film and how that can morph a face into a behavior; how the photographer's job is not only to capture a moment but to fill the moment with his perspective, his chosen composition and, ultimately, his taste of that momentary world of light. As it becomes more personal, light begins to have a personality that you project onto the image you're creating. Light starts to speak with you, and asks you how you would like for it to sit upon your subject. And the greatest photographers know, as all that is going on, that to wake up your eyes, to instigate a dialogue, is key to the final image so that it's not left dead and without a voice.

All that while lighting one of the biggest-budgeted films of the year.

Why?

Because he does it for the personality of art, and art is a personality if you sit with it for a prolonged while. Like with a meditation, you must allow yourself the honesty that your mind is distracted with a plethora of bullshit, and only in being honest about that are you able to strip it away, knowing that it'll be there later to distract you once again.

But for now, as the sun is coming up over a bed of millions of tons of sand, and the crest of a dune is throwing reveals of subjects and feelings and ghosts and an unspoken emotion that only you are perceiving, you must be in bed with art, inside the vagina of art, to impregnate upon art, that you are worthy of its presence. Only then will art gift you with a being who will be raised by the village that is your audience for as long as that image exists.

And that's one photograph.

That is the chrysalis in which transforms the butterfly.

These images sing that relationship with art. They prioritize art and in doing so reveal its subjects artistically: with light, with dark, with emotion, with behavior, with a word or a sentence that the viewer might attach to it that resonates most with them. Denis Villeneuve pushed for this because he knew that to allow art to win out in the end is to win. That's when the mystery becomes an obsession and the obsession becomes paintable.

So these are our paintings told through a potpourri of images and a swath of nomadic words to help you imagine our brief sojourn with Madame Art.

During the pre-production process of *Dune: Part One*, Denis approached me, aware of my long-forgotten history as a photographer, and requested that I consider informally documenting our journey as filmmakers. At first, feeling slightly overwhelmed by the magnitude of my assigned responsibilities, I gently declined the offer. "For the betterment of the film," I told him.

Quietly though, I started thinking about this assignment, and begun actually taking photos in prep, and on set, which Denis assured me would only ever be for our own private collections. Surprisingly, I started noticing a pattern emerging—a series of images that might not sell the film, but could convey the mood and atmosphere of our set. Contrary to my expectations, shooting stills on set turned out to be a fantastic tool that helped me focus and stay present during blockings and actor discussions, tuning out distractions.

But again, these images had no reason to be—no end goal, no purpose.

Then one day, during a hair and makeup test, in walked a five-foot, nine-inch, 190-pound reason to be.

As Josh and I got to know each other on Dune, we slowly started to share our writing and photos. Together, it seemed to me that suddenly these images took on a whole new life and reminded me why I became so attracted to filmmaking in the first place. Images, combined with words, can become greater than the sum of their parts.

In his writing, Brolin demonstrates a keen appreciation for nuance, skillfully crafting sentences that carry layers of meaning and emotion. Each word is carefully chosen to evoke a specific sentiment, allowing readers to experience a range of feelings, from joy to contemplation to introspection. Through considered phrasing he paints vivid mental images, enabling readers to immerse themselves in the worlds he creates.

However, it is not just the words he includes, but also the words he excludes that grant his writing its distinctive power. Brolin understands the significance of brevity, often saying more with fewer words. Often, through the omission of unnecessary details, he leaves space for readers to draw their conclusions, fostering a more personal connection with his work. This minimalist approach allows the reader's imagination to take flight, giving the images with which they are associated, more power.

The importance of what we were working on wasn't lost on me either. In his novel, Frank Herbert's words transport us to a realm of grandeur and complexity. The images he conjures are not merely static scenes but living, breathing environments that encompass the senses. We feel the oppressive heat of the desert, taste the spice-laden air, and see the shifting sands that shape the destiny of planets and civilizations. Herbert's words, which crafted the entire universe we were filming, also provided a remarkable starting point, helping enable us to discover our voices for this book.

In the realm of visual storytelling, the power of words and images is undeniable. The right word, carefully chosen and placed, can breathe life into an image, allowing it to break through its visual boundaries and to convey emotions, concepts, and narratives with unparalleled depth. Similarly, when combined with the right image, a single word can unlock a world of meaning, adding layers of interpretation and evoking a multitude of feelings within the audience.

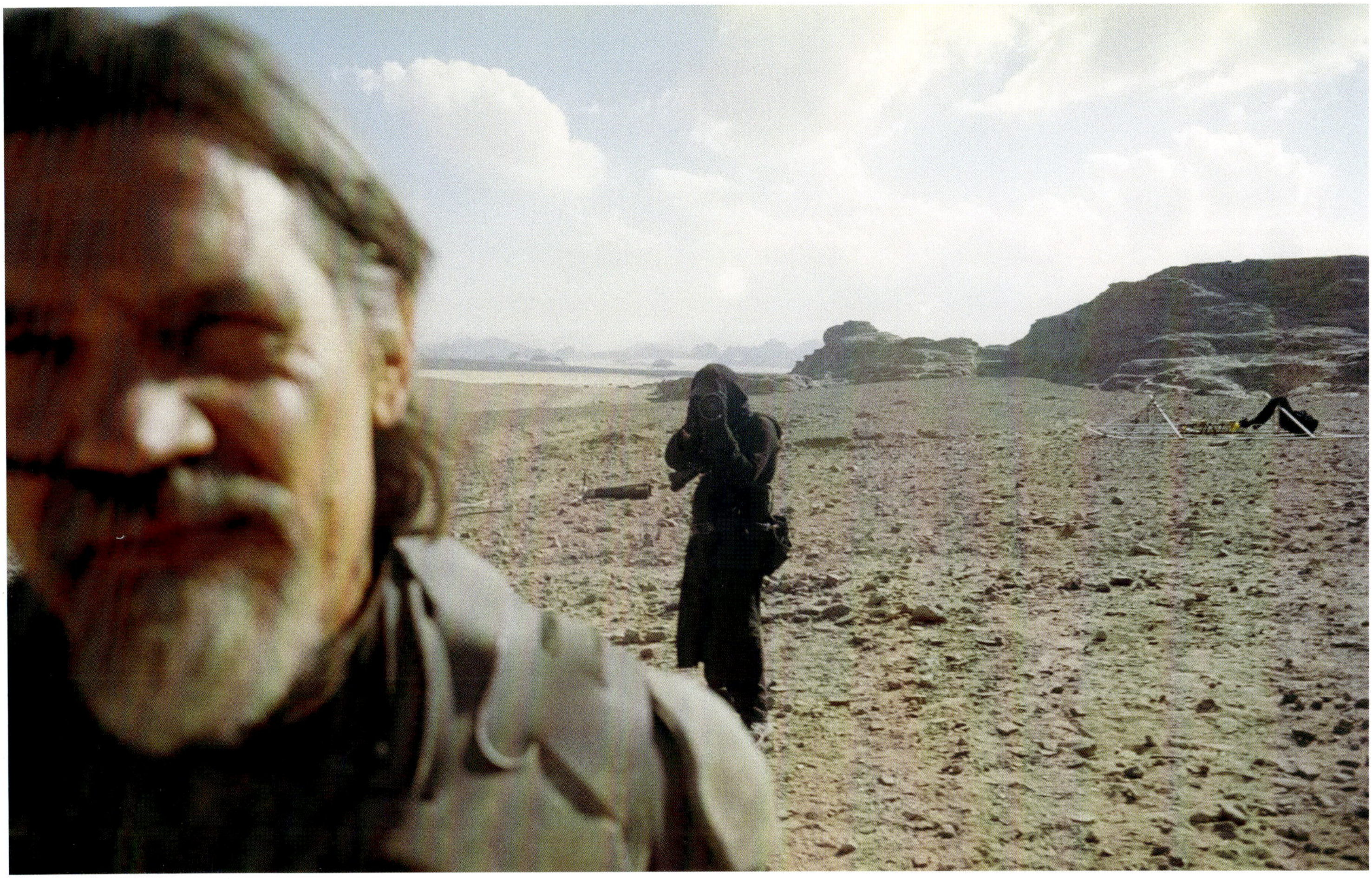

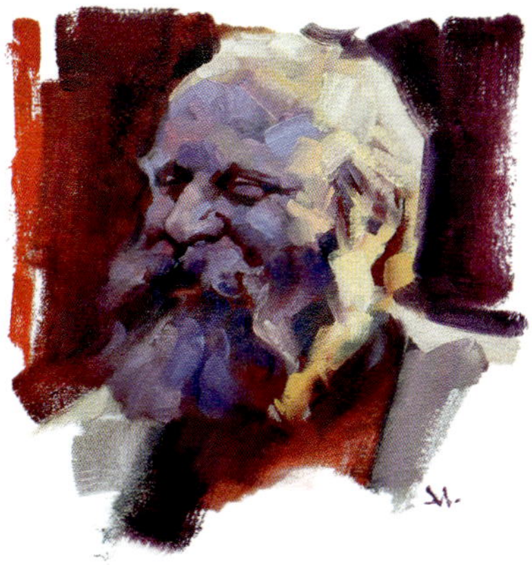

Frank Herbert (1920–1986) created the most beloved novel in the annals of science fiction, *Dune*. He was a man of many facets, of countless passageways that ran through an intricate mind. His magnum opus reflects this, a classic work that stands as one of the most complex, multi-layered novels ever written in any genre. Today the novel is more popular than ever, with new readers continually discovering it and telling their friends to pick up a copy. It has been translated into dozens of languages and has sold tens of millions of copies worldwide, in more than 40 languages.

As a child growing up in Washington State, Frank Herbert was curious about everything. He carried around a Boy Scout pack with books in it, and he was always reading. He loved Rover Boys' adventures, as well as the stories of H.G. Wells, Jules Verne, and the science fiction of Edgar Rice Burroughs. On his eighth birthday, Frank stood on top of the breakfast table at his family home and announced, "I wanna be a author." His curiosity and independent spirit got him into trouble more than once when he was growing up and caused him difficulties as an adult as well. He did not graduate from college because he refused to take the required courses for a major; he only wanted to study what interested him. For years he had a hard time making a living, bouncing from job to job and from town to town. He was so independent that he refused to write for a particular market; he wrote what he felt like writing. It took him five years of research and writing to complete *Dune*, and after all that struggle and sacrifice, 23 publishers rejected it in book form before it was finally accepted. He received an advance of only $7,500.

His loving wife of 37 years, Beverly, was the breadwinner much of the time, as an underpaid advertising writer for department stores. Having been divorced from his first wife, Flora Parkinson, Frank Herbert met Beverly Stuart at a University of Washington creative writing class in 1946. At the time they were the only students in the class who had sold their work for publication. Frank had sold two pulp adventure stories to magazines, one to *Esquire* and the other to *Doc Savage*. Beverly had sold a story to *Modern Romance* magazine. These genres reflected the interests of the two young lovers; he the adventurer, the strong outdoorsman, and she the romantic, feminine, and soft-spoken.

Their long marriage would produce two sons, Brian, born in 1947, and Bruce, born in 1951. Frank also had a daughter, Penny, born in 1942 from his first marriage. For more than two decades Frank and Beverly would struggle to make ends meet, and there were many hard times. To pay the bills and to allow her husband the freedom he needed to create, Beverly gave up her creative writing career in order to support his. They were a writing team, as he discussed every aspect of his stories with her, and she edited his work. Theirs was a remarkable, though tragic, love story—which Brian would poignantly describe one day in *Dreamer of Dune*. After Beverly passed away, Frank married Theresa Shackelford.

In all, Frank Herbert wrote nearly 30 popular books and collections of short stories, including six novels set in the Dune universe: *Dune, Dune Messiah*, *Children of Dune*, *God Emperor of Dune*, *Heretics of Dune*, and *Chapterhouse: Dune*. All were international bestsellers, as were a number of his other science fiction novels, including *The White Plague* and *The Dosadi Experiment*.

For the complete biography of Frank Herbert, read *Dreamer of Dune* by Brian Herbert

Photography: Greig Fraser

Words: Josh Brolin

Design, Handwriting & Typesetting by:
Manija Emran
Henry Hobson
for Me & the Bootmaker

Special Thanks:

Greig Fraser:
This book (and life in general) definitely would not be possible without my wife Jodie, and children Felix, Leo, and Poppy. Tanya Lapointe, and Denis Villeneuve for constant support and inspiration. Henry and Manija at Me & the Bootmaker, for everything you have experienced thus far. My shooting crew on *Dune*, for making it possible to balance photography and cinematography, without missing a beat for either mediums. My focus puller, Jake Marcuson. My assistants on *Dune: Part One* and *Part Two*. Nick Turner and Tamas Papps. Our team at Insight and Legendary for supporting our left of field ideas. And of course, Josh Brolin. Those words inspired much more than just the photography.

Josh Brolin:
I'd like to thank Greig Fraser first and foremost for creating photos that represent the real, the wool-lifted and the absurdist nature of what labyrinth we as storytellers travel. Through Frank Herbert's *Dune* we together have found a world that sings and in that Henry Hobson and Tanya Lapointe have both supported and helped create an aria that supports the opera that Denis Villeneuve helmed and make come true to life: tactile dreams. I'd also like to thank all the actors for inspiring what it is to have such talent yet still always being grounded and themselves. The crew, also: grounded, unrelentingly hardworking, and talented beyond earthly measure. And to my immediate family who perpetually inspires me to see it all anew, and steep in the gratitude on the platter with which it is presented. *Dune*: here and now.

Thanks to Frank Herbert and Herbert Properties, LLC

Paper:
Kinmari Dull-ex white matte art
Hopewell SDD210-24 woodfree
Hopewell BCL200-42 woodfree
New Xuan Ran Color Card
FaceBloom

INSIGHT
EDITIONS
PO Box 3088
San Rafael, CA 94912
www.insighteditions.com

Find us on Facebook: www.facebook.com/InsightEditions
Follow us on Twitter: @insighteditions
Follow us on Instagram: @insighteditions

LEGENDARY

ISBN: 978-1-64722-926-9
Limited Edition ISBN: 979-8-88663-583-6

We would like to thank Greig Fraser and Josh Brolin for their extraordinary work and artistry, the cast and crew of *Dune* and *Dune: Part Two* for their participation, and Denis Villeneuve, Tanya Lapointe, and Robert Napton for their ongoing support for our *Dune* publishing program.

Publisher: Raoul Goff
VP, Co-Publisher: Vanessa Lopez
VP, Creative: Chrissy Kwasnik
VP, Manufacturing: Alix Nicholaeff
VP, Group Managing Editor: Vicki Jaeger
Publishing Director: Ben Robinson
Art Director: Matt Girard
Editorial Assistant: Emma Merwin
Managing Editor: Maria Spano
Senior Production Editor: Katie Rokakis
Senior Production Manager: Greg Steffen
Senior Production Manager, Subsidiary Rights: Lina s Palma-Temena

ROOTS of PEACE REPLANTED PAPER
Insight Editions, in association with Roots of Peace, will plant two trees for each tree used in the manufacturing of this book.

Manufactured in China by Insight Editions
10 9 8 7 6 5 4